Fighting the Crusade Against Sex
Being Sex-Positive in a Sex-Negative World

By Jill McDevitt

Open Door Publications, LLC

Fighting the Crusade Against Sex:
Being Sex Positive in a Sex Negative World

The author has tried to recreate as accurately as possible
events, locales, and conversations from her memories of
them. In order to maintain their anonymity, the names and
identifying characteristics of individuals have been
changed. In order to keep the story moving, sometimes
events and conversations that took place over a period of
time were combined into one event.

Cover photo by Catheryn Ortiz
Cover design by Vanessa Kitzie

Published by
Open Door Publications℠, LLC
27 Carla Way
Lawrenceville, NJ 08648
www.OpenDoorPublications.com

ISBN: 978-0-9838750-1-7

To Ken,
Thanks for all your
support, for my career,
& against the Crusade
against sex!

Love,
[signature]

Acknowledgments

Thank you to RP for standing by me as I fought the Crusade, and still fight it to this day. Thank you for believing in me, loving me, and not being intimated by me.

Thank you to my entire family, in particular Mom, Dad, Gram, and Pooka, for being my biggest cheerleaders! Thank you for encouraging me to be self-reliant and take risks. Sorry you had to read about the intimate details of my sex life! Maybe you can skip those pages…

Thank you to RD and JM for loving me and supporting me. I'm proud to call you my friends.

Thanks to the following Feminique clients: Stacy, April, Robert, Angel, Jamie, Alisa, Alicia, Charlie, Jeff, Amanda, Susan, Zac, Ashley, Kelly, Nicole, Anna Marie, Brittany, Ken, Jennifer, Winter, Ruth, Jenna, Michael, Kevin, Barry, Amber, Ann, Katie, Landi, Heather, Megan, Jess, Leanne, Marah, Meredith, and so many more! You have helped me fight the Crusade Against Sex. Thank you for supporting me, my store, and my mission. Thank you for spending your hard earned money here and helping me keep my job. And most of all, thank you for being more than just clients, but friends.

Thank you to the whole Open Door Publications team: Karen for believing in this project and making me finish it. Thanks to everyone responsible for making me look hot on the front cover!

Chapter 1

"This from someone who freaked out at the word 'vagina?'" he said.

I sat behind the checkout counter that overlooks the baby pink and chocolate brown throw pillows decorating the seating area in my store – the store the media had dubbed "West Chester's sex shop," and I couldn't help but laugh at the irony. I had called to fill him in on all my latest excitement – front-page headlines, radio interviews, small town "scandal," – and although the voice was intimately familiar, the conversation was awkward. Strained. Emotionless. I had to wonder, "How did we get to this place?"

Rewind ten years. I was an ugly twelve-year-old with a bad perm and crooked bangs I cut myself, and Pat was a scrawny preteen with freckles and braces. At school I was known as the "dirty hippie" while he was known as the "dorky redhead." We had been classmates since kindergarten, but that summer before eighth grade – I don't know if it was sheer boredom, convenience, or our mutual rank at the bottom of the middle school totem pole – we became friends. One afternoon we were riding bikes down the alley behind my house, despite the crumbling cement and potholes that could swallow a bike tire, when he somehow discovered my prudishness. I was so straight-laced that I would actually cover my ears and squeal in disgust upon hearing sex-related terms, particularly the horrid "V" word. The previous school year I passed out in science class and nearly passed out again in Health when the "V" word was uttered, and once Pat learned of this he proceeded to torture me, as twelve-year-old boys will do, shouting "VAGINA" at the top of his lungs again and again until I flipped out and threatened to tell his mother.

Pat's memory of this story and how such a girl could grow up to own "West Chester's sex shop" was the comic relief the cold phone call needed. Really, how did we get to this place?

When I walked into the storefront that would become Feminique Boutique for the first time, the walls were neon green, and the floors were covered in warped and peeling macaroni and cheese colored linoleum. The electricity had been turned off for months, but through the darkness I could see an empty liquor bottle still adorning an otherwise empty bar. Most first-time small business owners with visions of setting up shop as an upscale women's boutique and no renovation budget would have passed this fixer-upper by, but I looked at the landlord as he scanned the dusty room with a flashlight, smiled, and said cheerily, "I'm definitely interested!" What else could I do? I was short on options, because *my* women's boutique was not going to be your traditional purses and knick-knacks kind of store. I was opening a feminist sex shop.

My Gram, Grandpop, parents, teenage sister, and best friend, George, spent a cold Saturday in March helping me slap some paint over the hideous green of my new store. I even recruited the help of strangers to get the job done, like a man named Tyler Mano, who I had recently met and who stopped by some nights to lend a hand. After pouring over the minute differences between Pastel Petunia and Priscilla Pink on the

8

sample tabs in the paint store, I found that when the first wet roll of reality went up, my decision actually looked absolutely perfect. I was overdue for a win, and after a year of setbacks in launching a career, choosing the right shade of pink counted as a big win in my eyes.

I had graduated from college in Canada nearly a year before with a unique bachelor's degree in Sexuality, Marriage, and Family. I moved back to the States, and it took me two months to land my first job interview. I was psyched. The job was with a university organizing its sexuality information website for teens. I thought it sounded perfect for someone with my degree and passion for sex education. I bought a suit, did a dry run to ensure I would arrive on time, and spent the night before the interview awake with those "I'm so nervous I'm gonna puke" butterflies. Luckily I didn't puke, and as I took a seat around the oversized conference table, I gracefully moved from nervous into my natural groove of confidence. This was my passion after all, and if there is one thing I knew, it was sex.

"Our culture has linked nudity with sexuality," I explained in a dignified tone, to the bored woman who sat across from me picking the dirt from underneath her fingernails. "And since our culture is rooted in erotophobia, now we see nudity being vilified. We see mothers getting arrested on child pornography charges for developing photos of their infants naked at bath time. It's absurd. I actually conducted my own research on this topic for one of the more popular articles I wrote for my...." She yawned, and my mind searched for a reason to not get up and walk out of right then and there. "My...sex column." I managed to finish the sentence despite my confidence being knocked down a peg with each flake of dirt that fell to the table in front of her. I was quickly growing to despise her. I don't know if she realized I was done talking, or even that I'd ever started, but apparently caked fingernail crud was far more interesting than what I had to offer.

I didn't get the job.

This went on for five hundred more resumes that I sent across the nation and a handful of similarly pitiful interviews.

More than once I had the "sorry, you don't have a master's degree" and the "sorry, you don't speak Spanish" doors slammed in my face, so I bought a Spanish learning CD and enrolled in a human sexuality master's program, meanwhile selling off the contents of my messy bedroom on Ebay to fill my gas tank. I even got uninvited to an interview with the sexuality education department of Planned Parenthood when they called to meet with me and then subsequently called to tell me not to bother coming in. Does that actually happen? This was my first go-around with interviewing in the "real world," but I had to imagine it wasn't a good sign. As if this process wasn't already bad enough, now it was moving backwards.

I wanted more than anything to be a sexuality educator. Ideally I dreamed of someday traveling the country on speaking tours, giving seminars and motivational speeches on sexual empowerment at colleges, conferences, and other venues. I wanted to pack auditoriums with a fun and quirky sex education comedy show or a stage show. It was my ten-year career plan. But in the meantime I would take any opportunity − if only one would present itself.

I got excited again when I received a call back early one morning from a pregnancy center. From what I read on their website, they were an organization that offered pregnancy testing and options counseling to women facing an unplanned pregnancy in order to educate them on all of their options. Once the woman had made a decision, she was referred to either an abortion doctor, adoption agency, or obstetrician.

The woman asked me a few questions about my degree and experience, and then she asked me in the same professional tone, not skipping a beat, "Jill, how do you balance your faith with your role as a sexuality educator and counselor?"

Come again?

I couldn't believe she asked me that. I was confused. And shocked. I was pretty sure it wasn't legal to ask questions about religion during an interview, but what was I to do? Should I call her out or answer the question? Would answering it honestly cost me a job that I *desperately* needed?

"Um," I started. "I don't. Um, I don't 'balance' my…faith, I don't really…" I was going to say I don't have faith but that wasn't entirely true, plus I thought saying that might screw me over for this job because obviously having faith was important to this women, otherwise she wouldn't be asking me. And then I thought, why should I have to defend myself? Not only was her question illegal, but completely inappropriate, and if I was going to not get this job because of my religious beliefs, then I was going to go down with an "up yours." Actually I didn't think about all that until after I hung up the phone and realized how pissed off I was. But before I did that, I said, "I don't believe one's religious beliefs, whatever they may be, should influence the way they educate or counsel others about sexuality. I think that's misleading and biased and unethical." Needless to say, I was not offered the job.

I later found out that this so-called pregnancy center was actually a covert Christian organization with a mission to steer women away from abortion while hailing themselves as a health center offering legitimate counseling and a variety of options. I had been duped! And I wondered how many women were also duped by this agency and manipulated into carrying a pregnancy because they trusted these people. The only thing more unethical than using your power and authority and personal bias to influence the lives of others is doing it without revealing your agenda.

After several more months of no callbacks from the resumes I sent to every clinic, health, community, or education center from Miami to San Francisco, my massive student loan debt came a-calling, and I was desperate for any type of paying gig, sexuality related or not. I was unfortunate enough to graduate college in 2007, on the cusp of the worst economic recession since the Great Depression. That, coupled with Bush's $100 million abstinence only agenda, was not going to make starting a career in sexuality education easy. "Just take what you can find for now," I told myself, "and when the economy turns around there will be more possibilities." Like the bitterness of a shot without a chaser, I grimaced, swallowed the pride of my Dean's List college

11

education, and applied to be a part-time receptionist, even a Hooters waitress, but despite my excellent telephone voice and 35-25-35-inch frame, I was not hired for either position.

I started to feel depressed, downtrodden, and was ready to give up hope. When I was passed over after yet another interview, this time for a job that paid barely above the poverty line and required me to stand on the street corners in the slums of North Philly handing out clean needles to IV drug users, I reached the end of my rope. "You were an excellent candidate," the interviewer said when she called me with the news, "but we decided to go with a bilingual applicant with a master's Degree."

"To hell with this nonsense," I thought bitterly after hanging up, realizing with an angry ball of acid turning somersaults in my stomach that all of my roads were officially blockaded. Snowed in. No outlet. I was fresh out of places to turn. So just like that, I decided if no one would pay me to be a sexuality educator, damn it, I would do it myself. I sold the Spanish learning CD at a garage sale for $4 and began writing my business plan. It was that impulsive a decision. Just like that.

All of these setbacks had brought me to a quaint little corner store in the winter of 2008. It had big windows and hardwood floors. The building was available for rent in the heart of West Chester, Pennsylvania, a bustling college town outside of Philadelphia, with trendy shops and restaurants. As soon as I saw it I began daydreaming about the finished product. I could already see in my mind where I would put the lingerie racks, where I would house the shelves with massage lotions, how I would create a comfortable seating area for the sexual empowerment workshops I would teach. I envisioned the sensual artwork, which I already had picked out, on the walls and the merchandise tables draped in pink satin. The commercial realtor I contacted about renting the building seemed delighted to have an interested renter, especially at a time when so many small businesses were having difficulty weathering the recession. Things were finally looking up. My hard work was finally going to pay off. Instead, I soon found out that due to the "nature of my business," the owners of the property would not rent it to me. Of course they wouldn't.

"I'm calling to give the daily report," I announced as I'd done a million times before. "What are you up to?"

Other twenty-one-year-olds were partying, drinking, and watching television, but with my fifteen-hour-a-day job of starting a business, the only form of entertainment I could squeeze into my busy schedule was a daily rehashing session with my best friend, George, where I poured over every detail and idiosyncrasy of mundane everyday life, a la an episode of *Seinfeld*.

"I'm folding my laundry," he said. For most people the conversation would veer into something like, "That's nice. So what are we doing on Friday night?" Ours went as follows:

Me: Folding? You're a folder?
George: Yes I'm a folder. What are you, a hanger?
Me: I've been known to hang, for the most part. And even though the rest of my place is a disaster, my closet must be organized with all the hangers the same color and facing the same direction.
George: That's because you're insane.
Me: No.
George: Ok, well what is hung and what is folded? That is the question.
Me: Everything is hung, other than underwear.
George: What about t-shirts? You hang t-shirts?

Conversations like this were a foundational part of our friendship. Not many eleven-year-olds fiercely debate politics, but on Election Day, 1996, George and I spent the walk to the sixth grade bus stop intensely discussing Clinton and Dole. He grew up a mere thirteen row homes away from mine, and since second grade I remember playing house with him on our small rectangular lawns. Other girls on the street and I used lawn furniture for a pretend living room, while George tried to bulldoze them down to build an imaginary courthouse in an effort to entice us to play lawyer instead. He was chubby, incapable of speaking in anything but a boisterous, bellowing Italian tone of voice, and talking with his hands. His incredible intelligence was offset by his cockiness, and growing up, all he could talk about was what he was being taught in school as if it should be the most obvious thing to everyone else who had yet to learn it. His strict grandparents kept him on a tight leash, so he became one of the girls, playing our games or playing by himself.

"So anywho.," I said melodically before any more of my life was spent discussing my laundering habits. "I do have news to report today. Since, as you know, I couldn't get that corner store with the big windows and hardwood floors, I decided to rent another one just two blocks away!" He was happy that I had found a place, albeit a rundown tavern with neon green walls, to house Feminique Boutique. Finally, something was going my way, although I think we both knew that the setbacks were only beginning.

Chapter 2

Like any young girl, I wanted my first kiss to be special. Not just special, but unforgettable and sweep-me-off-my-feet wonderfully romantic. When I was eight years old I played doll house and made my boy doll be so sweet and madly in love with my little girl doll. I played for hours at a time and always dreamed that their imaginary lives would be my own someday. When I was twelve years old, *Titanic* came to the theaters, and I was captured by the famous kissing scene at the front of the ship. How perfect was that sunset, that music, that kiss?

In my dreams, a summer pool party would conclude with Prince Charming throwing me into the water, while we both giggled flirtatiously. He would then push aside my dripping wet locks, moving towards me in slow motion, lift my mouth to his, and kiss me. Or better yet, at a school dance the man of my dreams would grab a microphone and sing me a love song before walking towards me on the dance floor. The audience, parting like the Red Sea, would leave me alone in the center of the room, everyone watching as he ran up to me and spun me around, locked in a kiss.

I had it all planned out, but unlike most of my eighth grade peers who were discovering the fine art of French kissing, I was hanging around with my best friends, Pat Abramowitz and George

Greccio, the two dorkiest kids in school, which wasn't exactly conducive to fulfilling plans. Plus, I had built up a romantic ideal so high that the thought of kissing a boy was downright petrifying. Despite all this, right before the school year ended, I took a liking to Pat's buddy, Mike. I knew he liked me too when I found myself being prompted for a kiss.

"Jill, we're dating now. It's no big deal."

He was tall for a thirteen-year-old and he seemed even taller leaning over me, my back pushed up helplessly against a chain link fence. With one arm on each side to block me in, we stood that way for three hours. His prompting became begging, and the begging became a frustrated mocking.

"What is the matter with you?" he demanded. "Don't tell me you've never hooked up before." *Hooking up.* Ugh. I loathed the new "cool kid" expression for kissing, which made something so beautiful sound so crude. My thoughts crossed between wanting to get it over with to panicking on how to get out of this awkward situation before making myself the subject of tomorrow's fodder with his friends. I decided on the former and begrudgingly leaned in. The nervous puke butterflies were upon me. My mind was racing: *"Am I supposed to turn my head to the left or right? What if we both go the same direction and we bump noses?"* My internal pondering was enough to make me pause mid-lean-in. He went for it anyway, and I turned my face away in disgust like a child trying to escape an incoming spoonful of strained peas.

"I can't believe you're such a baby." His anger was mounting as was my desire to get out. With my back still pinned against my neighbor's fence, I was relieved to see his mom's minivan pass by as she looked for her son who was now hours late for curfew. I watched him drive away with his mom and felt filled with an anxiety I couldn't express. The attempted kiss was neither spontaneous nor romantic as it had been in my dreams, but knowing that didn't make it sting any less when he dumped me a few days later via a degrading note he passed to Pat.

Pat showed up at my seventh period classroom before the bell rang on Monday with a folded up piece of loose-leaf in his hand. His khaki pants were flood high, exposing mismatched socks, but for once it was not his geekiness, but rather his concerned eyes that caught my attention. "Here, Mike told me not to let you see this, but I just think it's so wrong and that you should know," he said as he handed me the paper and dashed off to his own class before my teacher caught him in ours. The note was written in pencil, the lettering smudged and scratchy.

Mike: She's a bore.
Pat: Bore! I don't think so. She is very outgoing. I don't know how you get that.
Mike: Just because you like her doesn't mean I have to.
Pat: I don't but I do feel bad for her because of what you're doing to her.
Mike: What the fuck am I doing?
Pat: You're going to dump her because of nothing.
Mike: It was nothing to begin with.
Pat: On Saturday you were all over her! And you said yourself you're thankful you gave her a chance.
Mike: She can't do it for me.
Pat: Give her a chance. She wants to hook up.
Mike: Oh, hell no!
Pat: You were on your knees begging her to do it.
Mike: It was an act! Get that through your fucking redhead ass.
Pat: You don't act that out. I'm sorry but that is total disrespect.
Mike: I'm an actor, damn it!

Even though he denied it, it was no secret that Pat had a crush on me, and although it was also obvious he was one of the "nice guys" grown women spoke about there being so few of, I just couldn't stomach the idea of being seen with him in public in the capacity of "boyfriend." Our friendship was already bad enough for my image. A few days after he defended my honor in Mike's breakup note, Pat called me and asked me to be his date to the Eighth Grade Dinner Dance. This was the end of the year formal I'd been waiting my entire middle school career to attend. I turned him down, only half lying when I cited a desire to get back with Mike and go with him as my excuse.

"You want to go with Mike? After the things he said about you?" he questioned.

"Yes," I said, "I want my first kiss, and the Dinner Dance will be a perfect time to do it." I thought Pat would be hurt, upset, or at least have a bit of a bruised ego from my rebuff, but he wasn't.

"Well if that's what you really want. All I've ever wanted is for you to be happy." And to my astonishment, he called Mike and argued my case for me, trying to convince him to bring me as his date. Mike refused.

On the June night, after the obligatory photo session with our parents in my living room, I ended up going to the formal as a group with George, Pat, and my only female friend, Scarlet. The four of us were having a good time until I spotted Mike with his gelled hair and blue tie dancing in our gym under the canopy of streamers. He saw me looking at him, and nervous puke butterflies fluttered away in my stomach when he crossed the room toward me.

"You should dance with Abramowitz," Mike said as he approached, trying to pass me off, trying to distract my interest in him. I looked at our mutual friend, Pat Abramowitz, standing in front of me, his hands clasped, graceful pleading on his face. I didn't think about the time he got on his bike and chased away a group of older girls who were trying to jump me on the playground. I didn't think about how he was one of the only people who didn't make fun of my never-been-kissed status or my peace-love-and-happiness hippie bit. Instead, I was thinking about his kinky curly red hair and flood pants, his goofy laugh, his high pitched voice, his inability to keep up in conversation with George and I, his blissful ignorance of politics. It was frustrating. How could he not care what was going on in the world? I looked at Pat Abramowitz standing in front of me, in his Sunday best of a tucked-in flannel button up and no tie, and I just couldn't do it.

"I don't want to. I want to dance with you. Will you dance

with me?" I responded to Mike just as the first few notes of a love song began to play.

"Okay," he said. "Give me a second." He turned around, I thought to put down his glass of punch, but instead he walked straight into the arms of Brianna Benson, a plain-looking brunette I never thought twice about, but now envied. He never looked back. Just as the sting of such rejection was setting in, another couple walked passed me hand in hand to find a spot on the dance floor, and they noticed that I was upset.

"What's wrong? Are you gonna cry because they aren't playing your flower power music?" the boy said.

"Not that that matters. She cries even when they do," added the girl. They were poking fun of an episode in art class the year before in seventh grade. While we sat at the tables working on our shading-with-charcoal project, the art teacher put on the radio to the classic rock station. It made my day, and I began singing along loudly, even though everyone laughed at my enthusiasm for songs that were written before any of us were born. But then Harry Chapin's *Cat's in the Cradle* came on. That song always makes me cry. The last thing I wanted was to give them the satisfaction of seeing me be moved to tears by a song they dismissed as a meaningless old fogey tune. So despite my pleading with my teacher to change the station, which only made the spectacle worse, the song played on, and I inevitably cried.

I didn't know why the song affected me in such a way, and I wouldn't figure it out until ten years later, but nevertheless it did, and was yet another opportunity to be teased and bullied.

"Assholes," I thought. I tried to ignore their comments and turned to find Pat, who was now slow dancing with Nikki Russo. Nikki was a tall bi-racial girl with a sweet, naïve demeanor. Nikki Russo, Brianna Benson: these girls weren't in Pat or Mike's social circles. In fact I'd never even seen them in the same room until that moment. What was going on? The quintessential late 90s slow dance prom song, *Angel of Mine*, played on as I stood there alone. The couples danced against a backdrop of folded bleachers doused with glitter-covered star-shaped cutouts. Mike and Brianna, Pat and Nikki, the asshole couple, flowing gowns, curly up-dos, arm in arm, chest to chest. But I stood alone.

And so began the summer of bellyaching over my lost first kiss opportunity with Michael Higgins.

Chapter 3

If it weren't for the classic rock music coming through the massive boom box circa 1986, on the floor of my shop, I would have gone stir crazy. As it turns out, painting took five times longer than originally anticipated, and I was still going at it three weeks later. I was becoming very accustomed to figuring out the whole "how to run a business" thing as I went. I figured out how to make a website. And how to become incorporated. Figuring out that it takes eighteen gallons of paint rather than the projected four to cover hideous green was another piece of knowledge I picked up along the way.

I also figured out that one of the more frustrating aspects of starting a small business was setting up the credit card processor – finding a reputable company out of the millions of scammers, linking it up with a bank account, a cable line, and trying to figure out the complicated rate structures to see which company was offering the best deal. It took a lot of work. I finally signed a contract with a company through a national bank and was thrilled to get my card swiping machine in the mail. The dream of owning my own sex-positive feminist sex shop – my own center from which to travel and pack auditoriums and conference centers with my fun, witty, and educational sex seminars – was getting closer and closer to fruition. I couldn't wait to get that machine and swipe my personal credit card through, just for one penny, just so I could see "Feminique Boutique" come up on my statement. Ahh. I could almost taste it!

But…there was another setback. Of course there was.

A few days after I signed the contract I received an email from the credit card company.

"We took a look at your website, and unfortunately we will not be able to process any credit cards for Feminique Boutique due to the nature of your business," it read. There was that pesky "nature of my business" again. First the "nature of my business" precluded me from renting the storefront I wanted, and now it meant I wouldn't be able to accept credit card payments in my boutique or online. This was a major problem. Who carries cash anymore?

"What do you mean by 'the nature of my business?'" I asked in a follow-up phone call.

"Well," the man started, "we have a policy against servicing businesses in the adult entertainment industry."

Adult Entertainment? To me, adult entertainment was flashing neon "Girls! Girls! Girls!" signs, lime green lycra thongs, and a DVD collection of titles like "Back Seat Drivers 4" and "Bangin' the Babysitter 26." Teaching women about the power and beauty of their sexuality is "adult entertainment?" I did not like this blanket anti-Adult Entertainment clause.

When I was a kid, I thought sex was so gross and dirty that I had to cover my ears when hearing the word "vagina" – a part of my own body. My parents were open-minded and spoke candidly about sex during my childhood, and yet I still received the message that sex, my vagina, and all words associated with those things were bad. How did I come to receive and internalize these scripts if not from my parents? Perhaps because as a child I couldn't tell the difference between exploitative sexuality and pleasurable sexuality. Perhaps the person who wouldn't rent the storefront to me and the powers that be in charge of writing up policies at the credit card processors couldn't tell the difference either. Perhaps in our sex negative country, no one can. What a sad state of affairs that porn and sexuality are indistinguishable.

I felt like I was in a rubber band room being bounced around in a catch-22. Our society is sex-negative, but I was having a hard time setting up a business to try to fight sex-negativity because of the sex-negative social structures that were in place, and to combat those sex-negative social structures I needed a sex-positive education business, but I couldn't do that because sex-negative social structures…and back and forth and back and forth I bounced.

The most frustrating part of this setback was not the fact that I was being denied access to something because of sexuality, or even that I was being lumped into the same category as escort services and hardcore porn. My biggest frustration was that although they wouldn't live up to their end of the contract by accessing customer credit cards when swiped and depositing the money into my Feminique Boutique bank account, they held me to my end of the contract and required me to continue paying the monthly fee. For two years. For a service they wouldn't let me use.

"Don't you think that's a little odd?" I demanded after many rounds with customer service representatives. "If you don't want to do business with me because I sell vibrators, fine, but why do I keep having to pay this monthly service charge?" I never got an answer.

I chalked it up to one more thing I was learning along the way in the Business School of Hard Knocks: read a company's policy on adult entertainment *before* signing a contract with them.

With this newest lesson learned, I was getting highly anxious about the one step to getting Feminique up and running that I had continued to avoid. Dragging my feet. Dreading. That was getting a business permit from the Borough of West Chester, Pennsylvania, where my store was located. I'd already spent so much money, invested so much heart. After my dead-end job hunt in the months prior, I knew this business was my last opportunity. What if the borough of West Chester had a provision against "adult entertainment" too?

Bosses, lawyers, George W. Bush – few things make me

more uncomfortable than a man in a suit, and I was seriously stressing over how I would go about getting a permit to open a sex shop from the suits in the local government of West Chester.

When doing the research for my business plan, I had read online horror stories of sex shops and strip clubs, adult bookstores, and topless coffee shops forced to close or denied permits and not allowed to open due to little known loopholes of questionable legal merit in local zoning codes.

I started reading about a woman-owned sex shop in Pittsburgh that in 2005 was shut down one week after opening because it did not have a business permit. The owner had paid the fees for the permit and was given a verbal confirmation that it was in the mail, but town officials apparently decided at the last minute that her boutique selling lingerie, sexy costumes, and bachelorette party supplies should be considered a "sexually oriented business," and thus would have to close and reopen, if at all, in the city's industrial zoning district next to the strip clubs and porn shops. It took nearly a year to straighten out the legal mess, and it cost her countless thousands in legal fees, not to mention the rent she was paying for the store and lost business income.

Even worse, in 2007, a Lubbock, Texas, sex shop was raided by police officers who hauled away hundreds of vibrators. The female clerk, who sold a dildo to an undercover cop who asked to see the hidden display, was arrested, and at the time it was still unclear whether or not the state would make her register as a sex offender. An adult making a decision to use an instrument to touch their own bodies in one's own home: a crime. The person who sells them the instrument to do it: a sex criminal, in the same category as the person who forces scared children to pose naked for pictures and the person who forcibly rapes a woman as she kicks and cries for help.

Register as a sex offender. Fucking seriously?

The sexual world I was living in frankly terrified the shit out of me, as a woman, as a freedom-loving American, as a sexual being. The Lubbock area newspaper reported that the rationale of the police department for the bust was Chapter 43 of the Texas

Penal Code, which prohibits a person from possessing six or more "obscene devices," described as "a dildo or artificial vagina, designed and marketed as useful primarily for the stimulation of human genital organs." Texans have the right to own six guns, but they do not have the right to own six sex toys.

As I felt my mind starting to battle all that was wrong with these news stories, all that was inherently unfair and repressive, my stress about getting a permit to open a sex shop from the suits in West Chester mounted. Could something this preposterous happen to me? Were these just isolated, albeit outrageous incidents – the result of overzealous police or government officials up for reelection – and not the norm, not a true barometer of the lengths that those in authority will go to ease their discomfort about sex? The sex-negative structures I was fighting – the property owner who wouldn't rent to me, the credit processor that wouldn't do business with me – could the fear of sex really go this deep? Could the government really stop me from operating Feminique? I didn't think such an injustice could slap me in the face. No, that couldn't happen to me.

So although I couldn't shake the anxious feeling I had, not quite nervous puke butterflies but a dull nagging concern, I knew I needed to stop procrastinating. I left the shop that night with Jimi Hendrix blaring through the static on my radio with the intention of making getting the permit next on my to-do list. I just left the wet roller on the tarp. It would be hard as a brick the next day, but I didn't care. I was sick of painting.

Other small business owners in town stopped by from time to time to give me a hand and check up on me. I thought it was sweet, and I took advantage of their kindness to press them for information on my permit-seeking plight. "He's a real dick," one said of Anthony Ciccerone, the go-to guy in West Chester for such administrative tasks.

"He will destroy you," said another. "If Ciccerone wants you out of business he will find a way to do it. He hates my shop so he told me I needed $100,000 worth of work done to be up to code, which was complete bullshit." The young man with scraggly facial hair and dirty work pants didn't exactly fit into the upper middle class neighborhood, and it wasn't shocking that the suits would want him out. I was disturbed by the injustice. And scared.

"Well that's just fantastic...," I started. Sarcasm is one of my strong suits. "What the hell am I supposed to do now? I'm going to go out of business before I even start! This is ridiculous! What if that happens to me? I don't have $100,000!" Sarcasm may be one of my strong suits, but controlling my emotions – not so much.

I was looking for a comforting older brother-like response from my fellow business owners. Instead I got, "Just don't piss him off. Good luck."

As a child, my dad tried to teach me that you get further with honey than vinegar, and I had read in a self-help book somewhere that if you smile on the phone it resonates in your voice and the listener responds more positively. For some reason I actually thought this would work for me when I made the first phone call to the borough regarding permits and was thus surprised to be greeted with the bored indifferent tone typical of bureaucrats in response.

"Hello, Mr. Ciccerone, my name is Jill McDevitt," I said, enthusiastically smiling all the way. "You, sir, are a difficult man to get a hold of." I kept smiling and paused to wait for a response that didn't come, so I continued. "I was eager to get in touch with you last week but your assistant said you were in Palm Springs. That must've been an enjoyable trip." More smiles.

"It was on business, lady, give me a break. What can I do for you?" he barked.

"Well..." I continued. "I am opening a small business in the borough, and I understand I need a permit to do this. I wanted to make sure that this wouldn't be a problem given what kind of business I'll be opening. It's going to be a female sexuality boutique." Another pause. This guy was killing me.

"Send me a copy of your business plan, and I'll have the solicitor look at it. Good day." He hung up. I didn't even know what a solicitor was until I asked my disgruntled friend and fellow

West Chester small business owner and found out it's the attorney that represents a town. A lawyer. Ugh. Put that on the list of things I was learning along the way.

I was overdue for a daily report with George, and he called as I was neurotically reading and rereading the edited (I would say "censored" but I don't like that word) version of my business plan I had sent to Anthony Ciccerone in West Chester's Borough Hall. I was trying to determine how the solicitor could possibly find my business in any way unworthy of a permit. Was I just being paranoid? The wait was unnerving.

George: How goes it, my friend?
Me: Oh it goes. Fear not, it goes.
George: That is never a bad thing.
Me: You are correct about that.

It's amazing how long a dialogue can last without actually saying anything.

Me: So how was the job interview?
George: Tell me what you think of this one. I'm sitting in the office, and I'm yucking it up with the secretary waiting for the head of the math department to come in, and she offers me a pretzel.
Me: Ok...
George: The question is...should I have taken it?
Me: Is it a hard pretzel or a soft pretzel?
George: It's a soft pretzel, and she offered me mustard and everything.
Me: Was it the last one?
George: No, there was a whole platter of them.
Me: Then sure, you could've taken it. Why, did you?
George: I did but I still think I screwed myself. She offered it once, and I said "No thanks." Then she offered again, and I said no again. Then the Math guy comes out of his office, and he insists that I take one because otherwise they'll go to waste, so I oblige.
Me: That's so belligerent to ask three times. Who does that? Like

27

it's your responsibility if their food goes to waste. Would they not give you a job because you don't eat soft pretzels? How do they know you don't have a food allergy? To hell with them.

I was so glad I wasn't doing the interview thing anymore. What a nightmare.

George: Anyway, did you ever get a hold of that guy?
Me: Anthony Ciccerone? Yeah, a few days ago. I need to call him back to make sure he got my business plan. I should do that today, actually.
George: Can you believe we're talking about this? I'm going to be a teacher. You own a business. We're getting so old.
Me: I know. I know.

After I was finished talking to George, I grabbed some lunch and then put in the phone call to Anthony Ciccerone that would allow me to mark the permit off my to-do list and put my anxiety to rest. When I was done, I called every number in my cell phone with the news.

George: Didn't I just talk to you?
Mel: I CAN'T OPEN FEMINIQUE BOUTIQUE!!!!
George: Why?
Me: I called Anthony Ciccerone up and asked him if the solicitor (that's the attorney who represents a town, by the way) got a chance to look at my business plan. He was just so nonchalant about it. He said, "Oh yeah, the solicitor concluded your business plan is against our zoning code for adult entertainment so you can't open it. You'll be getting a letter regarding this matter via certified mail. Good day." Can you believe that? No "I'm sorry," no "Unfortunately this is the situation," he just said it like he's so used to dashing people's hopes and dreams on a daily basis that he doesn't even care anymore. Isn't this horrible?
George: Have you looked at the zoning code for adult entertainment in West Chester?

I could always count on George for a sobering, practical response to my emotional outbursts.

Mel: ...No.
George: Maybe you should get a lawyer to look at it. But that's the government for you. If that's their law then that's their law. Unfortunately, there's nothing you can do about that, Jill.

I could also always count on George for accepting the status quo for better or worse, like taking a soft pretzel he didn't want so not to upset some high school math teacher interviewing him for a job. But not me. I wasn't taking the "there's nothing you can do about it approach," and I knew someone who would encourage me not to lie down and take it.

I called my dad at work and told him the horrible news. My father is a dynamic two-sided character who is easier to describe with anecdotes than adjectives. A lover of pop-culture, he's a middle-aged white guy who knows all the words to the latest Kanye hit, and can also engage in a two-hour debate about moral relativism, metaphysics, or string theory while sitting around a bonfire. People like him. People like him the way they like Ferris Beuller. Whoever he meets tells me, "Your dad is such an amazing person," when he leaves the room. I often thought my definition of success would be people saying that about me when I left a room. Of all his fabulous qualities, he ironically wears a suit to his day job. No one's perfect, I guess.

He raised me after his divorce from my mom, and he often found himself in the role of surrogate father to all the neighborhood kids, including Pat, Scarlet, and George. He mended their family fights, attended their little league games and school plays, and was the wise ear to their woes when no one else would listen. He had the take-no-lip parental authority thing going strong, but was never out of touch with the tribulations of youth. He wasn't too good for us. We could even curse around him. I knew early on that the term "two peas in a pod" was written to describe us. We were always on the same page: about life, about what to order for take-out, about anything. And he always had my back, which for the longest time I thought all dads did. It wasn't until later that I realized many don't.

"You can be anything you want to be," he would say to me regularly. "Do what you love, and the money will follow. And if you do that, I will be proud of you no matter what." Being the smart ass that he raised me to be, I once countered, "Anything? What if I want to grow up to be a prostitute? Would you be proud of me then?"

He took a deep breath indicating an honest contemplation and then said, "If you did it because it made you happy, not because you had no other options. If you said, 'Dad, this is my calling, my dream job,' and you were the best prostitute you could be, then yes, I would be proud of you." You can see why I sought him out for straightforward advice during times like these.

"Dad!" I whined over the phone as soon as he answered. "What should I do? I tried the whole 'you get further with honey than vinegar' thing with the Ciccerone guy but it didn't work for me. I'm not diplomatic like you are."

"Well it's a good skill to learn, but when that fails, you gotta stick it to The Man," he said. "Don't let 'em get you down, Jill. We're all behind you, not just me, but your mom and Gram and the rest of the family too. You're strong, much stronger than I am, and you have to fight for what you believe in. It's going to be hard, and you might lose, but you know in your heart what you have to do."

He was right. Stick it to The Man. That's what I intended to do. I waited with nervous puke butterflies in my stomach for eighteen hours for the certified letter that carried my fate as a businesswoman to arrive, and then I put on my suit, the same one I had worn during my rejected job interviews, and marched to Anthony Ciccerone's office in West Chester's Borough Hall.

Chapter 4

School was out, and my obsession over Michael Higgins, or Mike "Asshole" Higgins as my friends maturely referred to him, became a huge source of annoyance real fast. George was spared the brunt of it since he spent all summer down the Jersey Shore with his dad every year. And although Scarlet and I had our girly sleepovers and carefree days at the neighborhood swimming pool, Pat seemed to be the only one who would stick around day after day during the dog days of summer listening to me carry on.

One day I would be hurt over the broken three-week relationship and sit in my room writing bad love poetry and changing the lyrics of songs to make them fit my adolescent dilemma. The next day I would be angry about the way I was mistreated and insist that I was too good to chase after a guy like Mike "Asshole" Higgins. Pat always agreed with this. Then the day after that I was back to being sad, thinking about the stuffed Mr. Potato Head Mike won for me at a carnival before school let out and agonizing over the lost kiss opportunity. It was enough to drive anyone insane.

Pat and I lay on the faded brown carpet in my living room one boring afternoon with our heads propped up against the bottom of my couch. Other than the air conditioner hum, the house was quiet, and I decided to break the silence. "Abramowitz, what was your happiest moment of eighth grade?"

"Probably making friends with you guys. You, Scarlet, and George, even though he's annoying and you two talk really weird to each other. And dating Nikki." Ever since the Dinner Dance Pat and Nikki had been an item, as much as thirteen-year-olds in two different towns on summer vacation can be an item, anyway. The conversation went on without even turning our necks to look at one another. "What was yours?"

"When Mike won me Mr. Potato Head at the carnival. It was May 24, 1999. And my saddest moment was..."

"Let me guess," he interrupted. "When Mike broke up with you."

"Yes," I said quietly. "What was yours?" Breaking with the tradition of the previous three minutes, Pat turned to look at me. Sensing his stare, I turned my head too. He was serious, and just like the infamous day he handed me Mike's breakup note, his eyes looked so big and so blue I couldn't help but stare back into them.

"It was the day you said 'no' to me, Jill." I turned back straight ahead with a jerk. He was so matter-of-fact, so honest, so unfearing of a rejection even though he knew one was coming. I was incredibly uncomfortable with the sudden intensity in the room, but I had to admire the balls on this kid. Me, turning him down to the Dinner Dance was his saddest moment of the year, and yet he didn't cry about his loss like I did. In fact he selflessly tried to get me a date with Mike instead. I was beginning to admire a lot about him.

"Why do you have to say stuff like that?" I responded in disgust. "I'm going to make some popcorn," and I quickly got up and scurried into the kitchen. A few moments later I brought the popcorn back in and changed the subject.

In mid-July George came home from the shore for a dentist's appointment, and I was excited that his stern grandparents actually let him out rather than making him go to bed early so he'd be well rested for his trip back the next day. As usual, we couldn't agree on something to do, so George, Scarlet, and I made the two-mile walk to McDonald's, our standard means of pre-driver's license entertainment. I wanted to bring him up to date with my summer, but in some ways I was embarrassed about what I'd been up to, all the time I was spending alone with Pat.

We walked along the streets lined with brick row homes and crossed busy intersections, all the while debating politics. We passed a gun shop and a rinky-dink discount store. There wasn't much in the way of recreation for teens in my town, which is why at thirteen years old some of my classmates were already pregnant and on drugs. Cute kids who I remembered fighting with over the next turn on the swings on the school playground in second grade were now vandalizing those swings with obscene graffiti and empty dime bags. It was never spoken, but George, Pat, Scarlet, and I knew we were too smart to give up on ourselves that easily. We were very different, but self-respect was the glue that held us together. So we stuck to our wholesome McDonald's hangout, our political debates, and our innocent musings about crushes.

"That girl in Texas – sucks to be her but the school has the right to implement uniforms," said George, referencing a recent political news story.

"Uniforms are not good. Not only do they repress individuality but they are also inherently sexist. Unless boys are required to wear skirts too, it's bullshit," I replied.

George rebutted, "Uniforms reduce violence because teachers can see if students are hiding weapons, and it reduces distractions and bullying of kids whose parents can't afford nice cloths."

We waited to cross on green, getting stares from a little old lady annoyed by our bellowing. We may have had impressive vocabularies for thirteen-year-olds, but we still had a lot of growing up to do. We had yet to master the art of debate, and our "debates" the summer going into ninth grade were more like screaming matches and battles of will.

"This girl wore a black armband to voice her protest about the dress code. She didn't disturb anyone. She didn't hurt anyone. Who is the school to dictate what she can and cannot wear?" I argued.

"Schools have the right to kick out students who disobey their rule."

"There is a little piece of paper I like to call THE GOOD OLE' CONSTITUTION! And it says that..."

"NO, NO, NO! I don't..." George interrupted.

"SHUT UP GEORGE!" yelled Scarlet.

When we started cutting each other off and screaming over each other, Scarlet stepped in to stifle George, whose voice was naturally louder than the rest of our voices combined. No one's feelings were hurt. It was all in the name of amusement. The discussion carried us to the next intersection, where I noticed a graying black woman driving a car that I didn't recognize, with a dorky kid with freckles and braces in the back seat who I did.

"Jill!" Pat yelled, "Wait up!" and he leaped out of the car just as the light turned green.

"Abramowitz, what are you doing?" I asked. Pat's girlfriend, Nikki, and her grandmother were driving him home after a date when the sudden action unfolded. "You just ditched your girlfriend in the middle of the street during a date to hang out with other girls! Are you insane?"

"I've never been on a date, but even I know that's stupid Abramowitz," George added. "And I'm not a girl!" We tried to resume our safety and order versus freedom of expression conversation but Pat was indifferent and carefree about it as usual, which to me was an invitation for more insults.

'You're such a moron, Abramowitz, don't you understand how this stuff affects your life?" Apparently he didn't. Despite my harsh tone, I was incredibly flattered that he wanted to see me so badly that he dropped everything at a second's notice and insulted his girlfriend in order to be in my presence. I would never admit it, of course. I just walked on to McDonalds with a little smile inside.

Chapter 5

West Chester's brand new municipal building stood on the outskirts of downtown. There were suits galore, but that day I was one of them. It's amazing how strangers look at you with an air of reverence when you wear a suit, even if it's a skirt suit with black pumps and no pantyhose. It's like you're suddenly part of their little club.

I tensely approached the Department of Building, Housing and Code Enforcement, written on a small plaque outside a service window on the second floor. You could see the office inside, with yellowing walls plastered in zoning maps of town, carelessly taped and tearing. The desks were covered with papers sprawled in something that was barely recognizable as piles, as well as the token personalized pen canisters and photos of children. The building was new but this office was already a bureaucrat's dream.

"I'd like a copy of the borough's zoning code of adult entertainment," I instructed the woman at the window counter. The department likely deals with hundreds of people a day, most of whom are nameless blurs, but she smiled at me knowingly. She returned promptly with a photocopy out of the law books and told me that Anthony Ciccerone would return from a codes inspection in forty-five minutes if I wished to discuss it with him.

I sat in the lobby and studied the carbon copy papers.

"Legal mumbo-jumbo. Rambling sentences. Circular wording. Value-laden ideology that has no business in the law," I said to myself. I feverishly scanned it a half dozen times before I even started to understand it. The code read:

An establishment wherein live displays of the human body without covering are conducted or an enclosed building used for presenting materials related to specified sexual activities or specified anatomical areas for observation by patrons therein.

If I hadn't been so angry and my livelihood hadn't depended on the seriousness of the situation, I would have laughed out loud. I was not selling porn, I was not opening a strip club or anything else involving "live displays of the human body without covering," as described in the regulation. What an odd way to write a law. And what was a "specified anatomical area" anyway? The language in this document was just so amusing to me, in a sick, disheartening kind of way. Would the chiropractor's office down the street be shut down because their clients exposed their backs and shoulders? What about all the people walking around with their noses and earlobes just hanging out for the world to see? No. While oddly never specified in the code, I assumed the "specified anatomical areas" in question were the ones that bring pleasure, and thus a bunch of people in suits had decided were dirty, and now illegal.

I continued to sit on the slotted wooden benches, reviewing potential conversations with Anthony Ciccerone in my head. I plotted out the stance I would take, the words I would use, I imagined him apologetic, tearing up the law ceremoniously after I gave an inspirational speech the way the antagonist always does at the end of movies. I *was* wearing a suit after all, and that gave me power.

Twenty minutes had passed, and the wait was brutal. The longer I sat, the more revved up I became. I knew I was doing the right thing; it was just a matter of getting Anthony Ciccerone to believe it.

While I was doing all the work to set up my retail store in West Chester, I was running the business out of my house, and I had seen how much my sex toys were helping people, in more than just the obvious way. Could I convince Anthony Ciccerone?

It started after I finished typing up my business plan. I purchased a selection of wholesale vibrators, lubricants, edible body toppings, and massage oils to sell and wrote the script for a workshop on female sexuality. My dad paid for the first shipment of products as a belated college graduation present, and although some may find it odd to receive a thirty-two-pound box of dildos as a gift from one's father, we thought of it as a business investment. I had decided that my new career would be as the proprietor of a sex education center and sex shop. Ironically, I still had never used anything one would find *in* a sex shop – no massage lotion, no thigh-high stockings, and certainly not a vibrator. In my lifelong prudish innocence I didn't even really understand the appeal at first, but I rationalized it like this: in a perfect world, I would love to get paid to spread the good word about sexuality and educate folks about things I am passionate about, such as evolutionary sexual biology and the role of concealed ovulation in human pair bonding, the restrictiveness and inherent sexism of the cultural phenomenon of "spit or swallow," genital integrity and the ethics of circumcision, the resiliency of the human heart and the process of grieving a relationship breakup…I could go on and on.

But in realizing no one was going to pay me to talk about these things, I discovered the first three truths about running a sex education business. People will *not* pay for knowledge. People *will* pay to be entertained, and people *will* pay for tangible things that are immediately beneficial.

I became inventive in finding ways to get people to pay me to provide them with sex education while entertaining them and selling them products. My philosophy became one of "edutainment" – get them in the door for a "girls' night out," and while they were in my grasp throw some schooling at them (entertainment), then sell them the corresponding merchandise (tangible items that are immediately beneficial), ensuring I could earn my modest living. "Workshops" became "parties," and I became so good at entertaining, no one noticed they were actually being educated. I sold pheromone-enhancing oil while educating the party guests about the use of olfactory hormones in evolutionary sexual biology. I sold an oral sex enhancing product while teaching how to make blowjobs more enjoyable by removing the subservient attitude. The goodies were a way for me to talk to people about sex, and when it comes to *talking* about sex, I am no holds barred.

I presented my first workshop/party at an old friend's bridal shower, followed by one for a former college classmate and her neighbors, and then for Gram and her friends. I placed an ad on Craigslist, and as word spread of my in-home sex education parties I got referrals and requests from strangers, and it wasn't long before that part of my business started growing.

If there was an opportunity to talk to a crowd about sex I was on it, which is why I was willing to drive over three hours to Penn State University when a student there hired me for my Orgasm 101 party recommended by one of her friends. I arrived at her apartment and made half a dozen trips from my car and up four flights of stairs carrying boxes and boxes of sex toys and other accoutrements, all while wearing heals and a gray pencil skirt. As I had learned was customary, I was barely acknowledged by the party guests, chatting amongst themselves and smoking on the outdoor balcony, writing me off as the "sex toy lady" there to give them a sales pitch like a Tupperware party, only with plastic penises instead of burping lids. They didn't yet know I wasn't just a saleswoman but a degreed sexologist on a mission.

I set up a small table in the middle of the living room, covered it with a white cloth, and displayed the bottles of lotions decoratively next to a pretty shoe case that hid the toys until the end of the presentation. A gaggle of twenty-eight pretty college women sat on hand-me-down couches, on the floor, and on lawn chairs that had been brought in for additional seating. I could tell they had primped before they came, with sexy clothing, hoop earrings, and knee-high boots, as if I was their entertainment for the night rather than going to the bar. I guess I was, except for one simple-looking girl in jeans with her arms folded guardedly across her chest and sitting in the back of the room.

"Is everyone OK? I didn't scare anyone off, did I? Can I move on to the foreplay products now?" I asked with a wink and a smile, mocking the fifteen minutes I had just spent showcasing PG-rated bath soaps and candles.

"Oh hell yeah!" the crowd shouted.

"Are you kidding me? You're not going to scare off this group of girls!" the hostess asserted, topping off plastic martini glasses with a concoction of cheap liquor as her friends laughed and nodded approvingly. "Jill, have another drink, honey," she added, taking my empty glass off the display table.

"No, no, that's ok…" I responded as she filled it and handed it back to me anyway. "Well," I said, lifting the glass as a toast to the room full of women seated in front of me, "The more I drink, the more fun this will be for you!" and I pointed at them theatrically before taking a dramatic sip. The giggling group followed suit.

I passed around a bottle of flavored massage oil that gets hot when you rub it and let everyone sample the edible gel that makes lips and nipples feel tingly. "Ooh, this stuff feels awesome," said a more outspoken girl, licking the watermelon flavor off her lips.

"You like that?" I asked, "That's the Dodge Neon of tingling. This right here is the Rolls-Royce." I declared, holding up a nondescript jar of green goop. I had their eager eyes and attention, amused by the metaphor and intrigued to learn what could be more sensational. "Who wants to try it?" The entire room, except for quiet Jane in the back with arms folded, jumped up for a Popsicle stick dipped in the jar of green clit cream and got in line for the bathroom. I can't adequately describe the sounds of nearly thirty young, tipsy women in various stages of rubbing arousal cream on their clitorises while their friends (and a stranger) wait on, but it's a sound of giddy amusement unlike any other. It's a sound of new bonds of friendship being formed. It's a sound of money, since I could count on anyone that tried it to buy it, so I could at least pay the gas to get myself the three hours back home. But most importantly, it's a sound of breaking down repressive barriers.

When everyone settled back down, taking their seats on the couches, lawn chairs, and crossed-legged on the floor in front of my feet, looking up at me wide-eyed like I was making animal balloons in front of a second grade classroom, I was high. I loved being the center of attention. I loved being in the spotlight of such fascination, but my favorite part was about to come.

"About seventy-five percent of women can't orgasm without clitoral stimulation. But there's nothing wrong with you, there is a biological reason for this," I started, immediately quieting the chatter. I had a way with weaving a tone of fun and merriment when I wanted to entertain and a tone of authority and wisdom when I wanted to educate, and I knew I succeeded with the transition when their heads cocked slightly to one side and forward, listening intently as if I were revealing a magic trick.

"When we are all in utero, our genitals are blank slates. As we develop, the same tissue that will become testicles for male fetuses becomes the ovaries in females; what becomes the scrotum in the male becomes the labia in the female, and what becomes the male penis becomes the female clitoris," I explained, using my hands as I spoke to demonstrate as best as I could and emphasizing the juicy words for added effect. "So all the nerve endings that are in the penis are in the clitoris, except packed into a much smaller service area. So essentially, the clit is your 'penis,' and how many men do you know who can have an orgasm without their penises being touched?" I asked with a chuckle. They chuckled at the punch line too, breaking the silent stares they had given me while I spoke. "That's why this gel is so amazing. That's why clitoral stimulation is so important." I could see it in their pretty young faces: wheels were turning and lightbulbs were going on. They had come to be amused by some vibrators and creams, but at that moment they recognized that what they had received was a little taste of their own sexual revolution.

And the madness ensued. The women formed lines with order forms in one hand and cash in the other, and I knew I had done my job. In some small way, I had aided in their sexual liberation. Soon the crowd died down, and guests started leaving with their goody bags. I sat at the foot of the hostess's bed with what was left of my inventory, a colorful heap of pink and purple bottles and boxes, scattered on the floor. A handful of party guests sat around their friend's bedroom watching me put the items into their carrying case. The plain, quiet girl who was sitting with her arms folded when I arrived, who I found out from her order sheet was named Katie, was now lying on her stomach on the hostess's roommate's pink and yellow flowered bed, her knees bent and her hands propping her head up.

"This is the best college party I ever went to!" she said. "And I didn't even want to come." I was thinking, "No, really? Your body language could've fooled me." Instead I replied, "Oh? Why not?"

"Well I'm just not comfortable with this kind of stuff. I thought it was going to be really vulgar, but you weren't at all." I was about to thank her for the compliment, but before I could, she added, "And that thing you said, about not having an orgasm without touching the clit, well that makes a lot of sense to me. I always thought I wasn't doing it right but...I can't believe I'm saying this but...I don't know, I just feel like I can tell you this... my boyfriend, I don't think he knows about the clit thing but I think I have the confidence to teach him about it when he visits next weekend – thanks to you."

Katie was now sitting up on the bed, and a blonde woman moved from the floor and sat up next to her. "Ok...I have a question," she announced. "Is it true that douching is bad for you? Because sometimes...I get really self-conscious about my boyfriend trying to go down on me because I'm worried he's

41

gonna think it's like...I don't know...like gross and smelly or something. Is that weird?" she completed with a nervous snicker.

"No, that's not weird; lots of women get self-conscious about that. But you don't want to douche, that just makes things worse. Just clean with mild soap, and I know it's hard, but try not to be embarrassed about it. So long as you don't have an infection, it's supposed to smell like that, and if he doesn't like it, then he doesn't like vagina," I responded. I paused with the packing up and settled more comfortably on the edge of the bed to answer the questions.

She replied, "Wow. I wouldn't even ask my Ob-Gyn this," We all laughed. Next, the hostess sitting in her wooden desk chair asked for clarification about the difference between transvestites and transsexuals, and then it was a free-for-all of asking and sharing everything they always wanted to know about sex, with me hanging around the tiny off-campus apartment bedroom like a big sister fielding questions at a middle school slumber party. We ordered pizza (they refused to let me chip in) and had some more drinks before crashing on the couches, and I thought, "Wow, I'm working right now." The next morning all the women and even a few neighbors helped me bring all my boxes down the four flights of stairs to my car and then hugged me goodbye. What a stark difference from when I arrived, when I was all but ignored by the party guests as I struggled with the boxes alone, flight after flight, trip after trip, and now had a line of appreciative helpers.

It was one of the most rewarding workshops (parties) that I taught until a few months later when a woman asked me to present my Sex Toys 101 workshop at a surprise sixtieth birthday party in New Jersey. Again, I drove several hours, this time to a mansion that sat right on the beach of a coastal town, and set up my table before the guest of honor arrived. A small gathering of just five women curled up on the oversized sofas in the den of the vacation home, next to a beautiful marble mantled fireplace and a unique vase that probably cost more than my Hyundai. As the party organizer served homemade Veal Florentine and Baked Crab Casserole, and offered me a glass of good white wine, I got the background story to the surprise party. Joanna, the birthday girl, was celebrating her first birthday as a widow, and the ladies, friends since they were sixteen years old, wanted to make her day extraordinary. So they took her out to lunch, enjoyed a day at the spa, and were now going to complete the evening with…me.

Just then, a short and petite redhead bolted up the steps, half covering her eyes with hands covered in glitzy gold jewelry, half peeking, unable to suppress her enthusiasm. "Oh, oh, who is this?" she cooed. "You're oh-so cute, but…who are you?" she asked me, grabbing my hands. I just smiled, trying to stay with the game and keep her guessing. Then she spotted my boxes of merchandise. "I know! We are making some kind of craft!" she exclaimed, and I burst into laughter at the deduction.

Her friends seated her, and I began somewhat apprehensively. Although my Sex Toys 101 party is on female sexuality, I speak a lot about ways the women can incorporate their partners into the fun, except Joanna's partner was gone. And the last thing I could imagine was how someone could enjoy themselves talking about sex when her lifelong sex partner, and love partner, and dance partner, and travel partner, and everything else partner had just died. But thankfully I got off to a smooth start, and before long I was on my usual roll.

They were such a fun group, reliving their carefree sixteen-year-old days and cackling like schoolgirls at everything I said. Halfway through the presentation, I cracked a one-liner about post-coital wet spots on bed sheets, and the already giddy group just lost it, roaring until tears rolled down the corner of their eyes. Tears began streaming down mine too, just watching them. It was the kind of laugh where the pit of your stomach starts aching to the point you have to literally hold your side or it might split. Abruptly they all just stop laughing, wiped their eyes, and looked at each other. Then at me. Joanna's face was red from the episode when she said quietly, "Jill, we really needed that. None of us have laughed that hard since Jim died. Thank you." And then just like that, they were back to their jovial ways.

Joanna called me the next afternoon. "Hey sweetie, it's

Joanna, the birthday girl!" she said, cheerful as ever when I picked up. "My sixtieth birthday would not have been the same without you. Thank you so much. You don't know how much it meant to me, to all of us."

I felt so overjoyed, so bemused at the idea that she could be so appreciative of me, when really it was she who had given me the gift that few people ever get: the opportunity to make a living doing their life's dream. I thanked her in return, wished her well, and then she said something I'll never forget. It was the only compliment I'd ever received that literally left me momentarily breathless, and coming from someone I'd only known for two hours and would never see again, it was particularly meaningful. I still remember her words verbatim. She said, "You are a special soul, Jill, and I'm blessed to have met you."*

"This, this right here, is what it's all about," I thought, feeling fundamentally satisfied and with just the smallest of tears in the corner of my eye.

But how could I persuade Anthony Ciccerone of that?

Anthony Ciccerone didn't care that my shop would be a place for people like Joanna to enjoy the now while remembering the bittersweet past, or young women like Katie to make discoveries that would empower them to enter a new frontier of womanhood, I thought, deciding that he probably saw me and my little Feminique Boutique as porno filth that didn't fit into his black and white, right and wrong law books. But I had come here in my suit and on a mission, and his forty-five minutes were up.

I headed back to the Department of Building, Housing and Code Enforcement. He was standing at the counter when I arrived, and as you guessed it, nervous puke butterflies were having a field day in my stomach. All the mental prepping I had done was no match for the presence of this man, standing nearly six-foot three inches tall with thick, broad shoulders, thinning slicked black hair, and a gold chain peeking from underneath his starched collar, a throwback to his South Philly days that was evident in his tough accent. I was visibly intimidated. Intimidated, but not bested. I approached.

44

"I received your certified letter, and I've been reading over the code, and I have to tell you, I'm not seeing the problem. There's nothing in this code that prohibits what I'm doing. Vibrators are not 'live displays of the human body without covering,'" I argued. And just like that, I knew I was done. I was too passionate, too emotionally invested. I was about to cry, I could feel it, he could see it, and although I fought like hell to stop it, I knew it was no use. I started to ramble about the dozens of workshops I would teach to help people, and got on my soapbox about how the code incorrectly viewed sex as unilaterally lewd, but it was just a lost cause. My upper lip was doing the trembling thing.

"Look, it's nothing personal…," he interrupted. I felt that his demeanor was so rigid, so consumed with the letter of his law. To me, he was that fellow who opened the door to the Emerald City, "Nobody gets in to see the Wizard, not nobody not nohow," with no interest in my good intentions or my struggles and triumphs over tornadoes and wicked witches that brought me to his mercy that day. But, "it's nothing personal," he said.

"You are telling me that the laws of this town state that the people who walk into my store for a lecture on how rape trauma impacts marital intimacy are the same as the people who walk into strip clubs, and that both are wrong, I TAKE THAT VERY PERSONALLY!" I yelled through slobbery tears. He just looked at me as I continued on. "Now I want to know why I can't open this shop!" I'm sure there were people there looking to get code permits for putting up a fence around their yard who thought I was a lunatic, but I didn't notice, and I certainly didn't care.

"Because, based on the business description you submitted to my office as reviewed by our solicitor, your intended use of the facility fits under our prohibited adult entertainment use."

Damn it. I wanted to shake him and scream, "BUT IT DOESN'T!" Just because some nameless, faceless lawyer had decided vibrators equal strip clubs didn't make it true. Anyone with two marbles could see that they were two very different things! But such a logical contention wouldn't help me now. Not when I'd already lost my composure. The show ended by me threatening to open Feminique Boutique with or without his worthless permit and storming out.

I knew I had an uphill fight to save my job, my company, my pride, my life's passion, but it was deeper than that. It was about shame. Shame made the suits in West Chester write the laws in the way that they had. I was determined in my accusation of injustice; I was not breaking any rules since my Feminique Boutique would not be a strip joint. But if it were, so what? Why is the thought of a naked body so horrifying that someone took the time to write its prohibition into law? I accepted that I was fighting for more than my job; I was fighting the capital "E" Establishment. And suddenly I was inspired, in a lofty folk music and peace signs sort of fashion; I had always wanted to fight the Establishment. I just didn't know how big the Establishment actually was until a few weeks later.

Two days after I finished writing this chapter, the woman who planned Joanna's sixtieth surprise party emailed me asking if I would be interested in presenting my female sexuality workshop again. She also informed me that less than a month after her party, Joanna died suddenly. My workshop was the last time the lifelong friends ever saw each other alive.

Chapter 6

When he was home that weekend, I did tell George that I had spent most of summer break joined at the hip with Pat. I even told him about the phone calls. But I was too embarrassed to admit the level of intimacy, the bond, the ritual that was our special thing.

It all began one night when Pat and I were yapping on the phone, as teenagers will do, except this time it was different. This time I was actually intrigued by the conversation, enthralled even. The next thing I knew three hours had passed, the lights in my house were all turned off, and my family was in bed. That's when the scheme came to me. "Hey, let's see how long we can keep talking," I proposed. "Let's see if we can make it til morning!" The idea was mischievous, borderline dangerous. If my parents found out they would be pissed. I still had a bedtime, and I definitely wasn't supposed to be up all night talking to boys, even if it was just meek and harmless ol' Pat Abramowitz. I didn't drink, or smoke, or have sex, so this was my courageous act of teenage rebellion. I gathered a few packs of dinosaur-shaped fruit snacks in hopes the sugar would keep me alert throughout the night and proceeded quietly to my bedroom, which was act of rebellion number two since I wasn't allowed to bring food in my room.

The exchange flowed beautifully and covered the gamut of

topics, from our preferred method of preparing Ramen noodles (he insisted it was meant to be a pasta dish while I did not concur with this assertion due to the fact that the enclosed seasoning packet made a stellar broth for soup) to God and the meaning of life. We pondered destiny versus free will, what it means to be a "good" person, and what happens when we die. Will we know we're dead? And how long will we be dead when the concept of eternity is both scientifically impossible and necessary? How could time go on forever, but if it doesn't, what's after it stops?

I started to learn that Pat was not exactly the simpleton I had pegged him as. Maybe he didn't share my passion for politics, but he was a thinker and a feeler. In his own way he had a mind on fire with a zest for questioning and wondering, and until now, no one had ever cared to wonder with him.

So we wondered. And we disclosed secrets. I told him that despite my outward strength, my external kick-ass-and-take-names façade, I was actually deeply wounded by all the teasing and bullying I was the beneficiary of at school. Wearing bell-bottoms and listening to The Doors made me the butt of relentless harassment. Being called a "dirty hippie" and having "Kumbaya" screamed in my face in the hallways, pushed off the lunch table bench and pelted with paper wads and erasers was a fact of my life, and although I would never conform to make the torture stop, I secretly wished people would like me.

He told me that despite the happy façade his family showed to the world, his home life was really chaotic and painful. His parents were divorcing and using the children as negotiable commodities; his dad never called to talk to him, only to fight with his mom. And if it weren't for the inheritance from his mom-mom, they would be on welfare. We fantasized about a better future for ourselves; lives that included a loving home in a world that accepts people for what they are.

We whispered our hopes and fears to each other until 5:30 a.m., when his mother got up to check on him, and he had to lie still with his eyes closed, pretending to be asleep. "That was a close call," he said when she left. "We should probably hang up now. I can't wait to talk to you tomorrow." And we did. And the night after that. And the one after that. While I can't remember all the subjects we covered, I can still recall the way the summer breeze blew in my bedroom window and how sweaty my coil-wired Elvis phone that danced and played *Jailhouse Rock* when it rang became after hours of holding it to my ear. And I suppose that remembering the things we talked about is not nearly as essential as remembering the feeling I was left with. At a painful, tumultuous, and lonely time called puberty, there is no greater feeling than knowing somebody "gets" you.

It was one hell of a summer, but ultimately the leaves began to turn orange, and that meant school, but this time it was high school. There were so many new people to meet, especially of the male variety, which was of particular interest to me. But as luck would have it, Michael Higgins was in four of my five classes, and I ended up getting back together with my old "kissing partner" by the crisp, beginning-to-wear-a-jacket-again days of October. Pat was vehemently opposed to this, and we went round and round about it, as we had so many times in the beginning of the summer. He told me I was a fool for going back to Michael, I said he had no business controlling my love life.

One day, my newly won back boyfriend and I walked home from school. As we neared my house he led me across the street near the scene of the up-against-the-fence incident and on to a less conspicuous area. I knew exactly what his plans were, and I felt like I was being walked down a corridor by the devil to the gates of hell. After a few overbearing words, he blatantly and shamelessly stuck his tongue straight down my throat, and scraped my lip with his teeth. I was appalled. We broke up a few weeks later to the delight of everyone, and that was the end of that. But it wasn't. My first kiss was forceful, disturbing, nothing like the way I always wanted it to be since I learned that kissing could be more than the small pecks my parents gave me as they tucked me in bed. But eventually I got over it, and life went on. I had a few other boyfriends in the months following, and I even kissed another boy, which was even worse than the first time. Still, I didn't need a

49

boyfriend – I had Pat.

"Do you...masturbate?" I mustered up the courage to ask George. Pat's bare-bones basement with an old brown and green woven sofa and wood paneling was our That 70s Show-esque Foreman's basement hangout at the moment, and we were entertaining ourselves one cold winter afternoon with a rousing game of Truth or Dare. It was no astonishment that George picked truth, he always picked truth, so I decided I had to turn up the bravado of my questions to level the playing field. Pat and Scarlet waited with hungry anticipation at the humiliation that was about to be revealed.

"And don't try to lie George. Studies show most boys have by ninth grade!" I had suddenly taken an interest in reading Cosmo and then spitting out stats from their articles like a little Dr. Ruth.

"Well....Yeah, I have."

I was shocked at George's honest reply. And I didn't like it. I didn't like thinking of my childhood friends in adult ways. But at the same time I wanted to know more, like how it was done, and what boys thought about, and what did they do with the...you know...stuff. I was stuck in that crux of adolescence where I was intrigued and curious about sex while at the same time grossed out and scared. Not to mention ignorant, hence the citing of Cosmopolitan magazine as a source for reliable sex information. But I suppose the knowledge I had gave me a certain basic thrill when we were talking about it, kind of naughty, like the staying up all night talking on the phone, but also powerful, and so although I was the priggish one, I was also the instigator of all the sex talk.

"Ok, my turn," George started with a devilish smirk. I knew he was up to no good. "Jill, truth or dare?" I played it safe.

"Truth," I responded.

"Tell us how you really feel about Abramowitz." Shit. Didn't see that one coming. Sometimes picking truth was more dangerous than any embarrassing or off-the-wall dare George could concoct.

George and Scarlet studied me, sitting on the brown and green woven sofa curled up next to Pat Abramowitz, my head on his shoulder, my hand on his thigh. In the safety of the basement, I could express this newfound affection I was feeling for Pat but would never show in school. I didn't verbalize the feeling either. No, never that. I wasn't ready to admit it to George or Scarlet, or especially myself. Instead I played it off. "How do I feel about him? I feel like he's a good friend." They eyed the cozy seating arrangement suspiciously, so I continued. "A good friend…with a really comfortable shoulder." They bought it…for now, I thought.

The truth was I didn't know what I was feeling. Or maybe I did but I didn't know how to label it. Sometimes I felt nurtured, and that felt good. His skills as a supportive friend who helped me get over my Michael Higgins kissing drama hadn't ended there. In his own scrawny way he beat up the bullies who threw rocks at me when I walked home from the bus stop. He brought me chicken soup when I was home sick with the flu. He even snuck out of his house late at night to tuck me in bed on nights I was particularly upset about my parents' looming divorce, when I struggled with which parent I would live with and if I'd have to move away. He would just sit on the edge of my bed, gently running his fingers down my hair while saying, "I hate it when you're sad," and then he would kiss my forehead and lock up my front door on the way out. Sometimes I thought I was in love with him, but then I thought it wasn't real love, whatever that means anyway. I thought it was a selfish love, thinking I only felt that way about him because he was bestowing all of this positivity in my direction, and it wouldn't have mattered who it was. And that's pretty profound thinking for me as a fourteen-year-old. That's profound thinking for me now.

But in addition to feeling nurtured, I felt passion; the sexy kind where warmth and tingles goes up and down your body and stop at your crotch when that someone touches you, even innocently like wiping an eyelash off your cheek. I had never felt that way before. And it kept happening. A hand resting on my stomach while spooning during a movie – boom! Tingles. A squeeze of the knee while riding the school bus home, squished in the narrow seats where no one could see us. Bam! More warm tingles.

51

"Here, have some of this," I said, giggling before smearing the powdered sugar from a hot funnel cake on his face.

"Oh Jill McDevitt, you are gonna get it!" he said, and took the plate from my hand and dumped the whole thing on my head.

"You know." I responded, "although I could kill you right now for just doing that, I'm actually really happy."

"Why's that?" he asked.

"Well, none of my friends were ever roller coaster people, and I'm really glad I have you in my life…to, you know…go on rides with me." We were walking back to his house after a night at the annual town carnival. This time last year, I had been giddy over Michael Higgins winning me a stuffed Mr. Potato Head at the dart throwing booth at this very carnival, and this year I was walking hand in hand with Pat, covered in white powder. I didn't care if everyone from school saw me because when someone makes your crotch get warm tinglies and makes you soup when you're sick, you'd be an idiot not to go with it.

"I promise that I will be your permanent ride partner. Forever. You can count on that," he pledged. "And how could I not? There is no one I would rather go on a Tilt-A-Whirl with than you. You are so amazing." Ugh. The blue eyes pierced through me again. I still didn't know how to respond to his overt proclamations of admiration, just like the day in my living room when he told me his saddest day was when I declined his date to the eighth grade formal. Like then, my response was to roll my eyes and look away. So hurtful and childish, but then again, I was a child. At the same time, I knew something was happening. When riding the Tilt-A-Whirl, there was more than just centripetal force pushing us together.

As we continued our walk home, a torrential spring rainstorm suddenly began splashing down on us. Within seconds my red top with the cuffed sleeves and denim shorts were soaked through.

"Hurry, c'mon let's run," he yelled under the booming of thunder, pulling my hand as I ran more slowly behind him, falling out of my flip-flops. "Here, I'll give you a piggyback ride," and he stooped down so I could jump on his back. He jogged surprisingly fast with my added weight, stopping only to let a car pass, splattering in a rain-filled pothole, before running across the street. My arms were wrapped around him tightly, and my chin rested on his shoulder, my wet cheek against his neck, inhaling the scent of his wet skin. I closed my eyes. With each bound he took, my chest bumped into his back, and his grip on my bare thighs got tighter and tighter in an attempt to keep me from slipping. My body and hips jostled and rubbed against his leather belt, up and down at each step until we finally reached his front door. When he dropped me back down I finally opened my eyes, reeling from these new sensations. I didn't know what sex felt like, but at that moment I started to understand why people love it so much.

His house was quiet and dark with the exception of the yellow street light outside making shadows across his living room walls. I stood in the middle of the floor, still dripping wet, and then I pushed him on the couch boldly and climbed on top of him, nose to nose in the dark. My heavy exhale was his inhale.

"I liked that," I whispered, feeling very womanly.

"What?" he asked.

"The piggyback ride." If this were an episode of "The Wonder Years," my grown-up Kevin Arnold voiceover would reflect nostalgically on the notorious raging hormones of adolescence. And it's true that part of the beauty of growing up is the memory of moments like these that are erotic in their innocence and powerful in their simplicity. Most people remember those times fondly, that moment when they realized, "Hey, this sex thing isn't yucky after all, in fact I kinda want it." But for me, that realization was more than that. It launched me into a world of wondering about the mysterious and complicated concoction of physical and emotional potions that were brewing in my body. *What makes people fall in love? Why do people in love want to have sex with each other, even though love and sex are two seemingly unrelated things? What was it about sex that was so good and blissful on one hand and dirty and embarrassing on the other? If it's true that sex is wrong sometimes, especially when*

53

you're a teenager, and it's the girls' job to keep the boys at bay because boys "only want one thing," then why wasn't Pat making a move, and most importantly, why didn't it feel wrong? I rested my head on his chest, in my soaking clothes, pondering precociously until the rain cleared and he walked me home.

Chapter 7

Lawyers are like cops, you love to hate them until you need one. When you don't need a lawyer, you can't escape the boring commercials and full page ads, but when you do, suddenly lawyers are hard to come by. When you need a lawyer you want a good one on your side. I couldn't afford a good lawyer. I couldn't afford a bad one. But it had to be done. No way was I giving up before I started. No way was I letting The Man dishonor a service so many women need and want. I planned to stick it to The Man, and I planned to start by calling West Chester area attorneys in the phone book – all two of them who specialized in business and zoning law.

One man called me right back after I left a message with his receptionist. This was promising.

"Ms. McDevitt," he started, "We won't be able to represent you in this matter. But if you'd like, I can refer you to another firm…elsewhere…in another county…," he said pleasantly but sternly. Could anything be simple or easy or straightforward? Could it be possible that my "sorry you don't speak Spanish or have a master's degree" setback, and my "sorry we won't rent this shop to you" setback, and my "sorry, your business can't open in our town" setback, and my "sorry, our bank won't do business with you," setback weren't enough? Was I actually, on top of everything else, also going to have a "sorry, we don't want to be your lawyer" setback? I asked him why he couldn't, or rather wouldn't, help me.

"Well, my family and I live in West Chester," he answered. I sat silently waiting for the punch line. "And..."

He continued. "And I'd rather not be involved in *that kind* of controversy."

I knew that sexual topics made some people uncomfortable. I used to be one of those people. I knew I was going to experience setbacks because discussing sex upsets prudish American delicate sensibilities. I understood I'd be met with adversity. But my conversation with the lawyer was the first time I thought of anything I was doing as "controversial."

They sell vibrators at Spencer's and massage lotion at Bath and Body Works and sexy lingerie at Victoria's Secret in every mall in America. So why was what I was doing controversial? I decided it was controversial because I wasn't selling these items as gag gifts to embarrass someone at their fortieth birthday party. I wasn't selling them as "massagers". I sold them for people to masturbate with. To rub on their lover's bodies and lick off. To wear to spice up the fantasy while they're getting laid. I sold them so they could bring *pleasure*. I was learning that it's not necessarily that vibrators, massage lotion, and sexy lingerie are controversial (although they can be), it is sexual pleasure and being sex-positive that is controversial. To me, the only thing controversial here was a lawyer unwilling to defend a blatant attempt by a government to prohibit a legal business from opening because of an erotophobic political agenda.

I decided that unlike my outburst to Anthony Ciccerone in West Chester's Borough Hall, I'd let this particular battle go and continue my lawyer search elsewhere...in another county...

George called me for the daily report on our respective job-hunting and business-saving escapades but I was in no mood for mindless chatter. I was driving to nowhere after storming out of my house. He could tell I was upset, that I'd been crying. It's not hard to detect. I'm not one to suffer in silence.

George: What's wrong with you?

56

Me: I was passing through my living room, half paying attention to this dumb Western that's on the TV, when all of a sudden this cowboy just grabs this woman, throws her under his arm, drags her to a barn, pushes her on the hay, pulls her dress up, and starts raping her. Just like that. I'm standing there frozen, watching this about to have a panic attack, waiting for the scene to cut but it doesn't. It just keeps going. And worst of all, he's not even supposed to be the bad guy in the movie.
George: Oh, here we go.
Me: What's 'here we go'?
George: Well, you tend to get a little nutso about this subject…a little overly emotional.
Me: I can't help it. Don't you think it's horrible? How could you not get emotional about it?
George: I'm not saying it's not horrible. I think it's a horrible crime. But I don't have panic attacks and drive around aimlessly making myself sick when I see a rape scene in a movie.

Logically, I knew he was right. And normally I was a sane and logical, albeit slightly neurotic, person. But a mere mention of sexual assault in passing could send me into a momentary catatonic state, frozen, nauseous, angry. The imagery seared passed logic and grabbed my emotions by the jugular. I'd spent countless hours with George and others trying to psychoanalyze the curiousness of this raw reaction, why it disturbed me in such a profound way, but figuring out the source was a puzzle I could never solve. I had never been raped or abused, nor was I ever a witness to it. Although, I could remember episodes when men were less than gentlemanly…

I rode down the sliding board at a playground on my belly feet first, and by the time I reached the bottom my legs landed one on each side in a straddling position. A young teenage boy with Converse sneakers sat on a nearby swing, watching me and smoking a cigarette. He shouted over, "Hey girl, you look like you're fucking that thing." I was six years old. My life was littered with these incidents – a vulgar catcall out a car window here, an unwanted slap on the butt there, but what woman's life isn't? It was unsavory, but not traumatic, at least not enough to turn me into a stark raving lunatic every time I watched the six o'clock news.

Me: Well of course YOU don't have outbursts. It's easy not to get enraged about something when YOU aren't the one that's going to suffer from it. No one is going to pull YOU into a barn and rape you.
George: And you don't know that it will happen to you either.
Me: Oh that's comforting.

Perhaps my fear, my panic-stricken feelings that made me so confrontational during these conversations with George, was the thought that it could happen to me at any time, and there was nothing I could do about it. Given the rape statistics of approximately one in four women, it wouldn't be unlikely, and I felt like the proverbial fish in the barrel, biding my time until it would inevitably be me on the six o'clock news. Every day that passed that I wasn't a rape victim was another lucky dodge of the shot. But how long could I keep that up? How long could any woman? This was the rationale that George considered over the top, pessimistic even for him. Maybe it was. Maybe he was right and I was crazy.

But of all this, the part that rattled me the most, of course, was the sex part. To take sex, beautiful, monumental, euphoric, pleasurable sex – the bringer of life and liberation – and use it as a weapon was in my little world the worst thing a human being could do. I was crying again. I had to change the subject.

Me: I don't want to talk about this anymore. So…I think I found a lawyer.
George: Very good. What's he charging?
Me: I don't even want to think about it. The important thing is he thinks I have a case.
George: Well that's a good start.

The evening left me more inspired than ever to save my business. People were all kinds of messed up; criminal sex was touted on primetime television, while touting good sex was criminal, in West Chester anyway. Anyone in the loop enough to see the insanity of this juxtaposition, those on the side of good sex, had nowhere to go for advice, no one to ask. People needed a Feminique Boutique. People needed me.

Like my crud-under-the-fingernails interview, again I found myself in a suit sitting around a conference table, except this time the person on the other side could help me – maybe. My attorney, Mark D'Ortone, a soft-spoken, gentle-looking fellow with salt and pepper hair, was perusing the copy of the zoning code and my business plan that I had brought with me. I sat on a chair with wheels in the bright room of a former beautiful estate that had been turned into offices, wheeling around anxiously.

"So you have the retail part of the business…" he started, reading down the list of items I intended to sell at Feminique Boutique. "*Lingerie.* Underwear is underwear if it comes in a shrink-wrapped packet of three at Kmart or it's lacy and sexy, it's still underwear, not adult entertainment. *Edible body toppings.* It's cream in a bottle. If someone washes their hair with it or licks it off someone's body in a sexual context in their home is their prerogative, and selling the bottle is not adult entertainment. *Lubricants,* it's a health use; you can buy it at a pharmacy. *Sex toys,* they're purchasing them from you and then taking them home to use them. So they will not be used, as the code reads, 'for presenting material related to sexual activities or specified anatomical areas for observation by patrons therein.' Sure, they'll 'observe' the box it comes in but that's not exactly titillating…to most people anyway. And you're not selling any pornographic videos or magazines." It was amazing how he could completely separate any emotions from the rational facts at hand. It was certainly something I couldn't do, and I was glad that without my emotional entanglements in the matter, I was still right.

"And then you have the services part of the business…," he continued. "The sex education classes, the parties, the workshops that you teach will be to private groups. Is that right?"

"Yes," I answered. Finally, I was getting somewhere.

"Here's what I think, Jill. I think this could go in your favor *if* you continued to fight it up through the court system, but that could be a very long and costly process. I know your finances are a concern for you. How do you think you'd like to proceed?" he asked. I had told him my budget practically the moment I walked in the door of his office, located in the next county over, and surprisingly, he didn't laugh in my face. Our only hope with my limited sum of money, he told me, was for him to call a meeting with Anthony Ciccerone and the Borough Solicitor and hope we could change their minds right then. If they held their ground, there would be no way I could afford to take West Chester to court, and Feminique Boutique would end there. The story would end there.

"I'll be honest," he admitted, "the chances of this going your way with just the meeting are slim." I appreciated him giving me a fair shake, an honest expectation that the line in the start-up expense section of my business plan called "legal fees" would likely be wasted on a fruitless effort. However fruitless, it was the only effort worth fighting for. What else did I have?

"Let's do it!" I exclaimed with a smile, and he smiled back warmly.

Chapter 8

It was the year 2000, I was fourteen years old and a freshman in high school. As Spring Break was nearing I was still the goody-two-shoes I had always been. I freaked if I got less than a ninety-five percent on a test, couldn't fathom ever getting a detention, I had never lied to my parents – not even a white one. I remember once I didn't finish my vegetables at dinner and was thus not allowed to have a bedtime snack. Later in the evening my dad offered me a pretzel stick as we watched TV together on our living room couch. "Thanks, but I'm not allowed to have snacks tonight, remember?" He took it back with furrowed brows, equally proud and disturbed that I was so frighteningly and abnormally honest. And to my peers, I was still that odd-looking, goody-two-shoes girl with thrift store Seventies threads and bad hair, although my perm and crooked bangs had thankfully grown out. High school had not made me any less dorky, or prudish, but there was one thing I was ready to stop being prim about, and that was kissing.

I decided I was going to kiss Pat, and unlike the gag-worthy encounter with Mike Higgins, this one would be special. So I began plotting, in the most non-spontaneous of ways, a memorable kiss that would take place in a memorable place, during a memorable song, so I could tell my grandkids someday how great it was. So when Spring Break finally arrived, the last one I would ever have that was not spoiled by part-time jobs or other adult-like responsibilities, I was home alone all day, footloose and fancy-free to make my move.

Apparently, Pat had a plot of his own because on the first night of the weeklong break from school, at his back door as we were about to leave to walk me home, he tried to give me a small peck on the lips. I turned away. My chance was missed.

"Oh, you're cold," he said teasingly. I couldn't believe it! I don't know why I dodged him, if it was my sheer surprise or if it was my desire to be the instigator, something I got a taste of that night of the rainstorm when I pushed myself on top of him. Maybe for once I wanted to be the kisser instead of the kissee.

"Well…I'll make it up to you," I responded.

In order to pursue my little scheme, I convinced Pat we should hang out under my dining room table. For some reason I thought this would be an eventful setting for the momentous kiss that was to be. So we spent the morning of day two of Spring Break under the table, lying on our backs side by side, staring at the particle board underneath of the table, talking and listening to the radio. The whole time in my head I waited for the right moment to jump him. Instead, we were interrupted by his mother beeping her horn out front of my house, ready to pick him up for an orthodontist appointment.

"Oh no, I forgot. I'm getting my braces off today," he said, slightly panicked at the thought of choosing between leaving his mom waiting in the street and leaving me waiting under the table, and then he concluded, "You should come with me." We rode together in the backseat of his mom's car. The new retainer made it awkward for him to talk, so we just sat there without saying anything, holding hands secretively under a throw blanket. Every once in a while he squeezed my hand, rubbed his thumb across my knuckles, laced his fingers around mine. I felt loved and cared for and fluttery. I decided this kiss *needed* to happen, can't-think-about-anything-else, every-muscle-in-my-body-will-not-rest-until-it-happens needed to happen.

So when we got home I insisted we promptly return to our safe but peculiar haven under the table. Before long I worked up the courage to go for it despite my nervous puke butterflies. I brought my face close in, slightly opened my mouth, reached for his shoulder and then – he pulled away. I was surprised, and he was embarrassed. He insisted that it was weird with the new retainer in his mouth, that it wasn't me. I told him he was cold. He said, "I'll make it up to you."

By day three of Spring Break I was an anxious wreck. Again we were under my dining room table, and I put on my Lynyrd Skynyrd CD and played "Free Bird" on repeat, hoping the nearly ten-minute timeless anthem of young love would be the "memorable" song of our first kiss. "Today will be the day," I decided. But as luck would have it, the phone rang at least fifteen times that day. Damn phone. First my mom checking up on me from work. Then a telemarketer. My sister's day care. Another telemarketer. A wrong number. Each time I paused the music, and then started it over again from the beginning once I hung up.

"Jill, why do we keep listening to this dumb song?" he asked as I crawled back under the table and pressed "play" again.

"First of all, Pat, this is not a dumb song, this is a classic rock 'n' roll masterpiece, and second, you'll see." But before I could show him, the damn phone rang again. "Geez, how long does it take to kiss a person?" I thought to myself, although I had to admit the chase and suspense was already more fun than my clumsy lip-lock with Michael Higgins. It was already memorable.

I was blabbering on to whomever it was, impatient to get off, twirling the curly phone chord around my fingers while I tapped my foot on the kitchen floor. For the millionth time, I hung up the phone and turned *Free Bird* back on. This time, he looked at me with bright blue eyes, and we started kissing. Just like that. No worries. No bullying classmates. No divorcing parents. Just two teenagers, under the dining room table, a song with passion and soul the soundtrack to it all. It was exactly the way I always wanted it to be – the epic moment that all memories are compared to before and after – the marked beginning of the best love story ever told – all those fantasies I'd been harboring since I was a little girl. I described the account in my journal as "the most natural thing that ever was – sweet, innocent, and not geared by an ulterior motive. His lips were soft, and his tongue was warm and welcoming."

A few days later back at school, Pat gave me a card in a white envelope. On the front of the card there was a pencil sketch drawing of two wooden rocking chairs on a picturesque porch in springtime, under which it read in stylized script, *"When I'm old and gray, sitting on my front porch, hearing nothing but the quiet breeze and the soft creek of wood against wood, I want nothing more than to be able to turn to you, take your hand in mine, and look into the eyes of the one I fell in love with long ago."* I opened the fold, and he had signed the inside, *"Jill, this is what I think about when I look at your face. Love always, Pat."*

It was sucking me in. The soup when I had the flu, the crotch tingles during the piggyback ride in the rain, the love letter, the nightly phone dialogues, the enchanted dream kiss come true, the artistry with which he exhibited his love for me. It was all a fluorescent bug zapper, and I was the insect, powerless to ignore the lure of dangerous pleasure that comes when another person simply adores you. Before the *Free Bird* kiss I feared that perhaps I should tread cautiously, that I was just getting enraptured in the egocentric thrill of being loved irrespective of the donor. Was I in love with love or in love with Pat? But after *Free Bird,* I gave up swimming upstream. For better or worse, I surrendered to the intoxication of bliss.

The rest of the school year flew by, and before I knew it I was out again for summer. The halcyon days of summer continued in this fairytale dream sequence, and for the first time in my life, I was at peace with the world – and myself. Pat and I did not want to waste any more time in a life without the other – I'd already squandered enough time writing him off as my nerd friend with red hair and freckles, so we woke up early every morning to meet. I left the house sometimes still in my pajamas, and he left the house in his, and we walked down the streets congested with double-parked Chryslers and station wagons with faux wood paneling trim, until we met in the middle.

Oak Avenue was a long block stretch, probably named for the strong beautiful oak trees that once lined it, but were now hacked back in contrived hoops around power lines. From down the long street I could see him approaching wearing a white beater undershirt and cotton shorts, walking slowing, probably still groggy from the fact that he was a teenage boy awake at 7:30 in the morning on summer vacation. "He looks good," I thought, admiring his broad shoulders and budding tan.

Just then I heard my mom's voice in my head. Like my friends, George and Scarlet, she detected the spark igniting between us long before Pat or I did, back when I still thought Pat was a detestable geek burger with cheese. "One day," she told me repeatedly in a mocking sing-song voice that only mothers can have, "you two will look at each other in a *whole new* light."

"That is vile, Mother," I cracked back at the time. I chuckled to myself thinking about it. I guess she was right.

As we inched closer to each other with each step, I would get all that psychosomatic fluttering in my stomach, like a fun version of nervous puke butterflies. Then I started smiling. I even, to my own surprise, giggled out and then looked around to make sure no one saw me. Good, no one around at this hour save an old woman watering the potted marigolds on her stoop.

"It's so amazing," I continued thinking as I strolled, "that the body and mind are so connected. Like love and sex, they are inexplicably twisted, commanding on their own and complicated when together. The body feels what the mind conjures. I just think of him, and my body reacts." And just then, my body reacted with a bolt of energy. I started running to him, a lanyard with the set of house keys I'd finally been trusted with clinking around my neck, and then I leapt up and wrapped my arms and legs around him, and we laughed.

"I have something for you, honey," he said as he plopped me back on the sidewalk, extending a hand with an offering.

"What is it?" I asked flirtatiously, eyeing the plastic sandwich bag containing small, pink candy marshmallows dangling from his slender fingers in front of me. I still couldn't contain the giggle-out-loud giddiness that had affected me moments before, and I didn't care to. Candy, love, youth, a summer day, a simple surprise. Did life get any sweeter?

"They're marshmallows from a box of Lucky Charms," he responded. "I picked out all the heart ones for you." Ooh. It just did.

We paraded down Oak Avenue and crossed the intersection with the gun shop and rinky-dink discount store. "Do you remember last summer when you drove by in Nikki Russo's grandmom's car and you jumped out here?" I asked him. He grinned in amusement, and maybe slight embarrassment. "I can't believe you did that. Wasn't she mad?"

"No, she knew we were friends."

"Yes, but you didn't leap out of that car on a red light because we were *friends.*"

"What can I say? I just love to be near you," he relented. And there it was, the psychosomatic stomach flittering again.

Our walk took us to a pancake house, where I enjoyed sausage and pancakes and a glass of cold milk. Pat treated me with his paper route earnings. We sat there for a few hours, holding hands across the table, and whispered sweet nothings over the clinking and clanking of silverware on dishes as a busboy cleared the tables around us. Patrons came and went with more clinking and clanking as their tables were cleared behind them as well, but we just sat there until it was nearly time for Pat's afternoon baseball game.

We went to Pat's house so he could change into his uniform, and then we headed to the ball field. We were early, so he laid on his back on the grass with his mitt next to him, apathetic about getting grass stains on his white baseball pants. I rested my head on his stomach, and our bodies formed a T. The field was a small oasis in the concrete jungle, a field that I had three-legged races across as a young girl, next to a playground where I spent half my childhood, the place of the "you look like you're fucking that thing" incident. It was on this field that Pat got on his bike two summers before and chased off older girls who were about to jump

66

me; I'd had red, welted handprints on my back from the shoving of spectators to the incident who kept thrusting me back into the ring of the thirsty mob. He happened to be there that day and cycled his bright orange Huffy into the commotion, breaking up the circle and herding the girls away. It was an anguished time and place, but now life was tranquil in the groomed grass on Pat's slowly rising and falling stomach.

Looking up at the clouds, I plucked a blade from the ground and fondled it in my hand, tearing it in strips down the veins like peeling a banana. As usual, he stroked my head and brushed stray dirty blonde strands from my face. If this moment was a scene from a romantic drama, there would have been violins and soft focus cinematography. Instead just then, "Oh Jesus. I think I just threw up in my mouth a little," said a loud, boisterous, bellowing Italian tone of voice.

George was crossing the gate toward us with his Phillies cap and a uniform that matched Pat's. "Enough kissy face, Abramowitz. Let's go," he directed Pat, and kept walking passed us in the direction of the dugout without looking back. George and Scarlet weren't the same people since Pat and I fell in love. They acted as though they were unnerved or felt neglected when they saw us together. Like we were breaking their hearts, somehow.

I sat next to Pat's mom on the metal bleachers, which were covered in a hodgepodge of different colored paint blotches that someone had done to cover all the graffiti. It was an effort of goodwill but a lost cause, it would just be replaced with even more graffiti soon enough. Sitting in the stands, sitting anywhere, without him was torturous. We simply could not endure being apart. So I watched him through the fence along the third base line as he squatted in center field. While checking out his butt in the tight uniform, I barely noticed George make a run in a rare departure from his usual lack of athletic prowess.

I was comfortable next to Pat's mom. She knew me well from all the time I spent at her home, hanging out in the Seventies basement and staying over for dinner. She liked me. And my parents knew Pat well and trusted him. They knew we were both good kids. Pat's mom and I chatted politely on the bleachers but my focus was on her son, now trotting back in at the end of the inning, waving me an "I love you" in sign language.

After the game was over, I didn't even know if they won or lost, as parents and grandparents and coaches and teammates milled around greeting each other and collecting equipment. Pat rushed to the stands like we were being reunited after months away, scooped me up, cradled me in his arms, and dashed back onto the dirt of the diamond in front of everyone where he spun me around, shouting "I'm gonna marry this girl!" Many of the grown-ups clapped, remembering their first puppy love, some of my peers smiled, but George rolled his eyes and looked away bitterly.

I had plans to spend the rest of the evening after the game with Scarlet, in the warm air of a June night when the sun takes longer and longer to melt into dusk. The plans fell through. Actually, I just ditched the plans. I don't remember how I broke the news to her or how I justified it to myself, but I decided I'd rather hang out with Pat. I'd rather be with Pat over anyone, or more than eating, sleeping, or anything else, for that matter. So he came over, and we cuddled and relived some of our *Free Bird* kiss moments, which were even more passionate in our entangled embrace on my living room couch. At curfew, he walked back home and called me for our nightly phone chat until I fell asleep with the phone in my hand around two o'clock. Then we woke up early and did it all again. This day repeated itself nearly every morning that summer like a blissful version of Groundhog Day – well, blissful for me and Pat, not so much for Scarlet.

It was late July, and George and I sat on his front stoop in front of his house, thirteen row homes away from mine, talking idly.

"Five and a half more weeks until school starts," George declared.

"George, you are such a dork. Can we not talk about school, please? It's the summer", I muttered in response.

"Fine. What are you doing later?"

"Watching a movie at Pat's."

George made a disgusted face and rolled his eyes, as I protested, "What? You can come if you want to."

"Yeah right."

"Why not?"

"Cause I don't want to be the third wheel while you're sitting on his lap making out and stuff. That's nasty," George said.

"It's not nasty. You just don't understand because you've never been in love before."

"So. Just because you are doesn't mean you have to ditch your friends and make everyone uncomfortable." George finally got to the crux of the problem.

"You're being immature. The only reason you think that is because you're a teenager."

"Hello. You're a teenager too."

"Yes," I agreed, "but do you think adults get mad when their friends want to spend time with their husbands and wives? Do you think they make faces when their friend kisses their husband? Affection is good for you, and the only reason you're upset is because you're too young to understand. You should be happy for me!"

Before he could answer his grandmother called through the screen door, "George, come get your supper." He went inside with a blank face, and I went to Pat's. I was right; George didn't understand. But I didn't understand either. I didn't know what it felt like to be so left out by my best friend.

That night when Pat and I had our late phone date, I mentioned the negativity that was bringing me down. "George is pissing me off," I told Pat through my Elvis phone. "He's always complaining about us. Why can't he just let us be who we are? And Scarlet is even worse!"

I read him a note she delivered to my house and left in my family's little brass mailbox. In it Scarlet composed a sad story that went, "I never really get to see you very often, and I want to know what's going on in your life. Your life, which consists a lot of Pat. Maybe I'm taking my feelings of hurt out on you and Pat…but you almost abandon me for something better, like somehow I wasn't good enough. I always think to myself, 'Is there something I could have done to make her want to leave me, and things could be the way they used to be'?"

Pat and I agreed our love had become distressing for those around us. But why the yanking of my heartstrings? Why did George and Scarlet make me feel as though in dating Pat I was breaking up with them? I didn't like my predicament. Not one bit. But in the end, I figured that if I was forced to choose, I'd rather be on that wooden rocking chair on my front porch when I was old and gray than with friends but without love, passion, and romance. I let the friendships whither. We still hung out sometimes, but it wasn't the same.

When yet another fall approached, I readied my schoolbag with fresh new spiral notebooks that had yet to be scribbled in and a packet of black pens that had yet to be lost or chewed. I was energized to start tenth grade with the other four thousand students who packed the hallways of Upper Darby High School. The building on the outskirts of Philadelphia was the same one in which my parents had met twenty-two years before. The high school was a real-life lesson on diversity that would shame any Human Resources department or college orientation training. It was a fusion of Greeks and Italians, Russians and Nigerians, Pakistanis and Puerto Ricans, all coexisting in narrow hallways. Little old white and blonde me was practically an anonymous punching bag no one noticed in the mayhem of thousands of teenagers trying to make it to class on time.

Maybe I had some small level of distinctiveness. To some people I was still "the dirty hippie" or "one of the smart ones." To others I was some ugly girl worthy of a little dose of ridicule every now and then. But mostly I was just ignored. Pat had the same problem. But together, we had a new identity. We were "the couple," "the love birds," or simply, "Jill and Pat," which rolled off the tongue in natural association like "peanut butter and jelly" or "shoes and socks."

Our peers, and teachers for that matter, detected our bond. Teenagers are notorious for their intense but short-lived love affairs, but somehow those around us perceived there was something different about us. And even though they still thought Pat was the antithesis of what they would consider as a cute and suitable mate, girls at school were envious and curious about our relationship. They noticed the heart-shaped love notes he taped to the locker we shared. They noticed that we walked hand in hand everywhere we went. They noticed one afternoon in the courtyard outside the cafeteria when Pat cradled my face in his hands and told me in a throaty whisper, "You look gorgeous right now. I mean really gorgeous. The way the light is hitting you, your hair, freckles, and eyes are all the same shade. It looks so beautiful." People act like such sappiness is repulsive, but deep down I think everyone wants to be loved like that.

Soon other tenth graders suddenly found me a person worthy of talking to. By Christmas vacation I was the go-to girl for dating advice. In the world of fifteen-year-olds, maintaining a six-month relationship without drama and tears, without rumors and accusations culminating in entire social circles getting into screaming matches at a school dance, was an anomaly.

"Pat treats you like gold. You're so lucky. I'm lucky if my man calls me when he says he will," admitted one acquaintance from school.

"Did you ever tell your boyfriend you'd like him to call you more?" I asked in response.

"No," she answered. "But he should know. He should know because when he does call me I say, 'oh, nice of you to finally call!' It's like 'hello, get a clue.'"

"It's frustrating but guys aren't mind readers. You have to speak up about what you want. You can't expect them to just 'know,'" I retorted. I eyed her sexed-up get-up of heavy eye makeup and garish jewelry from South Street, remembered her telling me stories of lay-there-and-wait-for-it-to-be-over sex with boys in an attempt to keep their affections, and I added for what it was worth, "And you know, it's ok to be yourself. You're worth being cared for just as you are. And if you are going to have sex with these guys, you need to make sure that you get pleasure too. It's not all about them."

In one boring lecture class there was a girl who sat in the desk behind me. She always kept her windbreaker on, half zipped with the sleeves pushed up even when it was warm in the classroom. It was some kind of security blanket or something. She always had her hair tied back in a simple ponytail. That's all I would have remembered about her had she not one day tapped me on the shoulder to grill me for romantic ideas for her boyfriend's birthday, and then each subsequent day fill me in on the latest installment of how she had created his homemade gift, and then got into a fight and nearly broke up before his birthday actually came around.

I was starting to really love my new role in my little world of Upper Darby High School. I was High School Sophomore Pseudo-Therapist Extraordinaire. I loved the detective work of finding the solution to the problem, giving advice in a way that was encouraging and sensitive, and best of all being trusted with salacious and juicy information the person had never told anyone before. But my suggestions were only based on my own limited personal experience, Cosmopolitan magazine, and a little measure of common sense. I needed more. I needed to do real research. I was famished with a gnawing hunger for knowledge of everything in matters of the heart. I guess you could call me a hopeless romantic.

By this time my parents' divorce was final, I had made my difficult decision. My mother remarried and moved across the river to New Jersey and took my sister to live with her, and I decided to stay with my dad and his new fiancé at home, close to Pat. After a year and a half of the nightly chats, my dad knew full well that I talked to Pat on the phone all night. When Pat would call in the evening, I would promptly leave the living room and walk up the stairs yapping, suddenly unaware of anything happening around me. The computer was no longer the object of my attention. The glass of milk I poured sat forgotten on the coffee table.

"Goodnight, Jill. I guess we'll see you tomorrow," my dad joked as I trotted up the steps, knowing that once Pat rang for me I was in a Pat-daze for the rest of the night. He teased that when he checked on me before he retired to bed, I could always be found conked out with a phone still on my pillow. Perhaps unlike most fathers, he didn't mind that I spent an inordinate amount of time with my boyfriend, at this point anyway, because it was a break from my usual uptight, fun-is-for-after-our-work-is-done, annoyingly well-behaved personality.

He wanted me to live a little, unwind my perfectionist coil. I arrived home late in the evening each day after school, volunteering, extracurricular activities, and the part-time job I took at McDonald's to save for a car, then I was up often until as late as four, writing and rewriting assignments. Unlike my freshman year, ninety-five percent wasn't good enough anymore. College applications needed to be bolstered. Scholarships needed to be earned. Resumes had to be sharpened. There were no excuses. I was often ill from exhaustion, but I went to school anyway. Once I was so sick from doing homework all night I stopped every few feet on the walk to the bus stop and sat on the curb to vomit in the street. But I didn't turn around and go home. I couldn't miss school. I didn't want to miss an assignment, or disappoint a teacher and lose the perfect student image.

"I'm so proud of how great of a student you are, Jill," my dad would say, "But at what cost? You need to live a little. What's the worst thing that could happen if you played a board game with me tonight instead of doing your homework?" The thought was preposterous. But he was right. I was so overwhelmed and stressed by my self-inflicted standard of success I started losing my hair. Big clumps would come out in the shower. It was an awful time, and any free pockets of time I found were devoted to Pat. He was my sole source of fun, of youth, of entertainment. He kept me sane.

When I got that phone call each night, when I put the dejected day behind me, climbed my stairs in oblivion, and rejoiced in the quiet connection of a strong love, it was the only time I thought the world was good. I spoke into the same Elvis phone in the same bedroom as always, but our conversations had evolved. Before, we dreamt about better lives for ourselves; now we plotted the details.

"You know what I think is sad?" I said into the mouthpiece, peacefully snuggled under my childhood comforter. "That people don't put thought into who they marry. I mean, I suppose they do, but it seems that they just marry the person they happen to be dating when they're of marrying age. They love each other I'm sure, but it's not the 'love of their life.' Not like we are."

"I know. We are so lucky that we'll never have to be alone. We'll never have to worry about trying to meet somebody in a bar. We'll have each other forever," Pat said, and then added, "You know what else is sad? People in school. They fight, they break up, they get back together. It's so immature. They don't know how to work things out. The guys are assholes, and the girls put up with it. I just look at them and think 'I feel sorry for you because you don't have what I have.'"

We were surrounded by miserable couples, divorce, pain, and heartbreak. We knew what we didn't want, and we strategized ways to avoid it, as if our forethought would save us from a similar fate.

"Dates are important," I stated. "I think married couples get into ruts because they stop taking time for their love to keep growing. They let chores like cleaning the garage and work and crap get in the way."

"We'll never do that," Pat agreed.

"So I think we should make sure we go on at least one date every week to reconnect," I offered.

"Yes, like every Wednesday or something would be our special date night. We'll find babysitters for Autumn Renee," he said. We had already picked out the name of our child, agreed we were only having one, at the age of thirty after we had time to travel. We had it all figured out, compromised on, and agreed on. In stone. We would have a cottage-style house with a white picket fence, bay window, and steps that go straight up, a small bed so we could cuddle more easily every night and awake to our cat enjoying the sun spot at the foot of our bed every morning. And sex, like the Wednesday night date, would be properly maintained and never allowed to get boring or fall by the wayside. We conspired about how we would spend holidays, how we would budget our money, what to do after retirement. We would die peacefully at ninety-four years old sleeping in each other's arms. We had our whole lives ahead of us, I couldn't wait to be done with dreadful school and get started. No way could it not happen this way. But just in case:

"Pat," I whispered. "The way I feel this moment, I want to feel like this always."

"Me too, Jill. More than anything," he whispered back.

"But what if we don't?" I asked fearfully. "What if we lose sight of this feeling, we let life, work, or cleaning garages get in the way?"

"We won't. It's impossible."

"Let's make a pact. We will go to the senior prom together no matter what. If somehow, someway, we forget the way we feel this second and we break up, even if we're dating other people and think we're in love with them, even if we hate each other, we will go together so we can rekindle. There is no way we could dance and hold each other and not want to recapture this. It's foolproof," I concocted, and I could hear him smiling.

"Well, it's silly to talk about because that's just never going to happen. I can't even imagine us hating each other. But just in case, I promise. It's a date."

I felt good about this. I felt smart. I felt like I understood things most people didn't about love and relationships and how to make them work. I was satisfied with my foolproof scheme, and after my taste of being a high school dating expert, I wanted more.

"Pat, I want to be like a, like a love guru or a sex therapist or something when I grow up."

"I thought you wanted to be a high school English teacher?"

"Well, I do. But I'll have the summers off to write self-help books about relationships. What does love mean? I want to study it. I want other people to understand it. That is what my books will be about."

"What do you think love means?" he asked me.

"I don't know, but I know life would suck without it. What do you think it means, Pat?"

"It means I never want to let you go." The words bounced around in my head while my heart pounded in rhythm. I managed to squeak out, "I don't want to be let go. Hold on to me, in every way you can."

Chapter 9

My first experience with song was as a toddler, watching music videos on MTV; a terrific benefit of having young parents in the mid-1980s. My favorite music video was by Billy Joel. There were very few things in his "We Didn't Start the Fire" list of historical events that I knew about back in 1989. Only three things actually: Elvis Presley, Disneyland, and baseball. Was I a quintessential little American or what? Just add apple pie in there, and I could've been on the front of a Wheaties box!

I asked my parents what the song was about, and their response confused me for years to come. They said, "It was when all those things were invented." *Invented*. Wrong choice of words. At one point Billy says the word "sex" in reference to a high profile sex scandal, and I knew that Elvis Presley was popular in the 1950s, so I for the life of me could not figure out how all the people older than Elvis came to be if sex wasn't invented until the 50s. Do not ask me how a four year old child has the wherewithal to analyze this, but that was me.

Of course I never asked my mom or dad for clarification. I never asked them about sex. I knew it was bad, that it shouldn't be talked about. I don't know where I learned this because it certainly didn't come from my family, but like most people, it was somehow ingrained in me at a young age. I closed my eyes during kissing scenes in movies because I didn't want people to think I was a pervert for being interested in seeing it. When I got my period at 11 years old I didn't tell my mother because I was too embarrassed to admit such an awful grown-up thing had happened to me. I was completely and inexplicably consumed with shame. When she found out a few months later and tried to talk to me about it, I sat on my living room floor with my hands over my ears, crying and yelling "LA LA LA LA LA," desperately trying to drown her out.

"You should be happy you have parents who tell you about these things," both my parents brought up at the dinner table. "Could you imagine how scared you would be if you didn't know why you were bleeding? If you didn't understand what was happening? We're trying to help you." I was so mortified I wanted to die. I would have elected to have my fingernails ripped off one at a time rather than sit at that dining room table at that moment.

"Oh my GOD! You guys are disgusting! What part of 'I don't want to talk about this' do you not understand?"

They looked at each other with great concern. How had I become so high-strung? In a household so open to frank discussion, it was a mystery to everyone how I managed to be the uptight black sheep of the family.

Fast forward eleven years as I was about to receive a phone call from my attorney, Mark D'Ortone. In retrospect, I suppose I was optimistic that he would bring me good news because while I was waiting, I continued to invest time and money into preparing for the opening of my business. The green walls were now completely a memory under the fresh Priscilla Pink paint. I purchased a cash register and satin hangers for the lingerie. I had flyers printed on nice glossy paper to promote my grand opening. I even had cute little pink and brown ribbon curtains hung in the small front windows of would-be Feminique Boutique. I opened several credit cards, with a total $8,000 limit, to pay for all these start-up costs and hoped for the best. The polka dot curtains in the charming square-paned window looked more appropriate for a beachfront cottage than a sex shop, but that was precisely the look I was going for: friendly, homey, welcoming, and natural.

It's unusual for me not to recall specific details, but I don't remember where I was or what I was doing when Mark called me with the news. "Anthony Ciccerone and the borough solicitor agreed to have a meeting with us." What? I almost didn't believe him, I felt as if I was watching a rerun of "Who Wants to Be a Millionaire?" when, for dramatic effect, Regis waits several seconds to tell the contestants they have the correct answer. With information as spectacular as "your dreams may actually have a fighting chance" you expect a drumroll or an exclamation point or something, but real life doesn't have a soundtrack or graphics.

The big day arrived, and yet again I found myself sitting around a conference table dressed in a suit. Mark and I entered the room and were greeted by Anothony Ciccerone and the borough solicitor, Brenda Beese, a young slender woman I thought looked prematurely bitter, as if the weight of the world and The Man had already beaten her down.

The mood was strangely friendly. Ciccerone complimented my white peacoat and mentioned his daughter had one that was similar, Brenda chatted up Mark about other attorneys they were both acquainted with. I got a warm, firm handshake from everyone. This went on for more than ten minutes. Obviously the boxing gloves were coming off, and I felt even more foolish than I already had about going in guns blazing on my last encounter with Anthony Ciccerone at Borough Hall. We were going to be professionals now? Equals? Ok, I could play along.

But soon enough the niceties were done, and it was time to get down to business. I took Mark's cue and found a seat around the table. I sat down and just sank right in, suddenly small. It reminded me of when I was little and I could barely see over the checkout counter at the store. I was the child in the room. The kid at the grownups' table. Everyone could sense it, but I pretended not to notice, trying to act as if I owned the place, that they were there at my mercy instead of the other way around.

Just as Mark's phone call is hazy in my memory, strangely so are the details of this meeting. I can't remember how long it took, and little of what was said. I do remember Brenda was concerned mainly about the "specified anatomical areas" portion of the adult entertainment code.

"Brenda," I said. "I think you have the wrong idea. You're thinking of the typical triple X store at truck stops off the side of the highway with the peep shows and porn videos. My store won't be like that. I won't be selling any pornography."

Again, for once I don't remember the conversation word for word, but I do recall her facial expression. She was trying to remain polite while also making it clear that she thought I was full of shit. She looked like she thought I would say anything or tell any lie necessary to get this permit. I imagined she didn't believe me because it never occurred to her that sex could ever be commercialized in any way except as raunchy and vulgar.

I told her there would be no pornography not to appease her but because I actually had no interest in selling it. It wasn't part of my business model as a sex shop and education center that teaches women to not be sexual receptacles for men, but rather agents of their own bodies and in control of their sexual empowerment. Although, I don't think I used this sexologist jargon. I probably said something like "I won't be selling pornography because it wasn't part of my business model as a female-friendly sex shop." That settled her down a bit. She and Ciccerone agreed that if they specified in writing those "specified anatomical areas" (which oddly enough were never actually specified in the code) to include "penis, vulva, anus, gluteal cleft, female nipple, or the depiction of a penis in a turgid state," and I would agree to not display any of those things, then I could open Feminique Boutique and go on my merry way. YES! I agreed. I promised. I swore. And I would honor my word. But inside I was laughing at the absolute absurdity. I shook their hands, and Mark's too, and went back to the shop. I needed to put on the final touches for opening day, now that I was actually going to have one.

Back at Feminique, I worked to make sure that my store followed the rules set out by Ciccerone and Beese. The anti-"anus," "vulva," and "penis" (whether in a turgid state or a flaccid one) statute was easy to comply with because I hadn't intended on parading them around the store anyway. The ban on female nipples was a little more challenging. Some of the tags on the lingerie might show a little something, and a few boxes of vibrators exhibited a woman's nipple or two, but no problem. I would just sell a different toy. Or put the price sticker over it, and make sure the sticker was big enough to obscure the areola too, just in case there was an areola ordinance I didn't know about.

I was so busy being resourceful in finding ways to shield the world from female nipples at Feminique Boutique that I didn't have time to get angry about the disconcerting sexualization of breasts that made public breastfeeding scandalous, the double standard of male versus female nipples, or the various other sexist boob-related social norms I was being forced to comply with.

In the task of making sure the "specified anatomical areas" rules were followed, the next thing I had to be rid of was gluteal clefts. Gluteal cleft? That's a butt crack, my friend! That ban in the code forced me to get rid of a beautiful piece of artwork I had purchased to hang over the shelf of chocolate body topping and flavored oil – a 27- by 36-inch sepia toned print of the back of a woman wrapping herself in a bath towel. I thought the browns and tans of the lighting and the womanly angles perfectly represented the sensual and feminine atmosphere I was attempting to project. But alas, her towel dipped down displaying her cheek and a shadow of her butt crack, or "gluteal cleft," and thus the art could not be hung. Because in West Chester, Pennsylvania, a butt crack is considered *legally* obscene.

After ensuring that Feminique Boutique was thoroughly butt crack- and nipple-free, I was ready for opening day. It was May 3, 2008, only twelve short months since I graduated from college. I opened the door, I put out my shingle, I set up a table for free food and tied up pink helium heart balloons outside. My mom and sister came by to show their support, as did my dad, and George, and my Gram and Grandpop who brought me pink flowers of congratulations.

"Good luck, kiddo," my dad said with a hug.

"I'm real happy for you," George told me while admiring

the dressing room he had helped paint a month before. It was now complete with a full-length mirror, clothes hooks, and hand-painted decorative accents. But soon enough all the well-wishes had been said, and my loved ones went back to their own lives, leaving me alone on the first day of my first real job. It reminded me of the way I felt on the first day of college after my family helped me carry all of my boxes to my dorm room, and then, just like that, were gone. It hit me that this thing I had spent so long preparing for was finally here, and I was in it all by myself.

So alone in Feminique Boutique I sat. And sat. And sat. And sat. I sat for nine hours and sold but one thing, a funky twisted purple vibrator with an attached clitoral stimulator for $31. So much for the idea that sex sells.

In the days that followed, my elegant New England-esque hanging scroll bracket sign was installed, and my dad made me a whiteboard A-frame sign for the sidewalk. In pink marker I carefully printed that I was open for business, but sales only slightly improved. I sold a few 99-cent trial-sized personal lubricants and a pair of panties. I ordered some pink t-shirts with two baseballs where the breasts are and the words "Save 2nd Base" as a fundraiser for a local breast cancer charity. I thought the combination of awareness and sexual humor and innuendo was quite clever, and apparently others thought so too because I sold a few of them. Mother's Day was a week after I opened, so I made a couple of bucks when men bought their wives and mothers last minute gifts of bubble bath or a candle. But that was pretty much it. I was starting to get worried. I couldn't make a living like this. I started thinking about all the credit cards I had nearly maxed out in order to start this business.

On my insanely limited budget, I looked into some cheap advertising. I thought about places where I usually noticed ads, and two that came to mind were the ads to the right of the screen on Facebook, and the ads on the back of the grocery receipt. As if the $500 I had to spend for the entire year on advertising wasn't a setback enough, I ran into even more setbacks. Go figure.

I loved the idea of Facebook advertising because you only

have to pay if it works. You can design the little ad in the box and link it to your website, and only pay if someone clicks it. The clicks are only pennies, and I thought this was an effective approach. I created a simple ad that said something to the effect of "Female Positive Sex Education Workshops" with a link to my website.

Not only did Facebook (which is supposed to be the cool force for social change) immediately take down the ad as being "abusive" but banished me from ever again running an advertisement for anything, saying any promotion of mine "should not be run again on the site under any circumstances."

With that effective and dirt cheap advertising idea exterminated, I tried the grocery receipt companies and found that my local grocery store, just on the outskirts of downtown West Chester, had an open space. It cost more than $500, but the ad would run for months, until the paper rolls ran out. I liked the idea because I knew I use the coupons on the back of receipts for oil changes and diners, so I was sure other people did too. Plus, the nice thing about coupons is you can track their success; when customers redeem them you know the promotion was successful. I decided it was worth the investment. Using the small margin I had left before my credit cards were maxed out, I went for it.

I designed a simple ad on my computer. It had a photo of me in a lingerie set because I was too poor to hire models and I look pretty damn hot in lingerie. In addition to my lingerie photo, the ad had the Feminique Boutique logo, the words "Smart. Sassy. Sexy," and a coupon for $5 off a purchase. This ad was shot down because of the photo of me in lace underwear. I changed the photo but it was denied again, this time for the words.

"We can't print the word "sexy," the ad representative wrote in his emailed response.

I was shocked that the word "sexy" was off-limits. It was becoming my routine: I was once again out of options and at another blockaded road. I begrudgingly revised my one- by three-inch advertisement yet again. This time, it said "Feminique Boutique: Lingerie." Like my eager agreement with West

Chester's nipple ordinance, I was getting so into the creative groove of finding ways to make this work that I didn't immediately notice that I was not being true to my mission. I didn't notice that I was compromising myself and my desire to promote positive sexual images. Instead, I was complying with social norms that I thought were hypocritical, norms that said that the female body was something to be ashamed of. Do the ends justify the means? Should I cover up and quiet down so I could get my name out there, and then proceed with my pleasure manifesto once my business was known and established? I decided that this was another worthwhile setback and submitted the "Feminique Boutique: Lingerie" ad.

"I'm sorry," the advertising sales rep responded. What could the problem be this time? "Apparently the word 'lingerie' is problematic to my boss," he said.

"You are kidding me!" I shot back. It's lingerie. LINGERIE! As in frilly sleepwear. They sell lingerie at Kmart. What is wrong with the word "lingerie" for shit's sake? Nevertheless, I revised the vetoed advertisement once more. This time to the most innocuous, asexual showing ever. It read "Feminique Boutique: Come take a peek" with a photo of me with 1940s style hair and dress peeking into a paper shopping bag. Unless one was already familiar with the fact that Feminique Boutique was a feminist sex shop, it would be impossible to determine it from this ad. This was a point that still somewhat unsettled me, if people didn't know what I was selling, how could the ad attract the clientele I wanted? But I'd come so far with this ad I didn't want to give up. I thought the ad made Feminique Boutique look like a consignment shop, but at least my name would be out there.

A few days later I opened the shop one morning, feeling good after doing an in-home party. I had done fewer parties while working to open my store, and I missed the laughter, the learning, the friendships that were formed with strangers during a quick three-hour event. It was easy to forget, while knee-deep in the mundane world of operating a retail store, that this was the reason I

84

had started a business in the first place. My day to day acti
included typing up the company budget, filling out state
government sales tax forms, and cleaning the toilet. Up until this
point I had never cleaned a toilet in my life, but alas, it was a warm
welcome into the world of owning my own business.

None of these daily activities are sexy. None of these things
set my soul on fire in my single-handed mission to start the new
sexual revolution. I was working ninety hours a week as a pencil
pusher with no income to show for it. The few customers that I did
have did not ask for advice or tell me their deepest darkest secrets,
like the women did during the Foreplay 101, Orgasm 101, or
Fellatio 101 parties. But why would they? There was no rapport
being built when a customer came in to buy a product, as there was
at a party, where friends chatted and sipped cocktails while
listening to my talk on the impact of female genital shaming or
penis anatomy. The customers who came to my store didn't know
me. I had not yet made a name for myself.

I had felt victorious when Ciccerone had given me the
permit to open my store, but my victory was short-lived. Not only
did I have to deal with the problems of marketing and advertising,
the West Chester Borough Council set a meeting to rewrite the
zoning code for adult entertainment to be more specific and
include the sale of vibrators among the prohibited uses so that they
would never have to worry about another Feminique Boutique-type
store opening again. As a sex-positive sexologist, I was saddened
that they were so hell-bent on repressing anything sexuality
related, but as a business owner, I was thrilled! Not only were they
effectively ensuring my monopoly by prohibiting a competitor
from ever opening nearby, but my meeting with Anthony
Ciccerone and the planned Borough Council meeting to rewrite the
code had made the front page of the local newspaper! Thank you,
West Chester! Everyone in town now knew about my store, and I
hadn't had to pay for advertising.

But when the front page story and my budget breaking
"come take a peek" ad did not improve business sales one iota in
the days following, my fear grew that not only was I going to go

bankrupt, not only was I going to be a failure, but Feminique Boutique was never going to be the leader in the movement, the advocate at the front of the picket line. I started thinking that I had allowed myself to get sucked into an idealized version of reality. I thought running Feminique Boutique was going to be all sexy, all passion, all monumental and life changing, all the time. It never dawned on me that there might sometimes be a customer who just wanted to buy a bottle of lube and not talk about the weighty socio-sexual quandaries that plague our world. This saddened me because I started Feminique to engage people in such conversations, not just peddle products.

If all this weren't enough, I got an email from the advertising representative from the grocery store register tape company. It read, "Hi, Jill. We received a call from the corporate offices of the grocery store chain asking us to remove the Feminique Boutique ads from the West Chester store. Unfortunately there is nothing I can do about this. You will receive a full refund on the money you paid."

"I don't understand," I responded, floored. "I thought you cleared this with both your boss, and the stores you provide register tape for, before it was printed."

"Our market relations department cleared it, but likely someone at the store (employee or shopper) called their corporate offices," he emailed back, and on that note the dialogue was concluded with an "all the best."

Someone was truly offended, insulted, and had complained about me posing in a knee-length dress and holding a paper shopping bag with the caption "Come take a peek?" My revolutionary spirit, which had gone into hiding under the weight of trying to open a business, regained its gusto as I realized how desperately it was needed. I was now anxious to get this new sexual revolution started and blow this little business up. I was a rocket with a lit fuse on the Fourth of July. My manifesto was written but I had no platform from which to deliver it, no audience, no listeners, and no followers. Yet...

Chapter 10

Fourteen turned into fifteen and fifteen turned into sweet sixteen, and as Pat and I grew, our love grew in intensity. Lots and lots of intensity.

He painted my toenails and showed up at my door late at night with a pint of ice cream. He knew I loved surprises, and on the morning of my sixteenth birthday, I was certainly surprised to see him standing over my bed. He handed me a birthday card, gave me a kiss, peeled my blanket down, and said, "C'mon honey, get dressed."

"Why? What are we doing?" I asked.

"I can't tell you yet. Just hurry up. It doesn't matter what you wear. Just throw something on," he said. So I did. He brought me outside where his mother and her new boyfriend were waiting in the car. We got inside.

"Where are we going?" I asked, confused. No one would tell me. After an hour of driving south, I finally discovered we were headed to the beach for the weekend.

"The whole weekend!" I exclaimed. It had been years since I had had such a treat, back before my parents' divorce when my family would drive to Wildwood, New Jersey, and eat waffles and ice cream sandwiches on the boardwalk and ride the bumper cars at night and spend hours and hours playing in the sand during the day. The salty seaweedy surf, the obnoxious overbearing seagulls, one of whom once had the impudence to land on my head and steal a hotdog right out of my hand, approaching the line for the biggest Ferris wheel I've ever seen while holding my dad's hand with my one hand and my mom's hand in the other – it was a flashback to the epitome of happy childhood memories. The spokes of the Ferris wheel lit up and danced in the spectacular show only a carnival could create. From the top, you could capture the perfect view of the ocean at night, black as far as the eye could see, nothing but water miles deep and thousands of miles out; a magnificent wonder, and I was on the brink of it.

How splendid it would be to experience it with the love of my life; more memories to build a lifetime on! "But what about work?" I asked, suddenly aware that life stressors and responsibilities don't care if it's your sixteenth birthday.

"I called in and requested off for you," Pat said.

"Well what about my dad? I have to ask permission," I interrupted again.

"Taken care of," Pat answered. "I talked to him about it a week ago. He gave me the key to your house so I could come in early and wake you up this morning." I was so amazed. Even though I'd been spoiled with his sweet and thoughtful gestures before, I couldn't believe Pat would go through such trouble for me.

"But Pat," I continued. The same neurotic impulse knocking in my brain that made me be obsessed with academic perfection would not let me relax and enjoy this amazing gift until I knew everything was in order, taken care of, prepared for. "I didn't bring any spare clothes. Or a bathing suit." He lifted a duffle bag from the floor of the car.

"I packed for you. Of course your room is a mess, and you have no clean clothes in any of your drawers or closet, so I just scooped up a handful of dirty clothes from your floor, washed them, and packed them."

I was speechless. What do you say to that? Through the rearview mirror I saw Pat's mom glance at her boyfriend in the passenger seat with a proud smile. She knew she was raising a boy who was going to be a wonderful man.

"But...but what about your brothers and sister?" I asked again.

"Pat arranged to have their uncle watch them for the weekend, so that we would be free to supervise," Pat's mom chimed in.

I really did not know what to say, or how to feel. The magnitude of his care and attention to detail, the finagling he must have done to convince my dad to let me go, his mom to drive us all the way there, his uncle to babysit two kids for a weekend, my work to let me have off, and the money to pay for the motel room and food and games on the boardwalk. It rained the entire weekend but in the end all I could do was wonder what I had done to warrant the love he had for me. Whenever I thanked him for all these grandiose demonstrations of affection he simply replied, "If it puts a smile on your face, it's worth it. All I've ever wanted is for you to be happy."

But it wasn't so much these gestures that kept me coming back, but rather our intrinsic bond. We were a part of each other, and the fibers of our lives became irrevocably woven into one cloth. Since the *Free Bird* kiss I had received daily love letters from him. One day he wrote me, "You are a part of me in so many ways. You can tell me how nice and good of a boyfriend I am, but without you none of it would be possible. Don't forget my niceness has a lot to do with your very being."

My school work and my perfectionism continued to beat the life out of me. I was unrecognizable as a teenager. I was more responsible than many adults, getting up while it was still dark, attending school all day, and then sweeping the floors of McDonald's at night for $5.15 an hour to pay for my own car insurance and cell phone bill. I was "on" all the time, always together, always self-sufficient and independent. And at the end of the day, all I wanted to do was collapse, fall apart, become unhinged, crumble and let someone else pick up my pieces. That someone was Pat.

Our bond, our interwoven fabric, became tighter all the time. Desire to be together became need, because when you are only half of a whole, you need both your pieces together to feel complete. When you put yourself in a cage the key of salvation becomes addiction. So wherever Pat went I followed, and vice versa. We worked at McDonald's together and lobbied to have the same shifts; we went to the guidance counselor at school to ensure that we could have the same lunch period. Our only time apart other than sleep was the hour and a half he ran with the track team after school. I did homework in the library instead of home on those days so that we could spend extra time together on the bus on the ride home.

One day at the library I took a break from my school assignments to read up on love and romance. Every chance I could I studied these topics; I longed to know the secrets to make love last, to learn everything about the positive sensations that flood through the body of those in love, both for my own interest and so I would be better at giving relationship advice to my classmates. I found a little book on a rotating wire rack, a small pink book all about kissing, and on each page was a description of a kissing technique and how to master it. I checked it out of the library and brought it back to Pat's house. In his bed, with the yellow street light from the back alley casting a sultry shadow, we tried out each one. His bedroom doorknob did not properly latch so we were always cautious, developing an acute sense of hearing as far as the sound of footsteps and an opening door were concerned.

By the light of the street lamp, I read the passages of directions. "The Vacuum Kiss" I whispered, reading from the text lying next to me on the pillow, the glossy page glistening in the dusk. "Suck on your lover's bottom lip and then run your tongue along the inside where their lip meets their gums." Without hesitation I leaned over Pat's relaxed body as he rested on his back with his head propped up on his open hand. I brought his bottom lip into my mouth and glided my tongue in his lip/gum crevice as the book prompted, I extrapolated the directions and moved my tongue along said crease of his top lip, then I integrated the

90

technique from the previous page, "The Hoover," and gently sucked on his tongue to pull it into my mouth, and then released it to again explore the underneath side of his lower lip. He had one arm wrapped tight around my upper body, and the other one hovered around my belt line, grazing the top of my hipbone exposed by my slightly lifted shirt.

"Ok...that's enough of that one," I said teasingly pulling away just as things began to get hot, so I could flip the page. I rolled off him to lie by his side on the narrow twin bed, covered in his simple navy blue fitted sheet and a yellow pig pillow that he had made for me back in a mandatory middle school home economics class. I gave him a seductive smile. Side by side on our backs, I held the book out straight in front of me, prepared and excited to read the next step of our exploration, when the bedroom door flew open. Pat and I scrambled to sit up and look innocent, like the mad dash to gather up picnic supplies when a sudden downpour interrupts an otherwise sunny day.

His mother had pushed the door open on her way to the bathroom, but hadn't looked in. I think she didn't want to know, but wanted us to know she was there. Despite our sensitivity to the sounds of parents walking upstairs, she had caught us by surprise that time. Thankfully, we were only "reading a book." On the way back downstairs, she scolded, "You know you are supposed to keep the door open if you want to be up here."

"Sorry, Mom."

Further trips to the library after school were even more fruitful. I settled in at a large table with wooden chairs, surrounded by two stories worth of books, thousands and thousands of volumes of texts and no one there but me and the stout little librarian who reminded me of Mrs. Potts, the teapot from Disney's Beauty and the Beast. On my table was a stack of books but I don't remember any titles. They didn't have fancy covers, but usually a hunter green canvas binding that smelled like it hadn't been opened since 1972.

The outsides of the books were simple, but the insides were pure gold. I found out a lot about love and enhancing relationships and romance. I read about Sternberg's Theory of Love, which is represented as a triangle, with intimacy, passion, and commitment at the three points. According to psychologist Robert Sternberg, if all three pieces are not present, it's not a consummate love. In other words, commitment without passion or intimacy is like an old married couple who started to hate each other years before but stayed together for the kids. Passion without intimacy or commitment is a one-night stand, and so on. I was pleased with myself, confident in thinking that Pat and I had all three. To better identify my feeling for Pat I read about the social attributes of love, such as theories of attachment and attraction. I read about bio-chemical components such as the hormone oxytocin, which researchers think is related to why people in love feel bonded to each other. I was completely engrossed, and before I realized it I had burrowed through hundreds of pages.

These old books were about more than just love, they also talked about sex, and I hungrily consumed all of the knowledge between the pages. I read all about the sexual response cycle discovered in Masters and Johnson's labs; arousal, plateau, orgasm, and resolution. I read that men and women don't have the exact same cycle. The stereotypical TV and movie scene of couples coming at the same time in a perfect crescendo is a myth. I discovered that part of the unfortunate reality that many women feel the need to fake orgasm is based on their desire to conform to what they incorrectly think is normal.

I sat in my high school library and read about the importance of foreplay and special attention during the arousal stage of the sexual response cycle (although I already knew that one). I read about the nature/nurture debate as it relates to gender. Do you learn to be masculine or feminine, or are you born that way? If you play with dolls as a young boy does that change something about you? I had always wondered what being a male or female actually *meant* anyway. I read about the sexually marginalized, the old, the young, the disabled, and filed it away mentally so the next time I heard an ageist comment, like an "ewww" about old people having sex or a "save the children" comment about children and sex education, I could accurately help the person who made the comment understand the misinformation. I learned not just about sex, but the politics of sex.

Most importantly, I read all about the clitoris. How amazing is this little thing, the only part of the human body whose sole and single function on this earth is sexual pleasure! Why had I not learned of this organ in health class? Why had I experienced hours of instruction over the years on fallopian tubes and not a word about clitorises? Who cares about fallopian tubes? I had never laid eyes on a fallopian tube; I never would. Fallopian tube, what have you done for me lately?

But the clitoris on the other hand…the erectile tissue, the blood flow, the premier mode of female orgasm – I was astounded. After reading more and more about it, my mind excitedly cast back to that night of the carnival, when Pat gave me a piggyback ride and ran through the rain with my legs wrapped around him, inadvertently jostling me up and down with each hearty step. The "crotch tingle" sensation I felt. Yes! Rapidly it was all making sense. It was the "no duh" epiphany that changed my life.

The clitoris was single-handedly the center of the female sexual universe – the focus of pleasure for women. It should have been something I was aware of, but no one had ever told me about it. My parents had always discussed sex with me, sometimes more than I wanted to hear. But neither of them had ever mentioned the clitoris. Were they ashamed? Was everyone ashamed of this one little piece of female anatomy? Despite my progressive upbringing and a comparatively robust sex education from my public school, the fact that I'd been left in the dark about the clitoris was for me the ultimate symbolism of sexual oppression. At that moment, I decided I would make a life out of liberating that oppression.

I didn't have the language to describe what I wanted to do with my newfound love of helping people by giving sex and relationship advice, and I didn't know how to translate it into a career. "Love Guru" sounded like a sham, "Sex Therapist" wasn't quite right because I wanted to educate, not provide clinical counseling. "Sex Educator" didn't seem to fit either because the term conjured up visions of teaching tenth graders about fallopian tubes, which wasn't me. Whatever my job title, I knew my family would support me, and I was right. When I mentioned my new career plans to Gram a few days later she said, "You go, girl!"

But at that moment there was only so much time for filling my head with such thoughts. It was now three o'clock in the morning, and I sat awake in my bedroom writing an essay on the Federalist papers for AP Government and Politics, a college level class I took instead of having a lunch. My stomach hurt from fatigue, and I grew angry. We live in a "seize the day" world, an ethos that celebrates the risk and adventure of living each day like the next will never come, and following your heart while screwing the rules. But that same world sets the rules, and I believed it expected me to be the sacrificial lamb working constantly now in order to have success later. Forfeit today for a bigger tomorrow, save money now for splendor later. "But if I die tomorrow," I thought bitterly, "I'll never get to enjoy that bigger tomorrow. I'll have spent my teen years, the best years of my life, reading about Alexis de Tocqueville."

I was pissed, and I wanted to slam the book closed on my computer desk, but I didn't. I deliberated about it in my monumentally weary and soundly somnolent stupor, but ultimately determined I had to keep at it. I had to get those college scholarships and be successful. I continued to work until 4:30 a.m. What was I going to do, tell the teacher the next day that I didn't do the assignment because I had decided to live each day like it's my last and go out and be a normal teenager? Ha. "Correction," I thought before returning to my textbook, defeated, "We don't live in a world that celebrates a 'seize the day' attitude. That's only in the movies."

The next day was Friday, and while I was moving slowly after the mere hour of sleep the night before, I was also a bit giddy because Fridays meant my curfew was extended from 9:30 p.m. to eleven o'clock; extra time to relish in Pat's adoring embrace. I made it through the day, and in the evening while Pat was at an away track meet, my dad took George and me to Scarlet's Color

Guard competition. She had taken up flag twirling to busy herself and make new friends after Pat's and my excessive PDA became more than she could handle. But the three of us could pretend that things between us weren't so sour when Pat wasn't around. So my dad and George and I sat in the bleachers and watched Scarlet perform.

I rode shotgun in my dad's boat-on-wheels Buick on the car ride home, prime location for control of the radio dials. *Sugar Ray*. Next. *Limp Bizket*. Next. *Backstreet Boys*. Ugh. 2001 was such a bad year for music. I flipped the station again and settled back in my seat when I heard the iconic climaxing guitar wail of *Stairway to Heaven*. My dad started drumming on the vinyl steering wheel, leaned over, looked at me with a smirk, and shouted over the music as he turned up the volume, "If it's too loud, you're too old!," and I nodded approvingly.

I looked back over the center console at George in the backseat, who was looking out the window like an anxious puppy, and asked him, "What does this song make you think of?" George and I had a running game of trying to guess when, of all the million times we'd heard any given song, which event our mind casts back to when we heard the song again. Maybe it was that by this point we had been friends for nine years, but we both always thought of the same moment.

"What does this song make me think of? That's an easy one. 'Always rocked, and always will.'"

"You are a beast, my friend!"

He was referring to a mixed tape I had made years before by recording songs off the radio, in the days before CD players, or at least in the days before we could afford one. I had recorded the end of *Stairway to Heaven* just long enough on the cassette to hear the DJ say, "Always rocked and always will. WMMR, Philadelphia's Rock Station." I loved it. I loved that I had a friend with whom I could share such obscure inside jokes. Who else in the world would know something like that? I started to feel the way you feel looking at old pictures, thinking about the things I was missing out on in my mostly self-imprisoned life, a life punctuated by a few Pat-filled paroles. And Pat didn't even like rock 'n' roll, which was perplexing seeing how he loved me so much, and rock 'n' roll represented everything important to me – sexuality and rebellion and revolution embodied in song. Not that I was doing a good job at the rebellion and revolution thing as I continued to slave away to The Man in hopes of high academic pursuits, but it was in my bones. It was saturated in my marrow. It wasn't in Pat's. I had tried introducing Pat to an assortment of different rock sounds, Neil Young and Tom Petty, Guns N Roses and Carole King, The Supremes, The Beatles, and of course, Elvis. He hated most of it.

I turned around to George in the backseat again and asked, "Ok, what specific event do you think of?"

"June 15, 1999, the last day of middle school, on your front steps; you blasting the tape on the boom box."

As if the conversation wasn't dorky enough, I extended my hand for one of our own special high five-type handshakes to congratulate him on sharing the same random memory. My dad, now playing drums on the dashboard while stopped at a red traffic light, turned down the volume and chimed in.

"That's weird. That you both think of something like that."

"We have good memories," I said.

"I used to have a good memory."

"Sucks to get old, I guess."

"Yeah well it beats the alternative. But getting older gets me thinking, all I am is a collection of my memories. I am who I am because I can remember the things that shaped me to be this way. You know?" my dad asked.

"What about your genes and all that? Don't they have a role of making you who you are?" I asked

"Let me explain it to you this way. If you were in a coma and in your dreams had all of your wildest fantasies come true. Every wish and every wonderful thing you could possibly imagine happened, but when you woke up you didn't remember a second of it, as if nothing happened, would you want to do it?"

"Definitely," I responded.

"George, how about you?"

George leaned forward with his head between the two front seats to get a better listen, a half moon smile on his face. He, like Pat and Scarlet, thrived on such stimulating conversation with an adult who had something to say to him other than "George, your supper is ready," and "George, is your homework done?" Most lecturing parents would be eye-rolled as verbose and out of touch, but not my dad.

"Absolutely I'd do it," George responded. "Would you?"

"No," replied my dad.

"Why not?"

"Because it's like it didn't happen."

"Yes, but while you're living it, you're enjoying it. So who cares if you don't remember it?"

"It doesn't matter if you enjoyed it or hated it. If you don't remember it, it's pointless. It has no meaning. This is why people believe in religion and an afterlife, to be remembered. People have a hard time accepting that all they have known and felt and experienced will die when they die, because then what would be the point of living? Someday everyone I have ever known will be dead. Someday all photographs and recordings of me will have decayed, my bones completely disintegrated, any proof that I ever existed gone. You may as well never live at all."

I countered, "Ok, so it's true that we'll all be dead and nothing someday. But each moment that you are alive is a moment you're alive, and if you live in that moment it's an overall wonderful experience."

"If you believed that Jill, that the past was done and the future nothing and that you had to take the meaning and joy from each individual moment, you'd be visiting new places and going on adventures, and climbing mountains, and riding roller coasters, and swimming with dolphins, not spending six hours a day studying. See, humans look to put meaning in life, because the alternative is that there is no meaning. Life is exactly what you think it is. No more. No less. If you think life is a worthless pile of shit, it is. If you think life is part of a bigger cosmos of space and

97

the universe, it is."

"So, if you believe that you make life mean what you want it to mean, are you doing anything extraordinary to give your life meaning?" I asked.

"I never said I take my own advice," he said and paused for moment. "Being a father gives my life purpose."

"Aww," said George from the backseat.

"How did we get into this conversation?" I joked.

"How do we ever get into these conversations with your father?" George responded.

My dad's Buick stopped in front of George's home. George said his goodbyes, and Dad waited, double parked on the narrow street until he watched him safely step inside his front door. Before parking at our own house just a few houses down the road, I noticed the green digital clock on the dashboard read 9:37. The Friday night was still young.

"Dad, can you drop me off at Pat's?" I requested.

"No, not tonight." he responded.

"What! Why not?"

"Not tonight," he said again, no louder or sterner, just repeated again as if I didn't hear him the first time. I knew all too well he was impervious to a whining teenager.

"You don't understand. I have to!" I said, and erupted into a crying fit that I had no more control over than a car can control accelerating when its gas pedal is floored.

"Why are you crying?" he asked without a hint of judgment or coddling, just concern and curiosity.

"Because. It's not fair. I work my ass of all day every day and hanging out with Pat on Friday and Saturday nights is the only time I have to actually enjoy my life and you're taking that away from me. Tomorrow I'll be up working the noon to eight shift at McDonald's while half the other people in my school are sleeping in after a night of drinking. This is the reward I get for being responsible. Would you rather me be a druggie, dad?" I blubbered. He was sympathetic, but unyielding.

"Jill…"

But before he could finish I interjected, "Dad, if you make me stay in, I'm gonna go crazy! I need to be with Pat. I *need* him!" By this point my father had parked his car in the gravel lot in the alley behind my house, and there we sat in the dark unmoving. I thought by the way he was listening to me plead my case, that he might actually understand my need for a little latitude. He understood something very different.

"You need him? Jill, Patrick is a very nice boy. But you can never depend on someone else to make you happy. You have to be comfortable with yourself because no one will be able to make you happy a hundred percent of the time. They are always going to let you down. I tell you these things because I don't want to see you hurt."

He was just full of these mini life lessons, spoken with the simple wisdom of a fortune cookie and the eloquence of a Hallmark card. And I knew what he was getting at. He thought Pat and I were too emotionally entangled and dangerously obsessed with each other, unaware of the havoc we could wreak on each other's hearts. We were a pair of untamed horses, and my dad was trying to pull back on the reigns.

The argument had moved from curfew to something much deeper, and by now it was 10:15 p.m. and there was not enough time to do anything anyway. I relented and got out of the car. I was still pissed, and I wanted to pout, but he always made it hard to stomp away.

"I love you," my dad said as he approached me, "Give your father a hug," and he reached out to embrace me. Pride is a grainy pill to swallow, but much easier when the other person has already completely let go of theirs. I hugged him back and then we went into the house.

I don't remember how it was that Pat and I found ourselves after school in his bedroom one day, why he wasn't at track and why I wasn't at the library or volunteering or any of my other activities, but there we were, home alone at three in the afternoon with sixteen-year-old hormones pumping through our veins like a river's roaring rapids after a rainstorm. I slammed the door behind us and threw my back up against it, pulling him against me by the collar of his Philadelphia Eagles t-shirt. We made out ferociously, hands wildly clutching at whatever cloth or the flesh beneath it we could reach. The *Free Bird* kiss, as we reminisced often, had been soulful and artistic. But other times, like that afternoon, it was sloppy and sexy.

I was often the instigator, the initiator of sultry moments of passion, but I knew he was on board when I felt through both our jeans his hard-on against my thigh. I liked it. The feeling invigorated me even more, and I wanted to keep riding the roller coaster's exhilarating upward climb, and in that carnal enthusiasm I grabbed his hips and shifted him into a better position, and pulled him closer yet, harder, then slightly back again in rhythmic motions. He got the hint.

After my self-education on the magnificence of the clitoris in the preceding weeks and months, Pat quickly became my apprentice on the subject. When I related the trove of juicy knowledge I found in the dusty pages of our high school library, he smiled knowingly.

"So that's why you're always trying to hump me!" Pat exclaimed aloud.

"I do NOT!" I hollered back, embarrassed at the barefaced exposure of my budding sexuality that left me feeling as though I was standing there naked. But of course I did always try to hump him. After the night of the carnival in the rainstorm, it seemed as though I always had an excuse to sit on his lap, "inadvertently" wiggling around to find a comfortable position, or as our love grew, straight out pushing him on a bed or couch and straddling him, arranged so that the seam of my jeans gave excellent clitoral stimulation, something he was oblivious to until I clued him in after reading the books. Sometimes I thought I may have actually had an orgasm from the writhing, although I couldn't be sure. And in my head, I thought this was the most absolute perfect arrangement, almost a deal with the devil. I could experience the pleasure, the closeness of having this person I loved be so close to my body without worrying about pregnancy or AIDs or any of that other yucky stuff that I was learning about in health class in lieu of learning about clitorises.

But I was ashamed of it. Somewhere along the line I learned that women don't initiate sex, they give in to it, and also that intercourse is "real" sex. Whatever weird body gyrating thing I was doing, therefore must be kinda perverted. I was sure no one else on the planet was doing this bizarre thing, and if anyone ever walked in or found out about it, they would think I was weird. At that moment, looking down at Pat with one thigh on either side of him, seeing his face, I felt like a part of a magical secret world for two. But when I looked over my shoulder at our bodies, I felt like a dog humping its owner's leg. Gross. I hung my head down in shame.

A chapter on sex acts other than intercourse was the subject one day as once again Mrs. Potts and I shared the otherwise empty library. I read about fellatio, cunnilingus, erotic massage, and then there it was – the subject heading of a brief paragraph: *Dry Humping*.

"I'll be a son of a bitch!" I said out loud. "So I didn't invent this!" I had been embarrassed because I thought this behavior was abnormal and I was the only one doing it. Now that I'd read that paragraph I knew women had been gyrating like this for clitoral stimulation since at least 1972, when the book was written, and I felt liberated. I became more determined that my future career should be liberating women from all this stigma and shame that I'd been inexplicably carrying around my whole life.

Now that I knew I was normal, my body was functioning just as it should, and that dry humping was a perfectly legitimate mode of sexual expression, dry humping ensued often and without shame from then on, and Pat's apprenticeship into the world of clitorises was complete.

But his apprenticeship was also short. A few guiding hands and a brief anatomy lesson was all it took, because in truth, he mostly learned by being attentive to my subtle body cues, like a breath that came from my throat instead of my nose, a husky breath that didn't require a textbook to understand. So by the time we were pushed up against Pat's bedroom door on that glorious afternoon, he knew what he was doing, he understood what my slight repositioning of his hips against me meant, and he drove his hips rapidly, so much so that the door, which didn't latch, banged against the door frame with each thrust. So I was in my jeans? Who cares? It was sexy enough for me.

There was lots of passionate dry humping, mouths, hands, tongues, and breasts, but no P in V intercourse. Not because there wasn't the opportunity, and certainly not because there wasn't the desire. It all stemmed from something that happened at school one day.

That semester I decided to fill my roster with classes that in any way incorporated something about sex. I enrolled in Health, Human Behavior, Adult Roles and Relationships, and Child Development. On any given day I was learning about sexual anatomy (minus the clitoris of course), or healthy communication in relationships, or sexual development or conception and so on. I was loving life. For once, my homework didn't feel like work. When reading textbooks becomes fun, you've truly found your calling.

One day, one of my teachers brought in a guest speaker from a local crisis pregnancy center located down the street from my high school. The young female speaker was attractive and articulate, and took immediate command of the classroom with her presentation on abstinence until marriage, which somehow managed to tap right into my romantic idealism about all things sexual. I became really engaged in the frank conversation about sex and love, two of my favorite subjects, because I related to her message about sex being "special." No one agreed more than I. My first kiss was delayed so long because I wanted the timing and the moment and the person and the memory to be perfect. The woman played that emotion like a harp.

Waiting is romantic.

Waiting will make you bonded to your future husband in a way that nothing else can.

I'd spent my whole life fantasizing about being bonded with my future husband. I didn't want to blow it on some teenage indiscretion, so she had my complete attention.

She began her presentation by asking us to list sexually transmitted diseases and their repercussions, like the gunky discharge of gonorrhea and the slow and painful death of HIV. She wrote them all on the chalkboard as we listed them, and she told us the story of a man who was seduced by a beautiful woman and had sex with her that night. He woke up to find her gone the next morning, but in red lipstick on his bathroom mirror he found she had written "welcome to the wonderful world of AIDS."

Then she asked the class to list the possible outcomes of an unplanned pregnancy: adoption, abortion, and unwanted parenthood, and why each one is terrible and completely life-ruining in their own way.

Next she asked what feelings sex can elicit. Ooh! Feelings! I raised my hand high to offer an answer.

"Intimacy," I responded.

"Excellent," she said and wrote it on the board.

Other students added "love," "trust," "embarrassment," and "slutty" to the list of feelings. After this catalog was compiled the young woman, who was probably just out of college, looked at the list and said, "Sex is a powerful thing. It has the power to create life." She pointed to the list of pregnancy options. "It has the power to cause death." She pointed to the STDs. "And it has the power to bring on the absolute best and worst of human emotions. Do you think something like this should be trusted to just anyone? Shouldn't it be only trusted to someone you're married to, who will love you forever?"

"Wow," I thought, sitting intrigued at my desk with my feet resting on the wire book basket under the seat of the desk in front of me. "Finally, someone who seems to understand the importance and dignity of sex like I do."

Next she took a piece of clear packing tape. "This is your

virginity," she announced. "But let's say you decide to have sex with someone...," and she stuck the tape on the forearm of a boy who was sitting in the front of the room.

"And then you break up," and she ripped the tape off him. "You start to date someone else, and you decide to have sex with that person, although you're still carrying around a part of this other person." She held up the tape with the boy's dead skin and arm hair caught on it and then stuck it onto another boy's arm and ripped it off. This went on and on to all the boys in the room until finally she got to the last one.

"And then, you find the love of your life, someone who will vow to love and honor you..." She tried to stick the tape on the last remaining boy's arm but it fell to the floor, having lost all of its tackiness from being covered with all the previous boys' dirt and skin and arm hair.

"You find the love of your life, and it doesn't stick."

To conclude, she told the story of her high school sweetheart and their beautiful love and romance and how his ultimate demonstration of his love and respect for her was that he didn't want to have sex with her, or as she put it "take the precious gift of my body" until they were married. He even got her a ring that was inscribed with "true love waits." And they did wait...and would wait forever because he was killed in a car accident before they could wed. But she still proudly wore his ring and told others about the value of waiting to keep his memory alive. Ah, how wonderfully tragic.

At this point in my life, I was not yet a connoisseur of logical fallacies, propaganda, and Aristotle's art of persuasion, and in my youthful ignorance I didn't see through the flimsy pathos that was being used as a mechanism of persuasion by appealing to my emotions. I didn't realize, for example, that the presenter's anecdote about her boyfriend was a sentimental fallacy, a deceptive tactic that is done under the belief that people will do and believe things they would not under normal circumstances because they are drawn by a sentimental or heartfelt story or visual.

I also didn't notice she employed the false dilemma fallacy, a flawed argument that falsely offers two solutions and demonstrates one is better than the other leaving the propagandist's solution as the best and only remaining solution. This is also known as the "you're either with us, or you're against us" logic. In the woman's lesson to my classroom, only two possible outcomes were presented: sex has wonderfully powerful consequences (within marriage) or terribly powerful consequences (outside of marriage), thus making us believe abstinence until marriage is the best and only way to protect ourselves from a life riddled with AIDS, unplanned pregnancies, and feelings of embarrassment and sluttiness, but the context is flawed. While the two solutions presented are certainly within the realm of possibility, what is not offered is the scores of other possibilities such as sex before marriage could be hot, pleasurable, and emotionally fulfilling while married sex could be boring and passionless.

I further was not astute enough at sixteen years old to recognize the propaganda of the tape on the arm demonstration. Not until after college when I was duped during a job interview with a similar fundamentalist Christian organization pretending to be a pregnancy health center did I begin to reflect on all the lies I'd been fed in sex "education" class. I did some investigating and found they're still using this tactic, but instead of packing tape, the lesson on "giving away pieces of yourself and having nothing left for your one true love when you find that person" is now demonstrated with a rose. A petal is given to each student to represent having sex before marriage, and by the time that one true love is found, all that is left is the stem. The tape and rose demonstrations are fallacies of false analogy. The false analogy argument erroneously compares one thing to another to draw an incorrect conclusion, for example, like comparing phones and televisions because they are both electronic, and then concluding that therefore televisions must make calls. The analogy doesn't work.

Likewise, the argument that rose petals are like sexual intercourse and rose petals are gone after you give them away, so sexual intercourse is gone if you've given it away is also a fallacious argument. Rose petals and sexual intercourse may be similar because they are both "precious," but rose petals are limited in number, whereas sexual intercourse can be had thousands of times. People do not "run out" of the ability to share sex with their spouse because they had premarital sex with others before.

And as for the horror story she told us about a man who had a one-night stand and woke up the next morning with "welcome to the world of AIDS" in red lipstick on the bathroom mirror – it wasn't even true, just an old urban legend.

I was pissed when I found out I deliberately was being sexually oppressed, misled, and lied to. But I didn't pick up on the rouse, and I never thought to question it at the time because I couldn't imagine teachers lying to their students to further their agenda. I never questioned the agenda of the guest speaker, because in my public school run by educated, professional adults concerned about my well-being, I assumed they vetted strangers before giving them hour-long free access to a classroom of children. I didn't know the speaker was from a covert fundamentalist Christian organization. I didn't know about the propaganda. All I knew at sixteen years old is that I desperately wanted romance and to hold on to the love of my life forever, and if abstinence was the way, then so be it. I bought the entire damn thing, hook, line, and sinker.

That afternoon, as soon as Pat got home, I excitedly recounted the whole no sex until marriage case word for word until I had him persuaded.

"Seems to make sense to me," he said. "All I've ever wanted is for you to be happy, so if it's that important to you, we can do that."

It was that important to me. I know some people preached abstinence because they thought sex was bad and wrong. I felt the opposite. I thought it was *so* wonderful and life-affirming that I didn't want to waste such a precious resource unnecessarily. I felt that as with kissing, my peers didn't take it seriously enough. They didn't analyze it, or emotionally examine it, or weigh the social and interpersonal implications – they just did it. These were the same people who claimed to like rock music because now that we were in high school, it was cool, but didn't feel it, connect to it, be moved by it, like I did. In a world of apathy, I felt like I was the only person who had any real passion for sex, love, music, anything.

The second semester that year came, and because I had taken all the fun (a.k.a. sex and relationship) classes the first time, I was stuck with Algebra II, French, and other dreadful things. Just as quickly as it had dissipated when I was taking all the sexy classes, my obsession with school and perfectionism, along with hair-falling-out stress, returned. And again, the more I isolated myself in my school work, the more I needed Pat as my only taste of salvation.

A few weeks into the new semester I realized I might actually, heaven forbid, get a C on my report card for the marking period. Only an A on the next day's Algebra II test could save me. The problem was that I didn't understand squat that would be on this test; the thought of being up another night studying and practicing math problems finally cracked my vase of perfection that had been three years in the making. I needed Pat. I needed him to help me, to hold me, to tell me it was all going to be okay. When I saw him after school at the locker we shared, I was in hysterics.

"It'll be okay," he said, holding me tight. Ah. I took a deep breath and sighed and felt the drug do its magic.

"Let's get you over to the math room," he said.

"The what?" I asked, feeling my eyelashes wet with tears when I looked up at him with my head hung low.

"The math room, for tutoring. Come on, I'll walk you, but then I have to go to track practice."

He took me by the hand and led me down the hallway to a classroom where all the teachers in the math department and peer tutors met with students after school for help with math homework. I hated the sight of it. It wasn't because I had some ego thing about getting help. I'm not sure why, but all the pressure and perfection and fretting that had been festering for years finally overflowed. I lost it. Freaked out. Burst into tears, had a temper tantrum in front of everyone.

Worried, Pat coaxed me to sit down at a desk by the chalkboard and crouched down in front of me, balancing his body in a squatted position to be eye level with me as I sat sulking on the chair, like parents dropping their bratty kid off at day care and trying to sooth them so they can leave for work without an outburst.

"You can't act like this, Jill."

"I can't do this anymore. I can't be perfect! I'm done!" I said loudly, attracting even more attention.

"I know this sucks but you can do it." He coaxed with a sweet and encouraging tone. "Just let them help you for an hour, and I'll see you soon." Pat kissed me on my forehead and stood up but I couldn't bear the thought of him walking out.

"Please don't leave me!" I cried out frantically. "Please. I can't do this by myself," and I jumped up and buried my face in his fleece jacket, partly because I was ashamed of my childlike behavior, and partly because I hoped the longer I stayed hidden there the longer I could hide the fact that my attempts to build a life of successful independence and prosperity had actually yielded the opposite, and completely blown up in my face. I also didn't want to see his face, although I didn't have to see it to know exactly the expression he had.

His lips would be pursed together tightly, the way one does when insinuating zippering one's lips to keep a secret. His forehead would be crinkled as he furrowed his brows. It was a look of fear of making the wrong decision; the wrong decision about how to best save me from this pain.

I had made me his responsibility. I had placed my ability to thrive in his hands, and he was faced with trying to keep the person he loved the most from falling apart. How does anyone rise up to such an unfair and impossible challenge, let alone a sixteen-year-old boy?

After the sting of the spectacle I caused died down, I came

to an immediate conclusion. I was sabotaging the relationship, and I had to stop. My dad was right. I had to be happy with myself first and stop depending on Pat to *make* me happy. When Scarlet and George warned us about being obsessed with each other or "being up each other's ass" as George so eloquently phrased it, Pat would retort, "Who cares if I'm obsessed with her, because she's obsessed with me back."

What we didn't realize when we proudly admitted our mutual obsession is that that's all fine and great while both parties are equally obsessed. But if one person clings tighter or lessens the grip, it throws the entire system askew like a wildly spinning washing machine with too many clothes on one side. I think the episode in the math room scared both of us into realizing that I had become more clingy, needy, and obsessive than he. I had to fix it.

My attempt at rectifying the shattering pieces of my young love affair was to suggest to Pat that he let me fall on my face. Stop coming to my rescue. If in my hectic morning I walked out without grabbing my lunch, no longer should he give me his so I didn't go hungry during the day. If in my frantic state I left a book in the locker that I needed for class, I set a new rule that he was no longer allowed to show up at the classroom door a few moments later to give it to me so I wouldn't get hollered at by the teacher for coming to class unprepared. And I also thought it would be a good idea if I had something good and redeeming and fun in my life other than him. That was the toughest part, because that meant time apart.

He started hanging out with his track friends after practice, and I started spending more time with George and Scarlet. Scarlet and I watched MTV and learned the choreography to all the Britney Spears and N'Sync videos (horrid, I know), and my parents were once again correct. When you spend time away from someone, it gives you more insights and things to share and talk about when you're together again. When Pat and I were once again together, I would perform my dances for him, and he'd practice dipping me in his kitchen while we waited for the Ramen noodles to cook. He'd tell me about his meetings at his track buddies' homes. It was fun. I felt we'd reversed the damage. My life was less stressed.

When I was arched back in his arms, my right leg extended in a silly overly dramatic dip after an impromptu three-step in his kitchen, reveling in yet another rebirth of his intoxicating, doting love for me, I was once again smug. Me and my wizardly sex and relationship expert ways were ahead of the curve. My plan to pursue other interests had worked, and I had outsmarted a situation that would have caused your average Joe high school relationship to tank – but not my relationship.

I had no clue that this safe world of Jill and Pat that had become my saving grace was about to tank worse than anyone could have imagined. Something was happening to Pat during those meetings with friends after track practice. Something worse than cheating, worse than any celebrity breakup gossip you've ever heard of. My life, my mind, my heart, was about to get fucked up, and badly.

Chapter 11

"I CANNOT WAIT for you to go out of business!"

A woman in her mid-fifties with unkempt salt and pepper hair growled this remark at me from the sidewalk through the shop door, which I had left propped open to attract passersby. Business had been slow, and I hoped a quick glimpse from outside would encourage more people to stop in.

"You should be ashamed of yourself!" she yelled again, continuing on down the street before I got a chance to rebut.

My dogged attempts at running a store during the first few weeks it was open were exhausting and excruciating. I could not *believe* I had put this building and everything in it on a credit card, and with no other income. I needed to sell over $50 a day just to pay the rent, let alone the inventory, insurance, credit card processing, internet, taxes, business cards printings, and whatever I could pay myself for my school loans and other life costs. This was not a well-thought-out plan. In order for one bill to be paid I had to wait for a sale. Instead of living paycheck to paycheck, I was living dildo sale to dildo sale. When sales weren't made (because let's face it, in the terrible recession I wasn't the only one tight on cash, and it's a bit hard to sell something when others don't have the money to buy it) I began digging myself farther into a financial hole.

I knew I had a winning business model. Maybe I had chosen the wrong time (the recession) and wrong place (a conservative area with "anti-adult entertainment" laws), but I knew I was on to something unique. I was the only known sex shop in the United States owned by a degreed sexologist. I was one of only a handful of sex shops that didn't sell toys with phthalates, a toxic rubber softener that wreaks havoc on the female reproductive system. I was the only sex shop I knew of that was started by a kid right out of college. One of the only sex shops that was feminist and didn't sell porn. One of the only sex shops that didn't sell cheesy penis macaroni and gag gift novelties. One of the only sex shops that started as a sex education business first.

All of the people who had been in the shop thus far had remarked how cute and welcoming the space was for women. The fun and educational parties such as Fellatio 101 and Foreplay 101 were a unique way for women to have fun while also having access to my expertise. Whereas most sexologists go into academia or private practice as sex therapists, I was making my knowledge available in a grassroots way to everyday women. Most importantly, I knew people could tell I wasn't just peddling dildos, but I was truly and from the heart passionate about female sexuality as a social justice issue, a human rights issue. Yes, I was a hundred percent confident I had a winning business model. But in order for the message of all these wonderful things about my Feminique Boutique to get out there, I needed advertising, and yet, advertisers wouldn't run my ads. Business was slow, and I was at another blockade.

I knew I needed some miracle to kick-start the revolution, to let people know about my crusade, my mission, my desire to eradicate erotophobia and advocate pleasure. That miracle came literally knocking on my door on May 27, 2008.

I had worked for twenty straight days, about sixteen hours each day, nine hours in the shop, a two-hour round-trip commute, and about five hours at home on the computer designing my website, answering emails, researching new products, and doing homework for my master's degree in Human Sexuality Education, which was now under way. On May 25 and 26, the Sunday and Monday of Memorial Day weekend, I decided to leave it all behind. I took Tyler, who had moved from painting helper, to crush, to full-fledged boyfriend in the past month, for a trip to Ocean City on the Jersey Shore. I decided I needed to take a break to remember who Jill McDevitt was and that there was more to me than Feminique Boutique and selling sex products, reading sex textbooks, teaching sex classes – sex, sex, sex. For two days I became Jill, the person who is an optimist when the sun is shining on my skin, turning my hair a honey blonde; Jill, a romantic and a sucker for new summer love, lying on the beach holding hands with that magical man, unable to hide my smile. I once again became Jill, the lover of seafood and intellect, cracking buttery crab legs over interesting conversation.

It was a perfect weekend and the mental and physical vacation I needed. I craved it so desperately that I left in a hurry and took off that Sunday morning with nothing packed but a bikini. I spent the entire weekend prancing around in an orange and white stripped halter two-piece. On Tuesday morning I peeled myself away from Tyler's warm hold as we curved around each other on our sides like spoons. Of course I couldn't wear my bikini to the shop, so I dug through my messy car trunk for something to throw on. I found a pair of denim capris and a too-big red polka dot tunic I had purchased a few weeks before. I didn't particularly like the outfit (which is why it sat in my trunk still in the shopping bag) but I had felt compelled to buy it because it was seventy-five percent off on clearance.

I looked a fright in this dreadfully ugly polka dot ensemble with windblown bed-head beach hair, no makeup, and a hint of sunburn. I didn't stress about it too much because it was all I had and there was nothing I could do about it, and I figured I wouldn't encounter too many people during the day anyway. Business was so bad I'd be happy if three or four people stepped into the shop all day.

I drove into downtown West Chester, farther and farther

away from Tyler's warm bed, and found a parking space along one of the tree-lined side streets. As I walked past the hipster coffee shop with the hippie kids playing guitar on the front sidewalk, and the metal restoration shop with the cobblestone façade and quaint awning, I gave George a call for our daily rehashing session.

George: Greetings
Me: And salutations.
George: How are you this fine morning?
Me: I'm doing quite fine actually.
George: And why is that?
Me: For one, I'm feeling very refreshed after my trip to the shore. And second, I think I'm falling for Tyler.
George: Really?
Me: We just had a good time together. Like a good time. Good clean fun. He's kind.
George: Well that's good; although to be fair anyone would seem kind compared to Justin, your last douche bag of an ex-boyfriend.
Me: True, but for real, George. We like have all the cliché stuff. All the corny "we just click" and the "I feel like we've known each other for years" BS, but it's true. We're hanging out, talking, singing, just being, and I'm thinking, I can't believe I just met you a few weeks ago. I'm very excited to see where this is going. I just have a good feeling that...

The conversation had carried me the next block on North Church Street, where I could see my little pink storefront quickly approaching. I could see the almost-noon sun glimmering off the metal bracket that framed my shop sign. I could also see an NBC truck parked out front, and a camera crew peering through the window and knocking on the shop door.

Me: Um...George. I gotta go. NBC is here!
George: What?!
Me: I don't know! I'll call you back.
George: You better! I gotta hear this one!

Me: Bye.

The pretty young reporter made eye contact with me as I neared. "Please tell me you're the owner of Feminique Boutique," she called out loudly as I walked briskly toward her.

"Yes, I am. What's going on?" I responded.

"We were covering the outcome of a murder trial in the next county, but after our boss read the letter to the editor in today's paper, he called us up and told us to come here immediately because there is a church-sex shop scandal happening!"

"What? What letter to the editor?" This is what happens when I take a forty-eight-hour vacation, I thought; big time, life altering drama goes down and I miss it.

"Ashley O'Malley wrote a lengthy letter to the Daily Local News about how your store is harmful to the children who walk by, and we were hoping we could interview you and get your insight on that."

"Ashley O'Malley? Who's she?"

"Ashley is a male, and he's the Republican candidate running for State Representative for Pennsylvania. He's making the closing of your store and the returning of West Chester to a 'family friendly' destination one of his campaign platforms. Would you give us an interview?"

"I'd love to," I responded with a huge smirk.

I knew right away that Ashley O'Malley, this stranger whose name I had learned just moments before, had given me the gift of a lifetime. I had been waiting for a platform from which to deliver my anti-shame, pro-pleasure manifesto, but I always assumed reaching that point in my career would be a long and laborious task that involved lots of pounding the pavement and slowly chipping away at the Puritanical block. I was only three weeks into my sexology career and this Ashley O'Malley fellow had given me the chance to put the issues I'm most passionate about in the world in front of a 5.8-million-person viewing audience across the entire Philadelphia, New Jersey, and Delaware

Valley. I jumped at the opportunity, and nothing could have stopped me from talking to the media that day. But inside I was thinking "does it really have to be on a day when I rolled out of bed with no makeup, beach hair, and oversized clothes?" Did my television debut really have to occur on my most physically unflattering day in my entire life?

Ashley O'Malley's pompous letter to the editor, I would later learn, read as follows:

Fears Shop Will Hurt Borough Image

I read with disappointment the coverage in the Daily Local News of West Chester's struggle with the new sex boutique in the downtown business district. I have spoken about this issue with many area residents and the principal of the St. Mary School, which is located near this facility. While new businesses are usually welcomed in West Chester, this shop has drawn strong opposition.

When I served on West Chester Borough Council in the 1990s, I proposed the Adult Entertainment Ordinance. Believing that adult entertainment centers featuring nude performers and pornographic materials should not be located in downtown West Chester, Borough Council passed my legislation, and the community has been spared from these kinds of businesses ever since.

Now a different kind of adult business, a "novelty" sex shop, has located in the heart of West Chester. Like most parents, I would not want my children to see this kind of business while eating in a restaurant, going to the nearby soft pretzel store or taking my son to our local barbershop for his haircut. This business may hurt West Chester's image as a family destination.

Perhaps most disturbing is the fact that this boutique is so close to the St. Mary Church and the St.Mary School. What will local schoolchildren think when passing this place on their way to visiting the nearby pizza shop or purchasing a warm soft pretzel across the street? As a St. Mary parishioner, I find this troubling.

As a candidate for state representative in the West Chester area, I have been speaking with people about the need for state legislation that would prohibit adult-themed businesses from opening their doors in close proximity to schools. Laws aimed at insulating schools from certain activities already exist. We should also examine prohibiting adult-themed businesses from marketing their products in neighborhoods where schools are located.

Like many parents, I believe common-sense legislation will help local officials regulate the location of these kinds of businesses and protect a community's character and quality of life.[1]

Despite all the claims that he feared for "the children," I thought that O'Malley's letter had nothing to do with protecting children. My guess was that O'Malley could give a shit about "children" or "families" or "the community" or Feminique Boutique. His letter was actually about something else. The use of expressions and ideologies like "won't someone think of our children?" is a powerful tool of rhetoric to push an erotophobic political agenda. And why would it be advantageous for a politician to push an erotophobic political agenda? Why would a politician want people to be fearful or modest about sex?

Because sexual repression is one of the many ways we keep society under control. Sexually repressed people don't question authority, they don't get in the way, they don't think outside the box. A sexually repressed society is a politician's dream. To the unquestioning eye, it would appear O'Malley's letter was written out of concern for children, but really it was an attempt at social control.

It sounds as if I am a conspiracy theorist, but hear me out. To better understand why the "what will the school children think?" argument is an attempt by politicians to pull the wool over our eyes while they steal away our civil liberties and censor our

---

[1] The Daily Local, West Chester, Pa., published by the Journal Register Co., May 27, 2008.

speech, a little lesson on the history of childhood, the history of erotophobia, and the history of the two together as a political argument is in order.

In the days following the 2011 Grammy Awards, the Federal Communication Commission (FCC) was inundated with formal complaints, like this one:

During the viewing of the Grammy award ceremony, we witnessed Lady GaGa (if you could call her a lady) show the viewing audience her mostly bare behind and frontal crotch area. I had children watching and I do not appreciate what I would consider inappropriate dress...Why am I subject to trash like this? What right do these "artists" have to subject my children to this type of material? [2]

Many more complaints were filed by people all over the country, all with a similar theme; the performances were sexually explicit, and this was a problem because children were watching. The same argument was made a few months before the Grammys when Adam Lambert kissed a male backup dancer during a televised performance. Protecting children from "obscenity" was also the rationale used by the FCC when they levied a fine of over half a million dollars to CBS after "nipplegate," the one half of one second that Janet Jackson's breast was revealed during the 2004 Super Bowl.

The history of using the "protect our children from moral corruption" argument as a political tool to censor sexual images, words, and ideas is a short one because the history of "children" and "childhood" is short. Obviously a period of chronological and

---

[2] The Smoking Gun, March, 11, 2010,
http://www.thesmokinggun.com/documents/crime/offended-beyonceacute-crotch-grabbing

biological time between birth and adulthood has always existed, but the concept of "childhood" as it is known today is a new idea only developed since the seventeenth century. Prior to that period, adults were largely indifferent toward children and viewed them as miniature adults. Not until the late seventeenth century did the socially constructed concept of "childhood" as a unique and separate entity emerge, the tenets of which were innocence, purity, and asexuality.

The history of erotophobia is not as short; erotophobia, as the name suggests, is the negative disposition, fear, hatred, or aversion to sexuality. It is a socialized, learned trait that is characterized by negative affective and attitudinal responses to sexual cues. I use the term interchangeably with "sex-negativity" as opposed to my eroto*philic* or "sex-positive" outlook.[3]

Since erotophobia is a learned behavior, societies and the individuals within those societies have historically run the gamut from erotophobic to erotophilic attitudes. For example, ancient Egyptians in 3000 B.C.E., on one hand, encouraged women to be sexually aggressive to arouse the gods, but also encouraged people not to enter a temple without first washing themselves after having sex, an implication that sexual activity was considered unclean or impure.[4]

Of a similar erotophobic/erotophilic dichotomous vein, in the fourth century the Kama Sutra was produced, which was an erotophilic manual on sexual positions, sex acts such as oral copulation and spanking, and how to attract a mate. But even in this text of erotic exaltation, the desire for Kama, or sexual pleasure, is described as a less worthy pursuit than Dharma and

---

[3] Fisher, W.A., White, L.A., Byrne, D., & Kelley, K. (1988). *Erotophobia-erotophilia as a dimension of personality. The Journal of Sex Research,* 25 (1), 123-151

[4] Manniche, L. (1987). *Sexual life in ancient egypt.* Routledge.

Artha, which are, respectively, virtuousness and material prosperity.

Also during the fourth century, Saint Augustine became instrumental in shaping erotophobic values about sexuality that continue to impact modern society to this day. He solidly believed the sole function for sexuality was procreation. While pleasure is a byproduct, desiring or lusting for the pleasures of sex, or engaging in sex acts that are not procreative such as oral sex or masturbation, was condemned by Saint Augustine. Lust became one of the mortal sins, and a quarter of Catholic canon law was written about sexual issues, setting the erotophobic precedent and the hybrid of sexuality and morality for centuries to come.[5]

To put it all together, if sexuality is accepted as a potential threat to morality, and children are regarded as keepers of innocence who are blissfully unaware of a painful and immoral world, then it posits that children should be protected from sexuality. But why is it a political argument?

The motivations for citing the "corruption of youth" argument are dubious. Knowing the sensitivity people have about protecting children and the public panic over intergenerational sexual contact, including the outrage over child pornography and pedophilia, the question needs to be asked if those sensitivities are being exploited to further political agendas, or if those who cite them truly believe a given idea or image will destroy that precious childhood innocence. Either way, the harmful outcomes need to be addressed.

During the Victorian era when extreme erotophobia and sexual repression was the cultural norm, a physician named Dr. William Acton wrote books and educated parents on the medical dangers of children masturbating. Following in Dr. Acton's footsteps, Dr. John Harvey Kellogg began writing books and advocating the eating of bland food, circumcising young boys

---

[5] Bullough, V.L. (1994). *Science in the bedroom: A history of sex research.* Basic Books.

without anesthesia, and putting carbolic acid on young girls' clitorises as a means to curtail masturbation.[6] Dr. Kellogg went on to invent Kellogg's Corn Flakes, making a fortune from the sale of his bland food.

In the 1950s, increased adolescent freedom, the Korean and Cold Wars, and the Red Scare bred social conservatism and fear. The average teenager's weekly allowance was often spent on rock 'n' roll records, magazines, etc. Elvis Presley, a pioneer in the culmination of sexuality embodied in song, was famously filmed from only the waist up after parents expressed outrage at his sexually suggestive dancing and hip thrusting on television. Less famous is the fact that some parents were so alarmed by the impacts Elvis would have on their children, they sent letters to the FBI, which started a six-hundred-page file on him. One letter addressed to J. Edgar Hoover himself and dated 1955, stated:

As a newspaper man, parent, and former member of Army Intelligence Service, I feel it is my obligation to pass on to you my conviction that Presley is a definite danger to the Security of the United States. [His show] was the filthiest and most harmful production that ever came to La Crosse for exhibition to teenagers. When Presley came on stage, the youngsters almost mobbed him…The audience could not hear him "singing" from the screaming and carrying on of the teenagers. It is known by psychologist, psychiatrists, and priests that teenaged girls from the age of 11 and boys in their adolescence are easily aroused to sexual indulgence and perversion by certain types of motions and hysteria,— the type that was exhibited at the Presley show. There is also gossip of the Presley Fan Clubs that degenerate into sex orgies. From eye-witness reports about Presley, I would judge that he may possibly be both a drug addict and a

---

[6] Kellogg, J.H. (1888). *Treatment for self-abuse and its effects. Plain facts for old and young.* F. Segner & Co.

sexual pervert. In any case I am sure he bears close watch,– especially in the face of growing juvenile crime nearly everywhere in the United States.[7]

Like the Kellogg anti-masturbation crusade, the censorship of Elvis was rooted in the political discourse of the time. The fear of overly powerful teens and anti-American activities became manifested in erotophobia. Similar persuasive tactics were used in both this letter to the FBI and the previously mentioned letter to the FCC regarding the recent Grammy Awards. In addition to the rhetoric of pathos and the protection of children, both letter writers drew into question the musicians' talent, using quotation marks around the words *singing* in the letter regarding Elvis and *artist* in the letter about Lady GaGa, in effect negating these singers' talents.

The 1970s saw a new social fear – homosexuality, and thus a new focus for a "save our children" campaign, this time literally. Save Our Children, Inc. was a political organization started by singer Anita Bryant, which lobbied to overturn legislation that granted equal housing and employment to homosexuals in Miami, Florida. She felt, in our free country, that certain people didn't deserve protections from bigoted employers or property owners, and that details such as skin color, religion, or in this case, sexual orientation, are a worthy reason to be fired, of course all in the name of the children. During this time a gay man was murdered while his killers yelled "faggot" and "here's one for Anita."

What is today's latest social fear? Terrorism? Muslims? The housing market crash? Same-sex marriage? Powerful women who have sex for pleasure, don't take their husbands' last name and remain voluntarily childless while pursuing careers or doctoral degrees? Whatever it is, it will be wrapped up in erotophobia because the powers that be can count on people getting all

---

[7] FBI File on Elvis Presley. May 16, 1956.
http://vault.fbi.gov/Elvis%20Presley%20

flustered and uncomfortable about sex and so will use that to show who is to blame for our problems – the sex perverts.

Look at how absurd this is: sex feels good, and it makes people happy. And yet folks at the top have taught us to be ashamed of it. It's completely counterintuitive. My philosophy is if you want to have bad, shameful, in the dark, under the covers sex that's your prerogative, but don't take it out on the rest of us. But erotophobes, the people who think sex is bad and shameful, *do* want to take it out on the rest of us. To loosely paraphrase Marty Klein in his masterpiece entitled "America's War on Sex," erotophiles (those who think that sex should be fun and pleasure is good for you) say, "I'd like to go to a nude beach. And if you don't, you can go to the clothed beach." But the erotophobes (those who think sex is dirty and shameful) will say, "I don't want to go to a nude beach, and so you shouldn't either. Let's close the nude beaches down." Erotophobes are the ones who try to push their closed-minded, Puritanical beliefs on everyone else, and yet ironically claim that they are the ones who are the victims.

Was I writing letters to the editor saying that Ashley O'Malley might have a boring vanilla, pathetic sex life and that this offended me? No. So why was he writing letters to the editor saying that I, and the people who shop at my store and the fabulous sex that we're all having, offended him?

It's a blatant double standard. We live in a world that has accepted the premise that sex is bad because erotophobes have managed to frame the debate in their favor. By making this a "protect the children" argument, the opponents are then logically "against the children" by necessity, and no one wants to be that. So erotophiles have spent decades countering the erotophobes within the context of their own argument. We agree to keep nude beaches far away from "family-friendly beaches," and adult bookstores several hundred feet from schools (because *Playboy* can walk?) and erectile dysfunction commercials on the television only at ten at night after the kiddies are asleep. We have fought them, yes, but only within the context of their "won't someone think of the children?" debate. Why don't erotophiles reframe the argument so that we are "pro-pleasure" or "pro-freedom of expression?" Let the erotophobes explain why in a free country as grand as ours, they are against freedom. Why do they oppose my freedom to see one half of one second's worth of a nipple during the Super Bowl? If they truly fear for the children, wouldn't they be more upset with the beer commercials scattered in between a violent sport that consists of people tackling the tar out of each other, rather than a nipple?

But that's not the conversation. The erotophobes have us by the balls (or ovaries) because they have made it much more socially acceptable to support closing a legal business in a recession because it makes them uncomfortable than it is to support freedom of expression and being pro-sex. That's a lot of power.

In Klein's book, he writes, *"There's a privileging of people's discomfort if it's about sex. If you're uncomfortable about blacks, you are a racist; uncomfortable about Jews, you are anti-Semitic. But today, if you're uncomfortable about sex, you're a civic leader."*[8] Being anti-sex is the only discriminatory platform in this country that is celebrated rather than condemned.

Those were all the thoughts that ran through my mind in the split second between the time the pretty young reporter asked me for an interview and me saying yes. Up until that moment my meager pro-pleasure manifesto had simply consisted of providing women a space to ask questions without shame and to arm them with the knowledge about their bodies they needed to ensure their pleasure and empower their sexuality. I was just a young woman who was angry about being lied to and misled about sexual pleasure, who was pissed that no one taught her about the power of the clit, who armed with a little formal education wanted to teach

---

[8] Klein. M. (2006). *America's war on sex: The attack on law, lust, and liberty.* Praeger.

other women about it. But now I was being delivered the opportunity to make that manifesto a revolution. Politics, religion, power, gender relations, bodies, pleasure, sex – everything that makes people awkward and uncomfortable in the world was on the table, I had the microphone, and everyone was listening.

Chapter 12

Even with our time apart, Pat and I still met on the phone each night, a tradition now three years old. His voice through my Elvis phone, in the dark, under my fluffy winter blanket, was the epitome of home. A mother's arms, being curled up with a good book while rain patters on the window frame, every image that conjures up the visceral feeling of "safe" flooded me every night in that bed.

"How was your day?" Pat asked pleasantly.

"My mom took me practice driving after school on the highway, which was exciting. I went fifty-seven miles per hour!"

"Nice! Look out world – Jill's driving on the highway!"

A few months older, Pat had already become accustomed to taking the car on the highway. For me, it was a big step in the grown-up world of driving.

"Oh be quiet." I responded. "And for the last six hours since I got back from my practice drive, I've been doing Algebra, surprise, surprise. And when you called I was on the other line with Scarlet. When I told her it was you so I had to go, she got all pissy. I don't know what to do about her and George, you know? Even though I have been spending so much time with them recently, they still get so jealous when you and I are together. It's like, what can I do? Why should I be made to feel guilty because I want to take a phone call from the love of my life? I didn't see you all day."

I was expecting something like, "Yeah, I know, I don't understand why they're being like that," or, "Gee, I'm sorry to hear you're still having a hard time with this." We'd had this conversation about three million times over the preceding three years, and in the three million times before that night when I had confided in him my hurt and worries about feeling torn between spending my little free time with him or my friends, Pat had responded with advice, compassion, and empathy, but this time it was different.

"Give it to God, Jill, just give it to God."

Say what?

Let's back it up a moment and recap. Pat and I were codependent and overly enmeshed, so we decided to explore other interests and spend time apart so the relationship did not implode. I began to spend more time with my friends (which apparently was not helping to smooth over tensions there), and Pat spent time with his track friends after practice.

His track friends had invited him to a Christian youth group meeting. I learned the local group met in the home of a couple named the Jared's in Drexel Hill, the part of town we considered rich because there were actually single family homes with driveways instead of row homes with street parking. This is where the "God" bit comes in. I thought nothing of it when he told me where he had been. At first, Pat called the meetings "weird because they sit around in a circle, clapping and singing Jesus songs," but he started going every week nonetheless for the free pizza and camaraderie.

I thought nothing of it when he and his track friends went for a long weekend at a sleepaway camp at the youth group's campground in upstate New York. Not only did I think nothing of it, but I continued to be proud that my brainy plan to spend time apart to strengthen our bond was working, and that I was able to "survive" three whole days without him, not even a phone call. I made it with no contact other than a postcard, on which he wrote:

Dearest Jill, how are you at home? I am having a great time. I really wish you were here! So far, I have gone canoeing for breakfast, went on a rope and mud course, water skied (very fun) and have an incredible entertainment here at every meal and at night. And in between I play basketball. I love it here. Next year, you must come! I hope you're not totally bored at home without me. I love you very much and would always love you. XOXOXO. PS: trust me, I don't go by the different zip code rule! I LOVE YOU!

What was not written in the postcard, and what I did not know about the sleepaway camp, was that after the canoeing and water skiing, and ropes course, there was a talk. Back in the cabin, after a fun-filled day of team building and new friendship bonding, older teens who served as camp counselors led a reflection on the day and what they learned about Jesus Christ. This part I learned when Pat came home, during one of our phone conversations.

Pat: The one night, Jill, they had a 50s dance. And the girls' cabin made poodle skirts, and the guys wore jeans and tight white t-shirts, and I slicked my hair back. I actually danced.
Me: In public?
Pat: Can you believe it?
Me: You never dance in public, even with me. I've never seen you dance except with me in your kitchen.
Pat: It's different with the people at camp.
Me: Well what do...
Pat: And the ropes course was AMAZING! Josh was the leader in my cabin, and he was the coolest. He wasn't like the normal idiot teenager like at school. He had a good head on his shoulders like we do, and he was so down to earth and a Christian.
Me: And how does...
Pat: Every night at the cabin we talked about the joys and blessings from our day, and learned about Christ.

Me:...
Pat: The last day Josh sent us out to walk around the grounds for twenty minutes and not talk to anyone, and just search our hearts and see if we want to let Christ in. I figure I have nothing to lose. It seemed to make sense to me.

I thought that going to the Bible study groups was kind of silly. And I thought this sudden conversion was odd. And I thought his subsequent "give it to God" remarks in response to my little adolescent dilemmas were peculiar and annoying, but what started to happen next was the unraveling of our relationship. I stopped thinking nothing of it.

It was a Saturday night at Pat's house, and his mom was out on a date, leaving us alone. Since I'd gone straight to Pat's from work I still smelled like greasy McDonald's, and the collared shirt of my fast food uniform was saturated in fry grease, but that was okay because the shirt came off soon enough. We were listening to the sexy saxophones of baby making music that plays on Philadelphia's soft rock station on Saturday nights, and we were enjoying a passionate make-out session that looked like it could be moving into dry humping territory soon.

We're one, but we're not the same
We get to
Carry each other
Carry each other...

One by U2 came on, and I lost my mojo because the song makes me think of September 11, which was still new enough to be raw. At the time, it was impossible to imagine it could one day be something you didn't think about and talk about and hear about every day. The song was played during the live "Tribute to Heroes" broadcast over a video montage of people giving blood, donating money, and collecting supplies for the victims. The video showed people of different ages, and races, and religions coming together to help, as one. The song always made me think of a common humanity, which is a warm fuzzy feeling in most scenarios, but not in sexy scenarios. The mood was killed, but we remained snuggled together during the ensuing discussion, one I'll never forget.

"This song reminds me of 9/11," I told Pat.

"I know it does, I remember talking about that before."

"It just makes me think. You know when you hear those stories of near misses, like someone who was supposed to be in the twin towers that morning but was stuck in traffic, or people who were supposed to be on one of the planes but missed their flight because they had terrible diarrhea? It just makes my head spin. Like, why were those people spared but not the others? Was it fate? Luck?" I wondered aloud.

"It's sad," Pat agreed, "but for reasons we could never understand, it was just God's plan."

"God's plan? I could never understand why people say that. What does that mean? Like God wanted them dead? That doesn't make any sense because God is supposed to be good!" I pondered.

Until this point in the relationship, Pat and I had engaged in dozens of conversations about destiny versus free will, what it means to be a "good" person, and what happens when we die. These philosophical musings and the safety I felt with Pat to freely think aloud and conjecture about my world were what lured me to him in the first place. But that kind of conjecture was not welcome anymore. Since he'd gone to camp, since dog-earred and post-it noted student Bibles lay around his bedroom, since he'd taken on Christianity, there was no more discussion, debate, or musing. There was one way, the Bible's way, and that was it. It wasn't up for discussion.

When I innocently questioned why a loving God would want his children to die, Pat huffed a condescending sigh, as if wondering how I dared to speculate about God's intentions. It was the first time I'd ever seen him exhibit snobbery. I didn't like it, and I found myself ever so slightly shifting my body away from his in our snuggling pretzel. I don't know if it was even enough for him to feel or notice, and I don't know if it was intentional, but my body distanced itself from him, even if just a millimeter.

"Did you just roll your eyes at me?" I demanded.

"I guess I did."

"Why?"

"It's just that you don't get it. People think that God is a nice old man with a beard and heaven is fluffy clouds, and if you do nice things and donate to charity and stuff then you go to heaven. But it doesn't work that way," Pat lectured.

"How do you know?" I asked, still eager to engage him in intellectual inquiry.

"Because the Bible says there is only one way to get into Heaven."

"And how's that?"

"Accept Jesus Christ as your Lord and Savior."

I'd never before seen Pat, who was ordinarily a gentle soul and eager to please, be domineering and absolute.

Even at seventeen years old, I knew that one of the premier qualities of intelligence is the ability to question. As far as religion goes, I was raised to follow the "Golden Rule" and treat others how I would like to be treated, and then use my noggin to question everything else. I was raised "Christian," as in trees at Christmas and chocolate bunnies at Easter, but my parents didn't speak much about religion in general as a child. My father's "stick it to The Man" family motto translated into a philosophical household aura that did not explicitly state, but gave the impression that religion was the "opiate of the masses," a means to have order and control over a population of savages and something people needed because the thought of rotting into the earth after death and life being pointless is too much to emotionally bear. The special occasions in which I did find myself at church had me forming a friendly relationship with the pastor, and we conversed politely about our shared love of creative writing. I even had him proofread a short story I wrote about Pat and my Free Bird Kiss.

Suffice it to say I wasn't "anti-religion." I wasn't "pro-religion" either. I didn't prefer or not prefer one religion over the other. In many ways, I didn't even understand the differences between them. I just didn't care about religion. Didn't think about it. It was inconsequential to my life. That is, until the love of my life got swallowed by it.

In hopes that Pat had not been entirely herded like a conformist sheep, had not had his senses completely dulled by the narcotic indoctrination of religious dogma, I continued to question, to put forth "what-ifs," hoping he would take the bait and engage me in a round of wondering like the good ol' days. He did not.

"Ok. If the only way to get to heaven is to believe 'Jesus Christ is lord and savior,'" I began. "What happens if a two-year-old child who lives in an African village dies of cholera and never heard of such things as Jesus or the Bible? And even if he had, he has no language skills yet so can he really even conceptualize and thus believe it. Does this child go to hell?" I speculated, hoping for a thoughtful, intellectually sound response.

"The Lord Jesus acts in ways that we cannot understand. We need to glorify God and be in fellowship with Him through his Son, Jesus Christ, our Savior. He died to save our sinning souls. If someone doesn't believe that, then why should He save them?"

Laughing, I responded casually, "Well I don't know if I buy that, I mean..." But I started to get a little nervous at his glare. I continued. "What? Does that mean I'm going to Hell?" Pat looked at me with terrible disappointment.

"Yes," he said.

I shot up like a cannonball, panic officially setting in. The anxiety of nervous puke butterflies had now flown up my throat and out of my mouth. I began immediately crying and screaming, obscenities discharging out of my mouth like water from a loose hose on full stream. I rushed towards the door, and then I stopped in the doorway and looked back at him still lying on the bed with the light from the hallway cascading in, my shadow creating a dark line across his body.

"WHO ARE YOU?" I snarled. "LOOK AT ME!" He lifted his eyes to mine. "You love me, Patrick Abramowitz. And you *know* me. You know my soul. If you truly believe in a God that would have me endure an eternity of pain and torture forever, if

132

you honestly think your God would send me to Hell, then you are SICK!"

I spoke in a voice that was no longer yelling or screaming or cursing, but was so full of jagged emotion it demanded attention without having to yell. "I don't know you anymore. You've been brainwashed."

I left.

Chapter 13

I unlocked the door to Feminique Boutique and invited the pretty reporter and the camera guy inside. As they set up the lights and camera tripod, I quickly ran a brush through my hair and rubbed a glob of gloss across my lips in an effort to prepare for my completely unexpected television debut. It didn't help much. I still looked like I had just rolled out of bed.

"Will you be counter-protesting tonight?" the reporter asked.

"Doing what?" I asked alarmed.

Turns out, the "church sex scandal" was bigger than goody-two-shoes Ashley O'Malley's prissy sex-negative letter to the editor.

"A local Catholic parish is staging a protest at the borough council meeting tonight," she responded. It made more sense now. The day before I had left my cares behind and headed for the beach, an old man had come into Feminique Boutique and handed me a piece of paper clipped out of a church bulletin. Because I was bummed about my terrible first few weeks as a business owner and eager to run away, I hadn't paid it a whole lot of attention.

But it was coming back to me. The man said that he had attended Mass at the church on the previous Sunday for a friend's daughter's First Holy Communion. He had been appalled when the Monsignor told the parishioners, from the pulpit, of my shop's opening, and encouraged them to protest at the borough council meeting. Printed in the Sunday church bulletin was a similar call to protest. "Keep West Chester family friendly," it read.

A few weeks before, after winning my battle for a permit to open my store, I had felt excited in a folk music kind of way, about fighting the Establishment. The Catholic pulpit, city legislative meetings, Live at 5 news broadcasts – it was becoming clear now just how big the Establishment was.

From the fact that I had had to go to a foreign country to study sexuality, to the fact that I could not find a job in the field of sexuality, from the property owner who wouldn't rent to me, the lawyer who wouldn't represent me, the zoning officer who hadn't wanted to issue a business permit to me, the advertisers who wouldn't print ads for me, the credit card processors who wouldn't do business with me, the town folk who made angry catcalls at me, the politicians who made campaign promises against me, and now the church that was going to protest me – the truth was becoming agonizingly clear. At every level of society, from every institution, there truly is a *crusade* against sex.

Chapter 14

A different kind of crusade had been waged back in high school – the battle to save Pat from what I perceived as a mind-controlling cult, the battle to help him recapture his beautiful mind from the clutches of blind conformity.

After Pat calmly told me he feared I was going to Hell, I decided to change; I was a mess, contemplating living life with his new ideas and attitudes. I was desperate to keep the Pat I loved and refused to even imagine anything other than us being together until we died together in each other's arms at ninety-four years old, even though I sometimes couldn't help but think he was already dead. His body was still walking around, but Pat was no longer inside. I didn't know who was.

The summer before senior year, I took all the savings I had diligently and responsibly collected from my McDonald's earnings and bought my first car! One mid-summer night, Scarlet and I drove to a nearby park with the windows down and the radio up. The park had an outdoor amphitheater and hosted a free summer concert series, and every summer we managed to find a way to get there with a spare blanket or set of lawn chairs to hear a Beatles tribute band. We catcalled "I love you, Paul" to the band until they would pull us on stage for a number and give us signed drumsticks.

It was our thing.

That summer we thought we were hot shit rolling up to the busy park parking lot in my junky little car. It was still light out, with a late day summer glow, and I was absolutely stoked. I had exactly one dollar to my name, and I used it to get a water ice, a Philly summer treat of flavored shaved ice in a cup.

Scarlet and I were laughing, plotting our strategy on how to get pulled onto the stage this year and reminiscing about our antics in years past. I felt close to her, and I blurted it out with a saddened tone, "So, you know Pat is a fundamentalist Christian now?" It was the first time I'd said anything to anyone about Pat to indicate things were anything other than perfect between us since we had fallen in love.

I don't remember her response or how the conversation launched from there, but clearly I needed to dump it out. I confided how Pat was always quoting scripture at me, how he went into the homes of strangers, like the Jared's, to hear "the word of God." I told her about the night Pat said I was going to Hell.

Scarlet looked at me, angry. Her dark brown eyes were brooding, and I got nervous puke butterflies. They were not nerves this time, like the first day of school or getting on stage in front of a crowd of people. The puke butterflies in my stomach were because her look confirmed what I already knew, something was wrong. Wrong with Pat, and wrong with "Pat and Jill," the unit. I couldn't pretend our high school romance, which until now had been the stuff of happy ever after movies, wasn't slipping through my fingers.

Scarlet's angry stare was particularly anxiety-producing because I knew it was sincere. I scraped a sliver of cherry ice onto the little wooden spoon, and I knew this was serious because she didn't say "I told you so." She didn't remind me that our relationship was too intense for people so young, or use it as a "serves you right" moment for choosing Pat over her so many times. She wasn't angry at me, and she wasn't angry at Pat's cruel belief that my soul would be tortured into infinity. She was angry that someone had fooled him into believing such nonsense, and that my heart, the heart of her best friend, would pay the ultimate price for it.

"That's....fucked up," she said.

"Yeah, I know," I was ashamed. I was embarrassed. I couldn't believe a simple after school club Pat attended had spiraled so far out of control and could have the power to make me feel this terrible about myself and uncertain about my future. I wanted it to all go away. I wanted the old Pat back, the one who loved me even when I was mean to him in eighth grade, even when I took so long to return his love; not the Pat who was condescending and judgmental and thought terrible things about the person he loved most in the world.

To squash that uneasy feeling in my stomach, in order to get rid of that nagging intuition that told me that Pat Abramowitz was in fact, not the love of my life, I had to do something. I walked around with psychologically-manifested pain in my stomach for the rest of that summer because I refused to allow myself to think there would ever be a time in my life that did not include being one with Pat. I adored him, and if the thought skittered across my brain, I pushed it down, down, down.

He would change back. He had to. If he didn't and I didn't fall in love with the new Pat, did that mean I never really loved him? You're supposed to love for better or worse and accept your lover for who that person is, aren't you? And if I never really loved him, or only superficially because he made me feel good about myself, and I was questioning everything because he no longer made me feel that way, did that make the last three-plus years a sham? My fears were crazy-making, and so down they went, into the pit of my stomach to be disregarded and locked away. Down, down, down. I filled the void with positive thoughts. He would change back. He had to. I believed it.

The first tactic I utilized in a futile attempt to change Pat back was ignoring the "God talk," as I called it. I just hoped he'd grow out of it. When he wrote me a love note one day, as he had at least once a day every school day since ninth grade, and it said "If God is for us, who can be against us?" and was signed with a Bible verse, Jeremiah 29:11, I said nothing. It made me sick. He sounded so phony to me, like a sad, lost puppy clinging to some nonsense. I felt bad for him. But I said nothing. I wanted to bring back the old Pat and have him read new Pat's love letter, so the old Pat and I could spend all night on the phone talking freely about how absurd it was. Alas, I couldn't do that, and ignoring the increasing number of insertions of "God talk" in every conversation was proving impossible, especially after my conversation with Scarlet, which forced me to reckon with the uneasy truth that I had ignored Pat's innocent God remarks in the very beginning and it had led us to this point.

The next tactic I tried was to express frustration and anger. When he gave me God talk, I argued with him about the absurdity of it and accused him of being brainwashed, sick, weird, and other insults.

When it was suddenly splashed across the news that scores of priests had been systematically raping children and that officials of the Catholic Church knew about it and not only did nothing to help these children, but actively covered it up by moving the rapists to other parishes, I was livid! The world's pain that I ache for most is rape, the ruin of something as beautiful as sexuality by wielding it as a weapon of destruction and humiliation. It's wholly immoral and against everything that is good. Normally we see rapists as wayward "bad guys" sneaking out from behind the bushes, or a douche bag boyfriend who gets his kicks from beating up and hurting girls. What happens when the rapist is a large scale international, billion dollar institution that people look to for moral guidance? The whole thing had me foaming at the mouth.

"Are you seeing what religious indoctrination does to people?" I scolded one Saturday while we were babysitting. We were watching the news and *not* in his bedroom rubbing and putting our mouths on each other. It was telling.

"Hypocrisy!" I yelled. "The same assholes who are preaching morality this and that are the ones out there doing the most immoral things possible!" *This and that*. I was so enraged I couldn't even formulate an articulate sentence.

"Well..." Pat started to offer a response but I continued to speak over him.

"Not to mention everyone supporting them. I mean some of these people are so programmed to be loyal to the so-called moral ideologies of the religion that when the religion takes part in one of the most patently immoral things possible, they ignore it and make excuses for it, and continue to donate money, and unbelievably, get mad at outsiders for daring to criticize it. Do you see what religion does, Patrick? It programs people not to think for themselves and makes otherwise good people actually defend and support kiddie rapists."

My face was hot as I thought about all the injustice. I was pissed and was getting more so about his cavalier response, the same "God talk" bullshit of a response he had given me about the people who died on 9/11 being part of "God's plan."

Of course Pat's religious conversion wasn't to Catholicism. He had been raised Catholic, not Fundamentalist. The non-denominational youth group that had warped his mind wasn't Catholic. It wasn't even a church. In fact, I didn't remember him attending church even one time since he had become a Christian. His entire faith system was based on the teachings at these private meetings at the house of the Jared's and the one-on-one guidance from his new friend, Ricky.

This second tactic took on a life of its own. I found it was easy to be critical and point out the faults in Pat's new lifestyle and new heart. By the end of the summer, after my August birthday but before school began, Pat started track and cross country practice again. I came with him to watch from the bleachers. And so did Ricky.

Ricky was a dorky, pudgy man in his mid-twenties. I don't know where he came from, or where Pat met him, but once again he showed up at the track field after practice and gave us a ride home. Ricky barely said two words to me. Maybe because he got the vibe that I was not impressed with his influence over Pat. Maybe he wanted to exert all his energy proselytizing to Pat and not waste his time on someone clearly not convertible.

They laughed and spoke about sports. Damn, I couldn't leverage myself into the conversation because I was clueless on the subject. Ricky encouraged Pat, asked him about his upcoming season, fed his ego, built him up, made him laugh, and then confronted him about a Bible passage. The propaganda was textbook and happening right before my eyes. Ricky was using the psychological manipulation technique called "the euphoria fallacy," which is done by heightening the emotions of the other through merriment, fun, or games, and then inserting the brainwashing content. The same thing happened to Pat at camp when they had him on the water skis and ropes course and then just when his endorphins were up from the pleasure of the sports, they introduced the "God talk." I may not have been able to detect the similar propaganda I'd been victim of in my classroom about abstinence until marriage, but I could see very clearly it being done to Pat. It was so obvious anyone could see what was plainly happening – except Pat apparently.

I sat together with Pat in the back the car
, holding hands, leaving Ricky as chauffer alone in the front. Ricky lifted his eyes to the rearview mirror so only I could see, and I looked back at him knowingly. I smirked and gave him the look of "I've got your number, I know what you're doing, and I haven't lost yet."

When we arrived home and got out of the car, I confronted Pat about Ricky.

"What the hell was that about?" I bitched.

"What?" Pat responded innocently, clueless.

"Why the fuck does that dude show up at your cross country practice?"

"Um, because he cares, and it's nice to have someone who cares," he said with an attitude. Then he softened his voice and continued, "My mom doesn't come to my sports stuff anymore since she took up drinking."

"I care. And I come to your sports stuff," I retorted. I tried to explain that Ricky didn't really care; he just wanted to find a way to reach Pat and gain his trust so he could infiltrate his mind with Jesus propaganda.

"I don't understand why you can't be happy for me, Jill!" he yelled. "You sound like such a conspiracy theorist. These are nice people and this is my new interest, and I want to share it with you without you criticizing me and saying I'm brainwashed all the time, because I'm not! I'm a Christian, and I want to spread the good news of salvation through Jesus Christ, and I wish you could just love me for it. Stop fighting me on this and just love me for it."

"Pat, it'd be one thing if you decided to be a Christian and stuff, but this is a cult, Pat. If you want to be a Christian, why can't you go to a normal church like normal people? This organization is crazy. They send grown men over to pretend to get involved with your life? What kind of twenty-six-year-old guy wants to hang out alone with a seventeen-year-old boy? It's creepy!"

He glared at me. He was insulted. By the time we reached his front door the tension was thick with anger.

"What the fuck are you trying to say? That Ricky is some kind of perv?"

"I didn't say…," but he cut me off.

"'Cause he's not! He's a good person and is mentoring and supporting the growth of my faith, unlike you, who does nothing but belittle it at every moment. Ricky and the guys from track warned me about you. They said to be wary of you because you're trying to pull me away from God. I don't want to believe that, Jill, because I love you, but it sure seems that way to me."

I covered my face in my hands and let out a cry. "Pat!" I was panicked. "I'm not trying to…" My horror increased as I realized the conspiracy was deeper than I imagined. The web of propaganda included convincing Pat I was the enemy, that I didn't understand him after we'd spent years of our lives getting to know every fiber of each other's souls. I was flabbergasted and became defensive. I went from angry to afraid. The conversation ended with me trying to explain that I didn't accuse Ricky of being a perv, and I wasn't trying to turn Pat away from God. The thought that our love could end because of this threw me into a fit of terror.

"I'm sorry!" I screamed, throwing my arms tightly around his neck and wiping the fat tears that rolled down my face on his shirt as I nuzzled my head into his chest.

"Jill, I want a wife who will pray with me every night. Will you do that?" I had a vision of closing my eyes and clasping my hands and saying "Hey God, thanks for my family and friends. Amen."

"Sure, I can do that," I said.

"I want a wife who is going to really mean those prayers and who can talk to me about God and pray with me to bring Jesus more into our hearts and continue to live through us. Would you do that with me, Jill?"

He saw the hesitation in my face and heard the lump in my throat. I felt so sick because I knew I was lying to myself in thinking I would ever do that for him. I wanted to so badly. To save this love, if it meant keeping us together and making Pat happy, maybe I could go through the motions of prayer. But I didn't think I could ever believe it. I didn't have to say anything. He knew my answer.

Chapter 15

I'm not one for celebrity gossip, but somehow I learned, or maybe I knew it instinctively, how to manage a media controversy. At least, I knew the secret of one very important maneuver – never publically say anything negative about what your opponent is doing because even if you're right it will be spun against you. Only say positive things about what you are doing.

Ready for my interview with the news station, I sat down on the couch in my shop where I'd offered a few sexuality workshops in my three weeks in business, and settled in next to the fluffy pink and brown decorative pillows. With the backdrop of a black and white print of the famous "Kissing the War Goodbye" photo set in a wrought iron frame stand, the camera crew thought this would be a nice background.

Why is Feminique Boutique here to stay? That was the question I needed to answer for the cameras. I *wanted* to say because after you Republican and Catholic prudes work your shaming over on your followers, their sexuality is part of the collateral damage. It breaks my heart to speak with women who have faked orgasm their entire married life because their husbands don't know what they like and telling them would make these women feel dirty and too forward. I feel sad hearing about how many people think their own genitals are dirty and disgusting because they were raised in a world that stigmatizes the human body. I cringe when I see parents cover their children's eyes when they walk by my pink store with a sign that says "Feminique Boutique," asserting their shame onto their children. I wanted to talk about how in some states one can buy guns but not vibrators, that it's legal to brandish a firearm in some public areas but not breasts. I wanted to say the obvious, and shout, "HELLO! At least I'm not raping little boys!"

But, I did not say those things. That would have made it too easy to vilify me. I'd be labeled the aggressor, attacking religion, unfairly categorizing all Catholics as rapists. They would accuse me of trying to lure children to Feminique Boutique. Instead, I tried to explain my goals for my store in a positive way. The key is to not insult the opponent but to say what you are doing well. In my excitement I did slip a little. I said "I'm not exploiting sexuality, like everyone else," (a negative and about them) instead of "I'm empowering sexuality" (a positive about me). I did point to what I felt was hypocrisy when mentioning that a candy store across the street offered children's birthday parties and attracted children to the store with an ice cream cone shaped bench on the sidewalk while also selling candy bras and g-strings, edible body paint, and cherry flavored oral sex cream. While these things were just as sexual as my store, their business tried to attract children who could see these products, and mine clearly was adults only. There was also a cigar shop and newspaper stand, only a block from St. Mary's, which sells Playboys and pornographic magazines. Why, I asked, was no one getting upset about either of these businesses?

Other than this little deviation of accusations and negativity, which the reporter largely glossed over anyway, I stayed strong, unwavering, and most importantly, positive.

I made these positive points, reframing the erotophobia/erophilia debate:

My business is about promoting positive female sexuality.

145

I provide access to sexuality education and products for women in an environment that is sex-positive and female-friendly.

I believe free expression of one's sexuality is a vital part of being human.

Promoting a shame-free world view of sex is a social justice issue.

After filming the interview and editing the segment in the news truck parked out front, the reporter informed me that in addition to the filmed piece, her boss wanted her to do this story "live at five." After that aired, she was told to stay to go live at six o'clock too. I called George, and he came by to give me support.

The Salem Witch Trials started because two girls went into convulsions. Whether they were actually ailing from some sickness or just faking it will never be known. But playing on the religious fears of a community, the idea of the devil incarnate in witches and claiming witches were to blame for the convulsions sent everyone into a frenzy in 1692 Salem, Massachusetts.

During the trials, people shouted and made blanket accusations based on impossible logic: to know for sure if someone was a witch, you tossed people from a cliff into the ocean. If they floated, they were witches and needed to be killed. If they drowned, they weren't witches after all, but, they were dead. In the court room there was chaos and mass hysteria, shouting, moral panic, and ridiculous overly dramatic claims. It's odd to us today to realize that nineteen people were hanged over such silliness. Because of *witches*? How could a civilized society allow mobs such as this to rule in court? Maybe because it was not, in fact, a civilized society.

In a way, the West Chester Borough Council meeting that night at 7:30 p.m. reminded me of Salem. They weren't calling me a witch, and they didn't want to kill me (at least in that way we've become more civilized), but finger pointing, yelling, name calling, and jumping out of seats to belt out outrage over sometimes silly things, and all based on strict religious beliefs, all occurred that night. Like witches, it may seem ridiculous to someone on the outside, but from the inside it was hard to ignore that these people were fighting for what they feel is the most important thing in the world – the family unit. They honestly think women having pleasurable guilt-free sex is the downfall of society as we know it, and I'm Public Enemy Number One for teaching them how, giving them encouragement, and the tools to do it. The people at the meeting that night were thirsty to protect what they thought was theirs and chomping at the bit to make their case before the council. The room was already packed with an angry mob when I arrived.

Still in my terrible oversized polka dot top and horrible hair, I showed up to the meeting almost alone. A young client had stopped in to make a purchase, and upon seeing a camera crew there and hearing of the impending protest by a church, she offered to go with me. My neighbor across the street, who initially warned me about West Chester's zoning officer, agreed to meet me there also. Inside West Chester's Municipal Building, where the meeting would be held, more of the media were setting up with cameras and lights. The local FOX affiliate was there, as was the local newspaper and the NBC affiliate that had filmed me live at five and six.

The scene was reminiscent of a TV courthouse drama – a group of all white, mostly male, mostly white-haired cranky pants fuddy-duddies sitting behind a long, mahogany lectern. The room was filled to capacity, with people standing along the back wall, however I managed to find a chair. There were nuns and priests in full garb, old women with coiffed hair, and stuffy men carrying folded newspapers. The entire environment, both the members of council high up in their presiding chairs, and the members of the packed audience looked to me like sticks-in-the-mud. It seemed like such a stereotype that I could hardly take it seriously.

The meeting came to order, with old business first discussed. The first order of business: a thirty-minute debate about whether four trees or five trees per block should be planted along the sidewalk.

"Four trees. Five will be too crowded," one person shouted forcefully from the audience to the council members. "Fifty feet between trees is the standard for city blocks in a town this size."

"Trees are what give West Chester the charm that people travel miles to visit," countered another from her seat. "I say we go with five trees. It makes a stroll through downtown whimsical and darling." I held back my giggling. Were these people serious? The state university and the forty-one establishments with liquor licenses within one square mile is why people travel miles to West Chester. Whimsical stroll? Get over yourself.

"Easy for you to say," another stood up to argue. "Sure the trees look nice lined along the sidewalk at first, but come on down to my block, why don't you, and see what happens to them in a few years. The roots rip up the brick sidewalks, and guess who will be sued when someone trips over the cracks? Not West Chester, I can tell you that, pal!" Several members of the crowd began clapping, and the head of the council lightly banged on the gavel for order. If people were getting this heated about trees, I was frightened to see what was going to happen once the vibrator conversation got started.

"Next on the agenda…" the head of the council finally said after reaching a decision and making a ruling on the tree matter, "is the adult entertainment ordinance for the borough of West Chester." There were horrified murmurs and gasps across the crowd. Drama queens. They acted like they didn't know what was coming, like their church hadn't sent them a memo to protest my store and that that wasn't why they were there that night.

"Currently, the code reads that prohibited uses for adult entertainment includes 'live displays of the human body without covering' or 'an enclosed building used for presenting materials related to specified sexual activities or specified anatomical areas for observation by patrons therein.' At the borough solicitor's recommendation, I would like to propose a vote to include more definitions of 'adult entertainment,'" he said.

They wanted to close that loophole and include the sale of

sex toys among other things. I assumed that the council members were now going to go round and round with each other and the audience in a discussion of the definition of adult uses, like they had about the trees, but instead an older man with sunspots and an unseasonable long-sleeved shirt stood up. His arms were rigid, and he stood tall and firm.

"I object to this smut! This so-called Feminique Boutique smut shop has no place in West Chester. God warned us about lusts of the flesh and to allow pornographic smut like Feminique Boutique in our town is an abomination! It's leading society down a path to sin. It's this council's and other government bodies' responsibility to help make sure streets are clean, and souls are clean. No one from here will be among the Lord's Chosen with this smut right on the main street with children walking by! You need to amend the zoning code to include the word 'smut' so there's no loopholes and debate about it. We shouldn't even be here talking about if something technically counts as an adult bookstore – smut is smut!"

My client and I looked at each other with "are you kidding me?" wide-eyed disbelief, and the newspaper photographers snapped a photo of our transparent bewilderment. I couldn't believe it. What surprised me the most was the facial expressions of those around him who were turned in their seats to watch him speak. They agreed with him. They believed these things. They nodded their heads in agreement. God punishes sinners. Sinners enjoy sex. Sex is smut. I sell smut. If they had torches and pitchforks I'd be in trouble. But they didn't, and so I smirked, trying to hold back laughter at the lunacy. I whispered to my client, "How many times can the word 'smut' be said in one paragraph of speech? That was like seven!" She giggled and then covered her mouth to hide it as the council began to speak.

"Mr. Shaw," a female council member responded politely but slightly ruffled by the outburst of the "smut" guy, who still remained standing. She knew him by name. Perhaps she was annoyed because he often went on "sinners" rants at these meetings. "A governing body cannot legislate against 'smut.'

That's not a legal term that can be qualified or quantified or defined. We can only legislate against the sale of particular items or services in particular places. Would Councilman Smith like to read the proposed list of prohibited uses in the zoning area in question at this time for the consideration of the council?"

Mr. Shaw sat down dissatisfied, and Councilman Smith spoke up. "In Zone C, the center business district, proposed prohibited uses include adult cabaret, adult arcade, adult novelty store, adult motion picture theater, escort agency, massage parlor …" he continued on listing several other prohibited uses.

I snorted a restrained laugh again. When I read about other sexuality stores who were shut down by governments, attacked by uptight citizens, and arrested by undercover police, I was hot with anger and raged at the injustice. I raged at sexual injustice everywhere. I lost my mind reading about the injustice of rape crimes. But here was injustice occurring right in front of me, about me, and yet instead of being angry, I couldn't stop snickering. I was so amused listening to Councilman Smith, a grouchy eighty-seven-year-old man with a whistling "s" speech pattern. He had seemed to get his kicks from the formalities of the meeting, calling for "nays" and "yays" and "seconding motions," with obvious enthusiasm, now he looked obviously uncomfortable as he was forced to say the words "escorts" and "adult theaters."

"So does that mean even after this new ordinance is passed, this type of garbage can still open on streets outside Zone C? It shouldn't be able to open anywhere!" Mr. Shaw shouted to more approving nods from the audience.

"It is state law that municipalities must provide a location for any business that is legal in the state of Pennsylvania," another councilman announced. The audience members looked at each other, appalled. They couldn't believe these things were allowed to exist, but they jumped on board quickly to do the next best thing – have anything related to human sexuality forced to the outskirts of town with the industrial parks and manufacturing plants, under a bush and behind a gated fence. They deduced that with the zoning change including "adult novelty store" among the uses not allowed in Zone C, West Chester's bustling retail and restaurant-walkable downtown, Feminique Boutique would be forced to the fringes.

Again I chuckled. I was entertained because I knew something they didn't. They were under the impression that if they were able to convince the planning commission at this meeting to include what Feminique did into the adult entertainment code, I would be forced out. They apparently did not realize that Feminique was "grandfathered in," meaning no matter what new laws were made, I would get to stay at my location because it was legal at the time I opened. For the remainder of my career, Feminique would stand in the center of "family-friendly" West Chester, between a pizza place and a gift and trinket shop, and there was nothing they could do about it. They did not know that insisting this ordinance be passed would not only *not* hurt Feminique or force me away, but it would actually *help* me by guaranteeing competition could never open anywhere near my store and ensuring my monopoly. They didn't know this, but they were about to find out.

I was really becoming an expert on the fallacious arguments of persuasion used by fundamentalist Christians. First from my abstinence-only-until-marriage indoctrination, then Pat's brainwashing, and now this. I recognized the "hell and damnation" ploys used by Mr. Shaw, the smut guy, as the "argumentum ad metum," also known as the appeal to fear fallacy, instilling fear by equating a feminist sex shop to the threat of eternal damnation. Next, the approach would be the sentimental fallacy, the heartstrings approach.

For the first time that night, someone raised a hand to speak. It was a younger woman who stood up, clasping her hands in front of her waist. "My name is Emily Mitchell," she started, "and I'm a mother of four. I live on Poplar Street. My husband and I moved to the borough of West Chester in 1995 because I thought it would be a nice place to raise our family. I recently was walking downtown with my children. My one son was attending a birthday party, and I was taking another child to get his hair cut. My other two asked to go around the corner to look in shop windows, and I hesitated because I knew Feminique Boutique was on that block. I don't want to fear that my children can wander ten feet away from me to another storefront and be exposed to age-inappropriate material. Now, I agree stores like this one should exist, but not in a walkable community." She graciously sat down and received a few pats on the shoulder from the people behind her.

"We are not here tonight to talk about Feminique Boutique," a member of the council said, but I suppose no one heard it or wanted to, because another person stood up, a younger man with a loud, confident voice to offer his opposition. The appeal to fear fallacy was used again as a persuasive technique, but this time, instead of using fear by presenting consequences, the speaker used fear by presenting graphic language and depictions. It works the same way at psychologically influencing people as drunk driving public service announcements that scare people to safety by showing graphic and gruesome car accident imagery.

"For those of you not familiar, the owner of Feminique Boutique teaches sex seminars. I went to her website, and this is what I read. This is a description of one of the seminars, right on her website." He smiled largely, as if about to revel in an "Aha, I gotcha!" secret that would destroy me, emphasizing the sex terms. "It's titled 'Going Down: *Fellatio* 101' and reads 'Did you know that one of the biggest bedroom complaints cited by men is that women don't give enough *oral sex*? Now you can impress him with skill and confidence! Learn all about his anatomy and techniques to bring *pleasure* with your lips, mouth, *tongue*, hands, *breasts*, toys, and more! Best yet, you'll learn how to please your partner without the pitfalls so many women dislike about *blowjobs*. After this class, you'll know how to please him without ever having to *gag*, *deep throat*, have jaw pain, or *swallow*. Participants will get to practice each move on a carrot, which will be provided with flavored *lube*. Sure to be a hilarious and enlightening evening!'"

The entire room let out several horrified gasps when he read this aloud, sucking air back into their lungs so regularly it could have had a melody. One woman actually covered her eyes with her hands, although I'm not sure why. It seems more appropriate to have covered her ears if she was upset.

"Just wanted to read that and give you an idea of the type of thing that is going on at Feminique Boutique, and I think we need to ask ourselves if this is what we want happening in our town," the man continued. So calm. So diplomatic. Sprinkled with frank and graphic sexual language, he showed them it was worse than what they feared. This was about more than just products. I was teaching people how to have good sex!

"Again I want to reiterate, that the function of this meeting is to discuss the incorporation of more explicit definitions for adult entertainment in the commercial Zone C. I can appreciate members of the community and members of St. Mary's expressing their concerns about Feminique Boutique, but that is really not a matter for this panel. Feminique Boutique is legal and will be allowed to stay at its current location as it's currently operating," the councilman said, attempting to bring the meeting back on track.

"Wait, what?" one person said with frustration. Others chimed in with remarks like "I thought that's why we were here. You're telling us there's nothing you can do to get Feminique Boutique out?" and "How was this allowed to happen?" One light bang on the gavel was needed to restore order and move the focus to zoning officer, Anthony Ciccerone.

He explained the concept of grandfathering and how legally there was no way he could have denied me the business permit to open, although the key now was securing a clearer set of rules so other "Feminique Boutique-like" shops could be denied. "But," he added, "residents can appeal any borough permit."

For the first time of the evening, I did not have the urge to laugh. Damn cockiness was going to bite me in the ass. Was there hope for these people? Could it be possible there was this technical little rule about permit appeals that would have me knocked out of West Chester like a pawn thrown from a chessboard after the winner slams a fist down in victory? How did I not know of these rules?

"They have thirty days to appeal the permit," he continued. This, I quickly imagined, was for a case in which your neighbor received a permit to build a deck on their house that would block your view. If this happened you would have thirty days to appeal to the zoning board for reconsideration. "Jill McDevitt was given her business permit on March 31. As today is May 27, those thirty days in which to appeal have since passed."

Whew. For me anyway. Massive amounts of chatter and groaning for everyone else.

"We didn't even know that she got the permit until recently when it was printed in the Daily Local. Had we known, we certainly would have appealed it within thirty days!" one old woman whined.

"I can't help that. Permit issuances are a matter of public record," Ciccerone said.

The meeting concluded with the council agreeing to take issues under advisement and reconvene the following month. I said nothing the entire time. It was all part of my strategy. I wasn't going to tangle with the seething erotophobic anger that was hissing in that room. Nothing good would have come from a hundred and fifty against one. I would have been verbally attacked by the mob, would have lost my cool, and gone on the defense. I couldn't afford it. Not with all the media there. I said not one word.

However, once I left the room and followed the flood of people into the lobby, I was met with the cameras.

"Jill, can we have an interview?"

"Jill, can we film your thoughts on how the meeting went?"

There were glares from many of the audience members, milling around the lobby. I don't think many of them had known who I was or that the "smut proprietor" had been there the whole time until I was pointed out by the reporters. Surely they assumed that if the owner of Feminique Boutique was there, she would have defended herself. I decided to let the media do that for me.

"As a sexologist, I think it's really important to be able to freely express one's sexuality without shame. We live in a culture that teaches that sex is bad, but I don't believe that. Women can come to Feminique and feel comfortable. It's not a 'sex shop' in the traditional sense. I can't tell you how many times someone has walked into my store, looked around, and said 'This isn't that store that's causing all the fuss, is it?' They stood in the store, looked around, and didn't even realize they were in a sex shop."

I went home that night, watched myself on the eleven o'clock news and went to bed.

Chapter 16

Maybe I was wrong, and violent criticism and opposition weren't the best methods to get Pat back. Or maybe Ricky and Pat's track friends and whatever went on in the Jared's living room were just too powerful. Either way, I lost the battle for my beloved's soul, to keep it safe from manipulation, to keep it functioning and free to think. Halfway through senior year, right before Christmas, Pat called me for our nightly chat, our one thousand and something late night phone heart to heart. But this time, he dumped me.

Moment One: Anger. I screamed "Have a nice life!" and slammed the phone down so loud my dad came to check up on me.

Moment Two: Sadness. My dad knocked on my bedroom door, and I was blubbering, crying, just wailing; my face was melting in tears. He hugged me until my hysterics calmed down to the point of random bursts of sniffling and gasping. Then I went back to bed not fully grasping the permanence of our separateness.

Moment Three: Despair. When I realized that Pat and I weren't together anymore and that it was in fact going to be permanent, I was despondent. As sure as the sun rises in the morning followed by the moon at night, there was Jill and Pat. I kept forgetting we weren't together. Our apartness seemed so arbitrary. Our togetherness occurred naturally; against active desire and social ridicule we had been magnetically pulled together. To be apart was forced and unnatural. When we both wanted to sit together on the school bus on days I didn't drive to school and we had to intentionally not because we were "broken up," it was unnatural. When during lunch a few days after the breakup I laid my head down on the lunch table and cried, Pat came over to comfort me.

"I'm always going to love you and be here for you," he whispered, wrapping his arms around my drooped over shoulders.

"I'm crying because of you. My heart is broken. I can feel it," I whimpered back. "You say you don't want to be together anymore but your first instinct when you see me in pain is to rescue me and comfort me. It's what you were meant to do so stop forcing yourself to tear us apart."

"I do want you," he said. I could smell him, and I loved it. I had been craving this. This felt right. This felt good. Why did it have to ever end? "But it's not that simple. You know that. We can't be together but you know I'll always be here for you."

Feelings of despair continued when we did the dreaded return of each other's belongings. Driving to his house gave me a bottomless aching, this cruel mental cycle that caused me to go from excitement because I got to see him, which gave me hope that something would change and we could be together, which circled into fear of how sick I would feel if something didn't change and we still couldn't be together, which let me to despair for my life without him, which led me back to excitement because I would get to see him, and that felt good. Fantasizing about being together was the only thing that sedated my pain.

He met me as I parked on the busy street out front of his house, and we opened my trunk. Everything had a story. A memory. His sweatshirt rumpled up in the back of my trunk that had been there since June and was still covered in sand from the time we used it to keep ourselves warm on a day we drove to the beach and it turned unexpectedly chilly.

He helped put my electric guitar and distortion machine in my trunk. The distortion pedal, which when hooked into the guitar creates a cool electronic sound, came in a wooden box. He laughed. "Do you remember 'the box'?" he asked.

"Yeah," I answered.

"That was so funny. You're carrying the box, we're walking to my house to jam, and all of a sudden you have this creepy look on your face and say to the box, 'Hello. Is there anybody in there? Just nod if you can hear me.' I was like, 'Who the hell is she talking to? Little people of the box? Is she possessed or something?' I could not stop laughing."

I was filled with physical joy. I felt as if my abdomen was a pitcher, and joy and hope and happiness were one liquid, and agony, anguish, and hopelessness were another liquid, and I could literally feel those liquids fill me up and saturate me with all of these un-ignorable, invasive emotions. When he reminisced with me about ninth grade, before we were even in love, when I convinced him we should start a band and become famous rock stars and we bought a guitar and bass but had no idea how to play them, I could literally feel the good liquid being poured, the levels rising past my belly button, my ribs, my chest. It was relief from the toxic liquid I'd been carrying around constantly for days. Well, constantly unless I was fantasizing that we were together.

"I wasn't talking to people in the box!" I said, with a laugh, flirtatiously. "I was singing a Pink Floyd song and just happened to be looking at the box."

"Uh huh, right," and he winked.

"And remember this, hon?" and he handed me a pair of flip-flops with the between-the-toe strap broken out. When the shoes broke while walking to get ice cream, Pat had given me a piggyback ride all the way home, just as he had the night of the carnival when I discovered the deliciousness of clitoral rubbing and intimacy and passion. Pat and I loved piggyback rides, and not just for that reason. They were playful and childish in some ways, close and intensely intimate in others, just like our relationship had been. But instead of basking in the calming warm liquid emotion while enjoying the memory, bad liquids suddenly were pouring in. I could feel rancid acid filling my belly, my chest cavity. It burned, it hurt. I don't know what it was, what kind of body chemicals, hormones, adrenaline, but it felt like acid. When it got high enough I clutched my chest. I thought the term "heartache" was figurative. Why did this organ in my chest *actually* hurt?

"Hon?" I growled? "As in "honey," as in a name of affection for someone you just dumped?

"I'm so sorry," his eyes got glassy.

"You bring me over here to pick up my stuff. I'm not getting it for vacation, Patrick, I'm getting it because we are out of each other's lives. We are not together. The point of breakups is that we leave each other lives. You're giving me my stuff so I can go and be gone from your life. No more memories to build. Gone. That's what you wanted, so why are you calling me hon?" I cried.

"It slipped. I'm just used to calling you that," he said, crying.

"Because it's natural. We're supposed to be together, but you want this relationship to be dead. Cease to exist. In five years from now, ten, twenty, I will just be a memory for you. We'll both be married to other people. We won't have vacations like we talked about, won't have our own house, we won't die in each other's arms at ninety-four years old. You'll be making all these memories with somebody else. That's what it means to break up, Patrick. That's what you're doing to us. Is that what you really want?"

He covered his eyes. "I don't know," he said. He reached out and pulled me into a firm embrace that almost made it hard to breath. He was crying hard, no holding back. Joy liquid started to flood my abdomen again, warm and comforting. It wasn't because he was crying, but because I was gaining confidence that he had realized what a terrible mistake it was to separate us. "I love you so much. I love you, Jill, with all my heart and soul. Completely. And I'm always going to love you. Even if this doesn't work out and in twenty years I'm married to someone else, you will always have a big place in my heart. Never forget that I love you," he whispered.

I was happy. "So that means we're back together? I grinned, hopeful, pleading with my eyes to say yes. Please help me stop this pain and say yes.

He looked down, unable to look at me as I shattered, and shook his head no, ever so slightly, to the right and left.

I went home and lost it. I threw myself on the kitchen floor face down, the bridge of my nose flat on the wood floor. I stared, blinked, dropped tears and watched them spread across the floor. I stared at the patterns in the wood grain, the tiny specks and swirls you never see unless your eyes are a millimeter from it, as mine were. I begged for the floor to open up and swallow me into a universe where this feeling didn't exist. Begged to whom, I don't know. Was this praying? I didn't know, I just knew I did not want to be submerged, drowning, in this pain. I remember thinking I would take physical pain over this heart pain any day. I began negotiating; with whom, I don't know. God? In my head I begged, "I'll get an operation with a rusty dull knife and no anesthesia. You can rip my toenails off. Anything, but please stop this pain in my chest."

This thinking got me even more upset. I got angry at God, at science. Why did this feeling even exist? How was it evolutionarily necessary to my survival? I felt trapped and started to hyperventilate. My breathing got faster and more intense, but it still wasn't enough to sustain me and I felt light-headed, like not enough oxygen was getting to my brain, which upset me more and caused more hyperventilation. I wanted to explode and release all this negative energy, all this toxic fluid that kept filling up my gut. I wanted to scream! In frustration I banged my head on the floor. It hurt so good, it was cathartic, like punching a wall or gritting your teeth. I did it again. And again. Harder and in more rapid succession. I don't know why I kept doing it. Maybe to release energy or to punish myself for driving him away with my lack of acceptance of his faith, or maybe just to feel physical pain to distract me from, and help me to release, this emotional pain.

After beating my own head again and again against the hard floor, I realized what I was doing, stopped and sat up, looked around. Even though it was perversely cathartic, I was immediately embarrassed about what I'd just done. I rubbed the growing bump on my forehead along my hairline and was so relieved that this self-mutilation tantrum happened while I was home alone where no one could witness how pathetic I was.

I called George.

Me: I can't go on. I forget who Jill is without Pat.
George: You're Jill.
Me: I can't stand it. We were so enmeshed that I…I just feel like we're one person and I'm walking around with my guts hanging out because half my body has been ripped off and is walking around somewhere else.
George: I really don't think that's healthy.
Me: I need him.
George: You don't need him.
Me: I used to have these dreams where all of a sudden, Pat hated me. I would try to say hi and he would ignore me, I'd try to ask what was wrong and he would turn away. No matter what I did, remind him of our love and how much we mean to each other, no explanation changed his mind. I would wake up absolutely terrified and I would go to his house at like five in the morning because we liked to have breakfast together before school. I would tell him about this dream and he would hug me and say, "That's never going to happen. But if it ever did, just hug me like this. I love to hold you, even more than I love kissing you, and I could never wrap my arms around you and want to ignore you." I still have these dreams, but now they're real! And some nights I have these dreams where we are together and we're happy and everything is like it was before, and then I wake up and I'm just so depressed because I know it's not real.
George: That sucks.
Me: I know. I just really want us to be together! And I can't make us together!

I began crying, and George said nothing. Did nothing. He just didn't know what to say. I was grieving, inconsolable, and my abysmal existence of life was making everyone around me uncomfortable as I moved from despair to desperation.

Moment Four: Desperation. In the crowded hallways of my high school or at the corner store, if a classmate or clerk politely asked "how are you?" I would forgo the socially acceptable "fine, how are you?" or "good thanks." I wasn't fine. I wasn't good. I said "really bad" as I sniffed back a runny nose.

Anyone who has been in desperation knows that social graces become meaningless. I no longer felt despair, the state in which I banged my head on my kitchen floor in a fit of heartbreak and anger, and then felt immediately embarrassed and ashamed about it. Social mores exist in the world to make such feelings of embarrassment manifest inside ourselves. Falling to the knees, convulsing, tears running down; crying is socially unacceptable. The fear of being socially unacceptable is a shield that forces those of us who are in anger, sadness, or despair mode to keep our act together while in public.

However, that filter gets lifted in desperation mode. I had worn my heart on my sleeve my entire relationship with Pat. Not a soul who crossed our path didn't know that Jill McDevitt and Patrick Abramawitz were in love. And now that I had moved into desperation and lost the ability to feel shame for acting out my pain publically, not a soul didn't know that I was completely and utterly falling apart without him.

On Christmas Eve day, I called Pat. I asked if I could bring over the Christmas gift I had for his mother. He was home alone, and when I walked in the door I was overcome with desperation. It smelled like him. I passed the table where we had shared a Valentine's Day lobster dinner. I passed the kitchen counter where he once left a tray of homemade cupcakes with the letters " I L O V E Y O U J I L L M C D E V I T T on each one." I missed his love, but I missed his friendship more. When I passed the couch where in eighth grade, before we began dating, we sat and put on a pretend TV show for his mother, I started crying. Not a cry of despair; a cry of desperation.

"PLEASE PATRICK!" I begged. "PLEASE don't do this! I can't live without you! I need you! I'll do anything, PLEASE!"

The shield of social acceptability completely deteriorated.

"Jill, don't do this," he said, crying. "It hurts me to see you like this."

It was the worst breakup I could imagine in my high school senior brain. I would have preferred if we hated each other. If there was cheating, abuse even. I wished I could yell "fuck you, and I want you out of my life!" and he could yell "I hope I never see you again," and we would be happy to part. Those are the best breakups. Short. Rip the band-aid off. Get rid of negativity, and move on in the world.

This, on the other hand, was the worst kind of breakup. When two people desperately love each other but it's a square peg and round hole situation. Despite all longing and heartache and love by both parties, it just won't fit. I wanted it to fit so badly. And his kindness and continued love and support and care and concern for my pain just made it worse. I wished we hated each other. It would have been far less painful than loving each other.

"PATRICK, PLEEEAAAASE," and I fell to the floor. I was so light-headed from intense bawling that I collapsed. On the floor, I held on to his ankles, wrapping both arms around them and resting my head on his foot. The bawling was so harsh that my screams were violently emitting out of my mouth beyond my control, black spots careened in front of my eyes from the light-headedness. I cried so powerfully I choked on the air and began violently hacking and coughing. Pat was scared, and he reached for the telephone on the wall and called my father.

Moments later I heard my dad's car pull in out back. Pat attempted to lead me towards the basement steps to bring me out to meet him but I refused to move. Dead weight. My dad came in the house. Part of me felt bad that I was putting my loving parent in the position to see his child so low, but the feeling wasn't enough to stop the compulsion to let my pain spill out for all to see.

I was sitting on the basement steps. Pat pulled on my legs while my dad worked to peel my clenched fingers off the banister, all the while I was screaming, "I love you! Why are you doing this to us? Can't you see what you're doing?"

It's embarrassing now to think of this, and write this, because of that shield to be "socially acceptable." But at the time, I didn't give a shit. I just wanted him back. I didn't "think" to do it, it just erupted. They peeled me off the steps, and my dad carried me down the hallway toward the back door, but I escaped and ran back to Patrick. This went round and round, somehow convincing myself in my head that I had the energy and stamina to do this forever. I could outlast them, and they would give up and I could stay. When all was said and done, I was being driven home, the palms of my hands cut where my fingernails dug in as I clenched my fists, and my left eye had a popped blood vessel from the crying, and I was no closer to reuniting with my love. Only closer to insanity. Epic failure.

In desperation, I had time. Lots of time. I didn't have Pat to occupy me, and I didn't have school either. I stopped caring. The years before I had slept as little as two hours per night so I could perfect honors and college level research papers. Now I didn't bother to write them; didn't hand them in.

Instead, to pacify myself and occupy the horribly long days of sadness and boredom, I drove my car to the local bookstore. I had read every sex book in the school library, and I was ready for more. At first I read about relationships. Love. Grieving. Breakups. Love loss. Depression. And of course, I read about sex. Every Friday and Saturday night when I would have been with Pat, cuddling in his bed, snuggled under his arm, enjoying soulful kissing and passionate grinding and clitoral rubbing, I instead sat in the aisle of the "Sexuality and Relationships" section and read every book. Sometimes Scarlet joined me. It was nice because I was so lonely that I enjoyed the company, but mostly I just read.

I also occupied myself with a part-time job. I quit McDonald's and began coaching gymnastics classes. I spotted back handsprings and taught balance beam dismounts. One afternoon after school I was so preoccupied with guiding the eight-year-olds around the circuit of gym equipment that for a quick moment I realized it had been the first time I had pressed pause on the pain. Since the breakup, my grief had felt as if I was being dragged across gravel, tiny sand and rock pieces cutting through my skin, muscle, bones, chipping away at them bit by bit. It couldn't go on like that forever. At some point, there would just be nothing left to drag. But that was the first moment it stopped. It was only about four minutes of temporary relief, but it felt so good to forget my hurt.

Another moment of goodness came at that gymnastics job. There was a ten-minute break in between gymnastics classes, and during this time I would tell the other coaches about what I had been reading, and my career plans.

"I'm going to be a sexologist," I boasted. I had finally settled on a title I liked. *Sexologist.* When I wasn't desperate and insane, before the Pat breakup, I was a powerful speaker. Whenever class assignments involved a presentation everyone else was shy and nervous, reading verbatim from their notes as they looked down anxiously. I gave impassioned, engaging presentations. It came naturally, and I loved the high that comes from being center stage, surrounded by a group of intrigued listeners. I loved being provocative and talking candidly about topics that were too uncomfortable for other people.

However, this bravado to talk candidly about sex was new to me. My entire life I had been horribly shy and ashamed of being a sexual person. I often had my fingers in my ears when my parents tried to educate me. When my mom was pregnant with my sister, when I was nine years old, she bought me a book on pregnancy that I refused to open.

I remember watching TV with my family in the living room one night, some early 90s sitcom, and a character said "masturbation" in a sentence. I'd never heard this word before, it sounded fancy and long so I turned to my parents and asked, "What's masturbation?" They just looked at me. Perhaps they were uncomfortable knowing I was probably going to freak out. Perhaps they were themselves uncomfortable, caught off guard at their nine-year-old asking them about self-pleasuring as they relaxed at the end of the evening.

"What? Why are you staring at me like that?"

"Masturbation is when people touch their genitals," Matter of

165

fact, stoic, just like that. Immediately I was red in the face for asking.

"Eww that's nasty!" I yelled, taking my embarrassment out in the form of anger at them. "Anyone who would do such a thing is nasty!"

"Jill, it's perfectly normal. Everyone does it."

"WELL I DO NOT!" I insisted, thoroughly ashamed that yes, I had touched my genitals. I didn't do it with conscious sexual intention, more out of something to keep my fingers busy, like the same way I would pick at my fingernails or twirl my hair. This fact did not stop my desire to die at that moment.

"You will when you're older," my mother responded, and this embarrassed me even more.

"No I CERTAINLY will not! And I'm sorry I even asked you. I only asked because I never heard the word before and I didn't know what it meant. If I knew it was about sex stuff I wouldn't have said anything!" I responded.

This is the way I had always been. But then miraculously, a switch flipped sophomore year while reading in the library. The books I read made me realize I had been a victim of erotophobia. I was terrified of being a sexual person because society had convinced me that sexual thoughts are disgraceful and bodies are dirty. So despite having open-minded, sex-positive parents and an opportunity to take so many sexuality related courses in school, I was STILL ashamed. What awful self-loathing shame were people with a less progressive upbringing carrying around? This question forced me to immediately overcome my shame and embarrassment about sex, fight that Crusade Against Sex that had manifested within myself, and want a career helping others overcome theirs.

So in addition to my four moments of insanity relief and a paycheck to pay for the gas and insurance for my little Pontiac Grand Am, Lola, I loved my gymnastics coaching job because the people there supported my little entrepreneurial sexology business.

I told them about my different business ideas for doing entertaining sexuality seminars for women. I ran by them one idea to have a long dining room table, make dinner, and have an informal discussion in that setting. I remember telling my manager about another business idea which I would call "Love Seats," where I would have sessions on various topics and participants would meet weekly as a small group in a room full of fluffy comfy love seat couches. I had binders full of notes and doodles. I designed the floor plan for the education center, wrote out the different courses I would offer, and outlined a lesson plan. I even knew then that the business would be more than just educating about sexuality, it would empower sexuality. Its mission would be to spread a sex-positive message into the world. I even had pages in my notebook filled with ideas for raising money for charities, like a raffle box which would be left at the reception counter, and a list of charities the raffle would support such as victims of rape, domestic violence, gay youth groups, etc.

I created a survey online, on a website called misterpoll.com where people can create polls, often silly things like "whose hotter, Jessica Alba or Britney Spears?" I used it to create something I later would learn is actually called a "needs and interest assessment." I titled it "A New Sex Business," and I described my business idea saying, "My plan is to be a sexologist and I want to start my business while I'm still in school. This is why I need your help." I asked questions like "Would you be interested in attending a sex seminar?" "If not, why not?" "How much time would you like to listen to a lecture?" I listed my catalog of over twenty class topics such as "Sexuality and the Lifecycle," "Love and Romance 101," "The Female Orgasm," and a support group seminar for parents of pregnant and parenting teens, and asked people to check off any classes that they would be interested in taking. I also asked "How much would you pay for a seminar if it wasn't paid for by your insurance?" Looking back I find it adorable that I thought a health insurance company might cover someone getting sex advice from a high schooler.

But in all these naïve musings, no one ever mocked me. No one ever told me I couldn't do it. My dad helped me put together a rudimentary website advertising my sexuality seminar business, a free site called *www.letstalkaboutsex.freesite.com*, Gram would announce as I walked in a room "Heeeereeeee's Doctor Jill!" saying I would be the next Dr. Ruth. Scarlet and George supported my dreams. My grown-up coworkers listened to all my ideas. No one ever doubted that I would become a sexuality expert, start my own business, and change the world – even as a teenager. So I confidently kept reading and studying and plotting and planning. I contacted a lawyer to learn about how to incorporate, file business taxes, and legally designate a business name. I was seventeen years old.

Then something else started happening to boost my confidence even more. My supportive coworkers became…clients, of a sort. One day, one of them pulled me aside at lunch and asked me for sex advice. I don't remember the details, I think something about difficulty with erection or orgasm or something of that nature. I responded with the information that I knew about it, and provided a face I can't describe well, a look of absolute judgment-free compassion, a look that said I understood her embarrassment in asking me seriously, a look that said I genuinely cared about her strife. The woman walked away feeling a little bit better, and I walked away certain that I had to keep making people feel this way for the rest of my life.

Planning the intricate details of a business offering sexuality seminars, lectures, and presentations and reading so many books to further my self-education about all things sex gave me the ability to live in my head for a little bit instead of my heart. It was a welcome relief from the heartsickness. In my high school classes I didn't give a shit about British Literature, Probability and Statistics, or Chemistry. I sat at my desk and sobbed the entire time; the bell would ring, I'd move to the next classroom, and sob the entire time there too.

Teachers were initially understanding of the woes of teenage heartache, especially one in particular who I imagined understood what desperation mode feels like after her daughter was murdered. She had experienced real heartache as opposed to my childish heartache, but I guess she believed heart pain is heart pain and was the most compassionate out of all my teachers. She excused me to go to the school social worker. Pat reportedly cried throughout all of his classes too. Not just the first few days, or first few weeks, but well into the spring semester, January, February, March – all day, every day, head down on the desk just sobbing.

At home it was no better. I came home after school feeling so hopeless, devastated, and desperate that sometimes even the sex books and business planning couldn't pick me up. So often I just lay face down on the living room couch, motionless. One day my dad came home from work and bent over to make eye contact with me.

"How are you feeling today, Jill?"

"I now understand why people are heroin addicts," I groaned, still staring straight ahead.

"That good, huh?"

"I was just thinking, I wish I wasn't such a goody-two-shoes so I could do some heroin just so I could numb myself to this pain. You grow up thinking that drug addicts are weak or immoral or bad people, but I just completely understand them now. I totally get it and empathize with addicts now," I told him.

"Absolutely. I feel complete sympathy for addicts. But once you've made the choice to do heroin, all your other choices are made for you. You don't choose to *keep* doing heroin. It's a sad, consuming life that I would never wish on anyone. But I certainly understand it."

"Well I'm not actually going to shoot heroin, Dad, so you don't have to lecture me. I'm just saying, I get it," I reassured him.

"So do I."

There was a pause, and I sat up on the couch.

"I know this hurts. But you will get over Pat, it just takes time."

"I don't want to get over him, Dad! I want him back! If I just get over him then that means it wasn't special. That means our relationship was just like every other stereotypical high school relationship where you date, you break up, you are sad awhile, and then find someone else. I don't want someone else. 'Getting over him' is taking the easy way out. Pat and I had a special thing that no one else had, and I will not give up on our love. I will dutifully keep suffering because when he gets un-brainwashed and comes back, I don't want to have moved on. It's like he's in a coma, and I will wait until he wakes up."

My father stared at me wide-eyed. I could tell that he thought I was crazy. That I was martyring myself. That Pat was not coming back, and even if he did, there were problems other than Pat's mental hijacking; we were codependent, emotionally reliant. I didn't want to hear any of it. I thought I was valiant.

There was a block in my neighborhood that I rarely travelled because it didn't lead to anywhere that couldn't be travelled via a more direct route. But whenever I did happen to find myself driving down this street, there was one house that always, no matter the time of day or the weather or how many years had passed, there was *always* an old man sitting alone on the porch waiting for his son to return from the Vietnam War. At the time, I admired this. I admired the dedication, the loyalty, the valor.

My dad, on the other hand, did not find this valiant. He thought it was terribly heartbreaking and sad to throw away a life in that way, and decided to bring up the proposition of sending me to a therapist.

I was agreeable to seeing a therapist, the same way I was agreeable to being sent down to the school social worker when crying became too disruptive in class, hoping they could say some magical thing to numb my suffering while I waited for Patrick to return to sanity and the world of intellect and curiosity. My therapist wrote me a prescription for Zoloft, an antidepressant medication. I was thrilled; a pain numbing drug that was legal and less dangerous than heroin! My experience with the social worker was less thrilling.

I entered her office one day bent over crying, desperate to unload the hurt seeping through me, destroying my soul and outlook and hope for living, frantic for help, for someone to lift the pain and give me relief. But she was on the phone at that moment, and I anxiously tried to hold on and not burst.

I could overhear her side of the conversation. She was speaking about arranging to have a bag of groceries dropped off for a student. I instantly felt worse. Someone in my school didn't have food to eat if not for the social worker, and my mind ran through all the tragedies of humanity like a rolodex.

"At this moment," I thought, "there is a human being on this planet who just found out they are HIV positive. There is a child being sold by her mother into sex slavery for enough money to buy a cow to sustain the rest of her children. There is tyranny and war. Someone right now is being hacked down with a machete as part of an ongoing ethnic turf war. Someone weighs forty pounds and is dying right now from starvation. Someone is lost at sea. Someone just lost their eyesight. Someone is being raped. Someone's life is so horrible that it's a 'good' day because the drunk driver who killed his wife was convicted."

I felt violently ill. This was the world I lived in? I felt awful because other people, like my teacher whose child was murdered and my classmate who had no food, had real problems while I was bellyaching over a high school breakup. I felt guilty that I was ungrateful for the good fortune that I had. I felt guilty that my life was comparatively wonderful. And yet my pain *was* real, which made me feel worse still. If this profound sadness I felt was living *well* compared to how bad things could be, then what did true tragedy feel like? I didn't want to live in a world in which how I felt at that moment was considered just a juvenile trial run, a get-overable human emotion.

And then, there was the tipping point. The final straw. The end of my rope. These euphemisms suggest an image where there is a physical entity, a bowl that is absolutely at capacity and cannot handle one more molecule without tipping over, a finite length of rope that has not another inch, not even a string of fiber left. It had been four months and my desperation had reached that moment. It was spilling out of me, and I was powerless against stopping it, or against controlling where the overflow spilled. And I was so scared.

It was the end of the day. I was getting my coat out of the locker I now shared with George instead of Pat, when he walked past me. Patrick, walking among the hustle and bustle of four-

171

thousand students pushing past each other in the dash to catch the school bus, was holding hands with *her*. I don't know who she was, but there they were. Laughing, pain-free, internal-torture-and-heartache-free laughing; they held hands and looked at each other, both oblivious to me standing there at my locker observing them, utterly broken. At once, the toxic liquids filled my abdomen again, burning me, choking me, making my head light. They flooded me, knocked the wind out of me, crippled me. I erupted into a fit of panic. For the first time since the heartache began, I tried to talk positively to myself. I didn't want to be a martyr anymore. I wanted to be well. I wanted to be rid of this awful sensation.

"It's going to be ok. Don't fall apart. This will pass. Just like all the other times, the feeling will go away," I kept repeating to myself mentally. But the feeling didn't pass. I walked outside to the school bus, feeling this despondent. The entire ride home, even when Scarlet and George put their arms around me, I felt despondent, aching to my core. During the walk home from the bus stop, it wouldn't relent. I wanted to stop hurting so badly, and it wouldn't go away. I could think of only one way to make it stop. I decided I was going to die that day.

I ran upstairs in my empty house and fell to my knees in the bathroom, frantically pulling out the contents under the sink, Comet, drain cleaner, ammonia, whatever harsh chemicals I could find, and dumped them out on the counter next to the sink. I urged my nostril towards the puddle, ready to inhale them and end my life. But my body fought me. Involuntarily, when I got close enough to smell it my head turned away, my throat gagged. My body was fighting it. It didn't want to die. I started thinking this would take too long, and probably be too painful anyway. Maybe it wasn't meant to be. But I was nevertheless still crawling in a muddy underground cave called desperation, and my fingernails were breaking as I frantically attempted to claw my way out, only to slide back down. Maybe detergent inhalation wasn't the way, but something had to give.

I decided to get in my car and run away. Drive south and just keep driving until I figured out how to manage this Hell. In my daze, I instead started north and found myself driving to my mother's house. I was hesitant. Clearly she would talk me out of killing myself, and I didn't want to be talked out of it. I decided to go there anyway. The thought was too comforting, too soothing.

On my drive, I listened to a classic rock station, as usual, and I had a moment of clarity. Why did I want Pat back anyway? What type of person wasn't moved by music and rock' 'n' roll, and groovy mellow sounds? What type of person's soul didn't get touched by the sound of passion, and tenderness and rising together to feel things, to fight the establishment, to win peace, to express human love? That was rock 'n' roll. And he didn't' like it. Did I really want to be with somebody that square?

Free Bird began playing. I listened to it. I listened to it more closely than I ever had before as Lola flew up I-95 through Philadelphia.

> *Bye bye babe, it's been a sweet love*
> *Though this is a feeling I can't change*
> *Please don't take it so badly*
> *Cause the Lord knows I'm to blame*

The bittersweet tone. The goodbyes. The mildly crying guitar. Why had I never noticed this before? This song, our song, wasn't a love song after all; it was a breakup song! And the worst kind! It wasn't the "good riddance, I hate you" breakup song, it was the "I love you, our love was sweet, but I just can't stay" kind of break up song. I was devastated, replaying in my head the six-second clip of Pat and a girl, some girl, a short, blonde girl, holding hands passing my locker and smiling, over and over. "Jill and Pat" the entity was gone. I had to get it back. I shook and trembled as I picked up my cell phone and dialed a number.

Me: Pat? I can't do this.
Pat: Jill. Stop.
Me: Pat! I saw you with her. Are you really done with us? You're so done that you can bear to have another girl hold your hand,

173

where my hand was? And you didn't even have the decency to tell me? I had to stumble upon you. Do you have any idea how much this hurts right now? I can't even function.
Pat: Jill, I didn't want to tell you because it would hurt you, but I'm not going to hide either. I have the right to date.
Me: FUCK YOU!

And the pot officially tipped. The rope ran out. I threw down my cell phone, hysterical, just as I approached an exit, and I floored the gas pedal.

My car lurched forward down the highway exit. I was ready to die that day. I was seventeen years old. The road made a sharp right curve as it merged onto another highway, but I didn't slow down. I didn't turn. I gripped the steering wheel straight and shoved my foot harder on the gas until the front of my car met the curve, launched me airborne, and I landed in a grass plot off the side of the highway. Alive.

"I can't believe I just did that," I thought, embarrassed, but tremendously glad to not be dead or injured. Sitting on the side of the highway, I couldn't believe what I'd just done. I couldn't grasp at why, despite my sorrow, it had come to this.

My dad went with me to my next appointment with the therapist and asked her, "Why would she do such a thing? I thought the medication was supposed to make her better?" She didn't really have an explanation. A year later, I saw a television advertisement warning of the link between the antidepressant brand Zoloft and suicidal behaviors in teenagers. I like to think that makes sense of it. I was too embarrassed to think I would have done that on my own.

It had been so long since I'd had felt embarrassment. The main tenet of this stage of desperation is not only the increased level of pain, but that the pain is so pervasive, you don't care about any social cues that dissuade you from displaying the pain

174

publically. Despair is stoic. Desperation is sloppy and messy and out there for the world to see without a second thought. As I sat in my car on the side of the interstate with three of my tires ripped to smithereens, noticing that in my suicidal outburst I had actually forgotten to remove my seatbelt, I felt wholeheartedly embarrassed – about other passing motorists that I could have killed, about explaining this to the police who might show up, about telling my parents.

Hitting rock bottom of desperation, there is nowhere to go but up, so at that instant of pure humiliation, I made the positive step back up to despair.

Chapter 17

After the council meeting, the interest by the newspaper and the film media and the thirty-day appeal laws that supported me, I was feeling triumphant. But I don't want to give the impression that I was not scared. I was. I let my high-strung emotions lose when I was home, in private.

"Dad! I can not believe this is happening! I don't know how to make these people see that what I'm doing is valuable and important for women, and people in general," I told him one evening. "And not only that, but I have no other choices. I put everything I have into this business after there were no jobs for me. If they shut me down, I'll have nothing!"

"And it's all your fault!" I added, jokingly blaming him. "I was debating between opening in West Chester or Philly, and you convinced me I should do West Chester! Why did I listen?"

"Don't blame me! I still think you can't beat having a Feminique Boutique in a college town like that."

"I know. I'm kidding. Besides, if I opened in Philly, a few million people wouldn't be at their dinner table right now having a conversation about sexual rights, and pleasure, and female sexuality. I wanted to become a sexologist so that I could break taboos, and get people thinking critically about female sexual pleasure – and that's exactly what's happening. But I'm still scared! What happens if they shut me down?"

I was scared, and I was also hurt. The next morning when I read the newspaper article on the website for the *Daily Local News*, West Chester's local newspaper, the people of West Chester were already flooding the site with comments, and my inbox was overflowing with emails.

One commenter wrote, "Ms. McDevitt is just one more in a long line of misfits who attempt to sell 'sexual education' in the guise of garbage."

I couldn't believe it! I was a misfit, socially ostracized? My passion and scholarly background in sexuality education, my formal education were just garbage? But it got worse! I sat for hours reading the message boards on the online news article. It was like a toothache; it hurt but I kept playing with it and poking it with my tongue. I kept reading and reading, and by the time I'd read through all the comments, more had been posted, and I read those. These were some of the posts, under screen names like "Conservative4Life" and "SoccerMom":

Abuse of children comes in many forms and such shops are examples of individuals contributing, unwittingly or not, to a culture of abuse.

Pleasure is part of it, but any attempt – including this shop and its workshops – to detach sex from life and love, is very dangerous...hence the out-of-control sexually transmitted diseases, marital infidelity, divorce, and much much more.

Ask yourself this question. If getting rid of Feminique Boutique would lower teen pregnancy and STDs, would you do it? Because that is what we are dealing with.

Perhaps the borough council should avail itself of any information from vice squads of all nearby municipalities to help

177

study the links between "sex shops" and sex crimes, and let us see for ourselves how truly innocuous such a place remains over time.

Too much sex, too much visual of sexual things and thoughts and images just simply takes all that mystery away and brings people into a boiling pot of indifference about sexual crime, sexual play and the long list of cultural demise that is tandem to this path.

"All of these people are just misguided and confused," I told myself, "because they probably haven't stepped foot in Feminique. They probably have never met me, or understand how I have no intention of degrading human sexuality. In fact my awe and respect for human sexuality is why I find it so important to educate people about it, and my advocacy for sex-positivity stems from my abhorrence of sexual violence."

I believed there was no way these people could still think Feminique was a bad thing if they knew how passionate I was about addressing serious issues regarding human relationships and sexuality. But then this comment was posted:

While the present shop aims to address serious issues regarding human relationships & sexuality, I and many others view it as a degrading assault on the dignity of the human person.

This person *did* understand my mission, and *still* found it not only a bad thing, but "a degrading assault on the dignity of the human person." Oh boy, those are some hefty, powerful words. This sexual empowerment thing was going to be a lot harder than I thought.

My email inbox was no less harsh. One email that really struck me was this:

Dear Jill,
I can't believe you are determined to destroy the morals of our young people. Shame on you! This will only bring the downfall

of family life and perversion for you and all concerned.
May God help you see the light.

I stewed for quite awhile on how to respond to this one. The others I could try my best to ignore as the ramblings of kooks who anonymously post on the internet, but here was this message, addressed to me personally, sitting in my mailbox, staring at me. I couldn't ignore it, but how could I respond? Rebuttals based on science, or research, or logic wouldn't change her mind. Criticizing her closed-mindedness and religious views wouldn't change her mind either; only further convince her that I was the devil. I was so angry, so frustrated, so hurt by the infiltration of negativity into my life that I had to do something with this energy, but what?

It was 9:45 a.m. and I shut my computer off in aggravation. I had been accused in a public forum of being personally responsible for child abuse, the downfall of family life, STDs, marital infidelity, divorce, teen pregnancy, sexual exploitation and sex crimes, child sacrifice, slavery and brutality and of course, assaulting the dignity of a human person, and I hadn't even had breakfast yet. How was I responsible for the impending downfall of humanity? Because I wanted women to love their bodies and enjoy their clits?

I drove the hour commute to Feminique and had just enough time to stop by a fast food restaurant and get breakfast; from the dollar menu of course because I was so broke. Next to the front door of the restaurant there was a newspaper dispenser, with my photo in full color taking up the entire top fold from the "smut" filled council meeting the night before. In the photo my head was turned so that my face was hidden, and I figured no one would notice me, until the man standing behind me in line at the fast food chain smiled in my direction.

"Hey, you keep fighting the good fight, woman!" he said to me.

"Excuse me?"

"Aren't you that girl in the paper today getting a hard time from the church?"

"Yeah."

"Well don't sweat it. Everyone's on your side. You keep fighting the good fight!"

"Oh...thanks, I will!" I stammered and headed to open my shop.

Once there, the phone rang almost immediately. It was a local radio station looking to bring me into the studio as a guest. When I finished with them the phone rang again; this time it was the *Philadelphia Inquirer* wanting to do a story. I was happy. I was even happier when sales that day were suddenly twice what they'd been each day prior. The store was full of shoppers giving me hugs, pats on the shoulder, and words of encouragement. I was happier still when I went home that evening to find the comment section on the online news article and my email inbox ten times fuller than when I left in the morning, but instead of hard insults and accusations, all the messages were energetic, impassioned words of support!

There were so many, I became obsessed with reading them. They lifted my spirits. I had three windows open on my computer: my email, the *Daily Local News* article message board, and the NBC10 message board. I would switch between the three, refresh the page, read the new posts, click the next window, refresh the page, read the new posts, and round and round.

When I was finished with that I did a Google search of my name and found that bloggers from all over the country had heard about my plight and blogged about it. New blog posts popped up rapidly. I refreshed the Google search every few moments to find a new post and smiled in amazement as I watched my story go viral.

The blog posts, written by strangers from all over the country, quickly garnered hundreds of comments themselves. I felt supported, but more than that, I felt protected and cared for. These comments were not like the ones made by people trolling the internet making off topic, inflammatory, or indifferent remarks, as is often the case with anonymous, online forums. These writers were insightful, articulate, angry at the injustice I was facing, and they were ready to fight for me and my cause.

Everyone was supportive, but for different reasons. As I read and read, I noticed one's rationale for support fell into one of nine different categories:

There was the "I Agree!" argument:

I just want to say thank you for having this shop so close to where I live and I support your beliefs on human sexuality. I will be visiting your store very shortly.

Sex is a wonderful gift and sometimes needs a little "help" to keep things hot. Your shop is perfect for this!

The "Misplaced Outrage" argument:

I am a lot more concerned for my five-year-old daughter about the images portrayed in any number of television shows (e.g. murder, drugs, etc) than anything she would encounter in your store.

Leave this woman's business alone. Aren't there more important issues to worry about (i.e. the war in Iraq, impeaching an inept president, etc...)?

The "What's The Big Deal?" argument:

The fact that it is near a school...who cares? The storefront displays nothing crude.

The storefront is harmless. Do you feel the same way when at the mall and you pass by Victoria's Secret???

The "Economic" Argument:

Cut us a break! This is a legitimate business with a license to operate.

Let the shop owner do her business. If she is legally registered, and pays the same business taxes everyone else does, then she should be allowed to operate.

The "Double Standard" Argument:

This is the old double standard. Men get to frequent their nudie bars and watch porn, but God forbid a woman should offer a store where other women can feel comfortable exploring ways to get in touch with their sexuality.

Oh please. The church is just pissed because the shop caters to women.

The "Bully/Underdog" Argument:

I saw you on MSNBC this morning and I just have to say WAY TO GO! Don't let anybody get you down!

Don't let them get you down! If they begin protesting at your store and you need counter-protesters, email me and I'll be there along with as many of your supports as I can muster. Hang in there! We're all on your side.

The "Separation of Church and State" Argument:

It's called America. It's called free enterprise. If we let religion dictate everything it will destroy this country.

I find organized religion offensive, but that doesn't mean I get to legislate it out of my neighborhood.

The "Live and Let Live" Argument:

The prudes that disapprove of her store obviously haven't

had a good time in a long time. But don't ruin it for the rest of us!!!

To those who are offended, the answer is quite simple. Don't patronize the store.

The "Hypocrisy" Argument:

Hmmm…I wonder what would happen if an adult boutique sued to close down a church for "corrupting the morals of children." As far as I know, there are no recorded instances of children being molested in an adult toy store…

Last time I checked, vibrators don't RAPE people. Talk about the pot calling the kettle black.

I couldn't believe it! My stay positive tactic had worked! I had said only what I believed, what I was doing well and the positivity I had to offer, and other people had picked up the other pieces. I didn't have to say inflammatory things or call people prudes or bring up the child rape scandal within the Catholic Church. Others had done it for me. The points had been made in the public discourse while I continued looking innocent and bullied, which rallied people around me even more because everyone loves a good underdog story. It was all coming together beautifully.

Chapter 18

I was a first-generation college student. No one in my family had received a higher education, and I knew nothing about college, or how college could help me become a sexologist. I didn't know the difference between a college and a university, an unsubsidized Stafford Loan from the Federal PELL Grant program. I didn't know how to pick a school; there were thousands of colleges in the United States and they all seemed the same, and I certainly didn't know how to pay for one.

When I wasn't moping and crying face down on my living room couch or sitting at the bookstore studying sexuality and filling spiral bound notebooks with ideas for my sex education business, I was surfing different college websites with great irritation. I clicked the drop-down menu for available majors.

Secondary Education
Social Work
Sociology

Damn. No sexuality. I visited the next college's site and scrolled through the "S"es.

Safety Sciences
Sociology
Spanish

What the hell? I tried another school's site.

Science Education

Soil and Watershed Science

Studio Art

And on and on it went. But that was only part of the problem. The tuition for these schools was $14,000 a year, $22,000 a year, $29,000 a year. Even if there was such a thing as a sex major, which there wasn't, I wouldn't be able to go. I couldn't afford it.

Despite living with a single father who was recently laid off, I didn't receive any grants for school. And despite my absurdly perfect grades, volunteer work, and extracurricular activities, I didn't receive any scholarships, not a one, save ironically a one-time $500 scholarship that the congregants from the childhood church I hadn't attended in years had raised for me. My four-year degree would cost me $70,000, and all but $500 of that I would pay myself – plus interest. I had worked so hard all of those years for nothing; rewriting papers, staying after school in the library, taking honors and college level courses, staying up until four in the morning doing school work, vomiting on the way to school from exhaustion. It had all been for *nothing.* I applied to the cheapest school I could find and was accepted.

Senior year eeked by slowly, day by day. I woke up. I cried all through school. I came home and read sex books. I cried a little more. I went to bed. Sometimes I saw Scarlet and George, but all I did was cry to them too. This went on until June. Until Senior Prom; my last ditch effort to change Pat's heart.

Before we had broken up, before he was brainwashed into Christian fundamentalism, Pat and I had made that pact to go to the Senior Prom together.

Now, he changed his mind.

"I'm sorry, Jill. I don't think it's a good idea," he told me when I brought the subject up.

"Why not?"

"With all the hurt we've been through this year, I just don't think we should put ourselves through that."

"But we promised each other," I protested. "That was the whole point of the pact; that if a situation happened like the one we're currently in, we could let go of all the drama and remember how it's supposed to be between us."

"How about this, I'll save you the last dance."

That part of the promise he kept, and we both cried the entire song. A few days later we graduated, and I couldn't wait to get to college and escape.

In the fall of 2003, I started at East Stroudsburg University, a state college in Pennsylvania's Pocono Mountains. It was far below my academic level, but all that I could afford. I loved college. People were nice. They didn't start shit. There were no bullies and no one throwing rocks at me, and certainly no one mocking me for being a "hippie."

Back at home, listening to the Grateful Dead and being a vocal peace and social justice advocate made me an outcast; in college it made me cool. It seemed like anyone who was anyone in college listened to the Grateful Dead and was a peace and social justice advocate, so I fit right in. I joined the Gay Straight Alliance Club, marched in Washington D.C., New York City, and locally against the war in Iraq, protested against George Bush's corrupt administration, and attended Take Back the Night rallies on campus to speak out against rape and sexual violence, sitting on the quad around a bonfire singing Crosby, Stills, and Nash as someone strummed on an acoustic guitar. I had a lot of school work, but I was not stressed or losing my hair or sleeping two hours a night while writing papers as I had in high school because I enjoyed what I was learning.

I decided to major in Psychology, the closest major to sexuality I could find, and developed my own interdisciplinary curriculum by picking out the sex related courses within different majors. I took Psychology courses called "Human Sexuality" and "Social Psychology II: Interpersonal Relationships," a Communications course called "Gender and Communication," a Sociology course called "Marriage and Family," English courses where I elected to write all of my papers about sex topics, as well as two public speaking courses where I, of course, chose to write speeches about sex and hone my skills as a dynamic and engaging speaker as I gave my presentations to the class.

I absolutely LOVED college. My favorite part was when I had visitors in my dorm room. The dorms were ugly rooms with tan painted cinderblock, but my roommate and I had decorated ours with so many colorful fabrics and pillows and warm lighting that it felt like home. The bookshelf above my desk was full of nothing but sex books that I had collected throughout my many trips to the bookstore in high school, as well as books Gram and my parents had picked up for me over the years at yard sales. There was "The Guide to Getting it On," and "The Pocket Book of Foreplay," and "Satisfaction: The Art of the Female Orgasm" by Kim Catrall, "Don't Sweat the Small Stuff in Love," plus all my porn, such as "Letters to Penthouse." Before long word got out about my little sex library, and I would get knocks on my dorm room door from curious visitors wanting to see it for themselves. Soon after the start of the school year, people would regularly gather in my comfortable, homey freshman dorm room asking my advice about sex and dating. I was a busy girl, and between it all whenever I got a quiet moment, I would continue designing my business educating women about sexuality.

Life was good. I even had a new boyfriend, Derrek. His mother was a pastor at a Presbyterian Church and his whole family seemed as if they came out of an episode of Seventh Heaven – loving, pacifist, and feminist do-gooders. The family was so happy peachy-keen: Derrek and his siblings even lovingly referred to each other as "sister" and 'brother" just like the feel-good sitcom, as in "Hey sister, you relax, it's my turn to walk the dog today." It helped soften my anger about organized religion as I realized that not every Christian was a brainwashed sheep and that many, like Derrek's family, are full of love and compassion.

But as a Christian, Derrek was a virgin and had never had intercourse, just like me. But unlike me, he was not a connoisseur of *outer*course. I changed that. I made him skinny dip with me in his pool after his parents were asleep. I made him skip church so we could take a bath together, knowing we'd be alone for awhile as his whole family stayed late for the after service luncheon. I also made him learn about the clitoris.

"You know, we don't have to actually have sex to get pleasure…" I said.

"What do you mean?" he asked nervously.

And I launched onto my clitoris soapbox: the clitoris is biologically the same as a penis so rubbing and licking clitorises gets women off, and it's actually better than sex because penis-in-vagina thrusting pretty much ignores the clitoris.

"You mean, we can still come and stay virgins, not have to worry about pregnancy, and it actually is better than sex for you because more of the orgasm nerve endings are in the clitoris, not vagina?" he clarified, bemused.

"Precisely," I said.

"So why the hell is everyone all about regular sex then? And how did I never know this?" he asked.

I responded excitedly, "Exactly! This is my frustration! What's considered 'regular' sex is because it's most pleasurable for men, and what's most pleasurable for women is considered 'foreplay,' like it's lesser and not 'real sex' if it's *only* outercourse. I'm sure sex is awesome and wonderful, but when it comes to actual *orgasm*, it physiologically just makes more sense to do things like dry hump or oral, based on all the books I've read. But as far as why you didn't know about this until now, why was I and why were you and countless other people left in the dark about this? That part I haven't read in a book. I have my own little theory about it. I think it's because penis-in-vagina sex has a 'purpose,' procreation and the like. But flicking a clit has only one purpose – pleasure. Keeping this information hidden is a tool of oppression designed to keep women as receptacles for men, just a vessel to dump semen in without anyone knowing or really caring how women orgasm. And people wonder why women fake it?"

He stared at me.

"What?' I asked.

"You're going to be an awesome sexologist," he stated, and

188

I chuckled.

"No, seriously, listen to you. You have passion, you have knowledge, and the way you speak, I mean 'flick a clit,' it's so funny. I think people will really relate to you," he complimented. Then I taught him how to go down on me.

We never had anything to talk about unless I was on a rant about sexuality, or he was on a rant about Bush's latest inept policies. We dated for an entire year, and when we broke up the summer after freshman year in college it took me about two days to get over it. I loved him, but it was not like the love I had for Pat. This scared me. If it took me only two days to get over a yearlong relationship with a perfectly nice person, I believed it was because no matter how nice the person, or how long the relationship, I would never have love like I had with Pat. I was doomed to pine for Patrick Abramowitz for the rest of my life.

Truth be told, even when I was with Derrek, even when I was happily sitting in a college classroom having stimulating conversations about gender based violence or the proposed anti-gay marriage Constitutional amendment or reading from my sex books to a dorm room full of girls, I was always thinking of Pat.

Things were calmer in my brain. I wasn't in desperation mode anymore. I had even progressed past despair and into ordinary sadness. Without the panic and the pain and the toxicity of seeing Pat every day and being reminded of my heartache, I was able to have some semblance of coping. But make no mistake, I still wanted him back more than anything. Now that I was sane again, I could think of a plan to win him back that was more rational than collapsing on his basement steps, clinging to the banister, and refusing to leave. Now my plan was to become a Christian too, so we could fit back in. Square peg, square hole. Jill and Pat.

When Derrick and I were dating, I sometimes went to the non-fundamentalist, non-cultish church where his mother preached, and after we broke up, I decided to keep going to church. A different one of course, but every Sunday morning, I went. I also started reading the Bible. I hoped it would enchant me. I hoped I would read it and buy into it. I wanted to be brainwashed so I could go to Pat and say, "Do you remember when you said you wanted a wife who could pray with you every night and keep Jesus in her heart? Well I can do that for you!"

That summer, the summer before sophomore year of college, Pat and I met up once or twice, and it was as if we were magnetically attracted. We were both back home, on the old streets where we used to ride bikes, where we used to meet early on summer mornings. After a year apart, the skin had started to crust over old wounds. I was stronger, but we were still drawn to each other like that bug to a bug zapper, just like we were the first time around. We went for walks and found ourselves holding hands as we toured our old stomping ground. We cuddled. We flirted. We stayed up late talking, except this time in person curled up on the couch, instead of on the phone because now we were eighteen and allowed to. It had been over a year and a half since the breakup. A year of that time I was dating someone else who was wonderful, but the moment Pat and I were together again the rapture was instantaneous; it was as if we'd been apart for only a day. Everything was so natural and good and the way it was supposed to be.

For my nineteenth birthday, in some of the last few days of summer before it was time to head back to college, Pat and I sat in his car. He handed me a card and gift wrapped in paper. As always, he handwrote the card. It said:

> *Jill,*
>
> *So, who would have thought? We never know what God has in store for us. We've been through a lot, and I only predict that there is more to come, good and bad, but one way, or form, or another, we'll be together somehow.*

"I hope he's right," I thought. We didn't have a label for the love we'd grown into. It was stained with a history of adoration, obsession, and attempted suicide, but there we were.

I excitedly unwrapped the crinkled paper package. It was a leather-bound Bible with my full name inscribed in gold letters on the front. I closed my eyes and sighed as I realized I did not want this gift, realizing that for whatever reason I *couldn't* believe this book and Pat *had* to believe this book, and all the pretending and wishing I did to make either of us convert would never work. Square peg, round hole, and nothing I could do to change it. I didn't say a word.

"Jill," he started, looking at me as I'd always remembered, piercing me with his deep stare. "I know we've had our differences. But I hope you know I'm always here for you, and I'm always praying for your happiness. I don't know what we're doing. Maybe when I study abroad this year we will go our separate ways, or maybe someday we'll find ourselves together like we used to be. I'm not saying that's going to happen, and I don't want to give you a false hope. I'm just saying, even though we haven't talked in a year it does not mitigate the fact that you are, and always will be, one of the most important people in my life." The tears started welling in his eyes as he pointed to his chest and said, "No matter what, you'll always be right here."

George: To what do I owe the pleasure of your phone call at this hour of the night? Or should I say morning?
Me: Pat and I are sorta back together again but not really.
George: Oh shit.
Me: You don't sound very happy about it.
George: The two of you are crazy and you're setting yourself up for a world of pain again. Why put yourself through this?
Me: I don't know, it's total insanity! But listen – I'm so confused. It's not forced. We just are drawn together. We were meant to be a union. But at the same time, I'm afraid because I started to open my mind to being a Christian a little bit but that, unlike my union with Pat, it's a bit forced. I want to be a Christian so bad, but not just for Pat. I think it would make things easier. Not to question, not to worry. To actually believe somebody is going to take care of everything, it must be so freeing. But then, he gets me a Bible for

my birthday and I'm like...I can't do this. I've been reading this book. It's not...it's evil. There's slavery, and murder, and cold-heartedness, and God kills his own people with plagues and locusts. It's ridiculous. And there's rape. Which I just can't even.... You know I can't even handle. I just don't believe any of it.

Plus Pat took me to one of his meetings at the Jared's. I got to see it for myself, George. I want to do good things in the world. I want to love others and not judge them. I asked for people to give to charity instead of getting gifts this year for my birthday. I thought these things would make me Christian enough for him, but they don't. I don't like what I saw at the meeting. I don't want to be brainwashed. I want to question. I want to think for myself. But not doing these things is the only way to get to Pat.
George: You're insane.

I was insane, when it came to Pat anyway. I was not a good person around Patrick. I was a person who ditched my friends and was clingy, obsessive, suicidal, willing to change my values. When I said it out loud I couldn't stand how pathetic I sounded. Without him I was a strong and determined young aspiring entrepreneur.

Me: So anyway, are we still on for a midnight movie tomorrow?
George: Actually, change of plans.
Me: Why, what's up?
George: Samantha and I are going to her parents' for dinner and then she wants me to stay over...
Me: My, my, how the tables have turned. George is in love and ditching his old best friend.
George: Well, I...
Me: Don't worry about it. Have fun. Just make sure you don't forget the clitoris, George. Clit, clit, clit!
George: Yes, Dr. Jill.

I started my second year of college in the fall of 2004. Pat was studying abroad and sent me gifts from around the world as he studied in Kenya, China, and India. I took great comfort in

192

believing what he wrote in my birthday card "we'll be together somehow." In the back of my brain I thought we'd wind up together in the end, just like in all good love stories, but I tried to keep that thought for the future and concentrate on digging in even deeper into the college scene. I volunteered for John Kerry's campaign in the Presidential election in the hopes of defeating George Bush. I worked even harder on planning my future sexuality education business. I sucked the marrow out of life and enjoyed every minute.

While Pat traveled the world for school, some very interesting things were happening to me back at my little one-horse college. First, I got hot. It was as if overnight I blossomed from an ordinary girl to a sexy confident woman. And second, I got my first break.

Early in September, when it was still warm out and school assignments were not in full throttle yet, I came back to my residence hall late after a night class. I was in a different building this year, and I didn't really know anyone yet. I walked up to the second floor, and as I scurried down the long hallway to my dorm room, I passed the student lounge. A few people sat at a table reading, and a group of five others were curled up on the couches, wearing sweatpants and college hoodies. I so wanted to keep going to my room, desperately tired from a long day, but I decided to once more suck that marrow, live in the moment, and attempt to make more friends. I wanted to bask in every college moment. When else in my life would I live in a space where strangers gather in a common area to socialize? I had to be a part of it.

I boldly walked in, introduced myself, and found a seat in the circle. Someone quickly noticed my Kerry/Edwards 2004 button.

"Nice to meet you, Jill. Nice button," said one of the girls.

"Thanks! This is a big election. You're all registered to vote, right? Because if not I have voter registration forms in my room."

"Absolutely!" one of the guys answered. "This election is so important. That's cool that you keep registration forms on

193

hand."

"Just doing my part to get this fascist, war mongering moron out of office," I said.

"I just met you, and I like you already!" another of the guys chimed in.

"I think I've passed your room before. It's the one with all political signs on it, like, 'If you're not outraged you're not paying attention' and the gay marriage one," added a third.

"Yeah, that's me!"

"Gay marriage?" asked one of the girls.

"Yeah, it's a tongue in cheek list of reasons gay marriage would ruin society, like marriage will be less meaningful if gay marriage were allowed because then the 'sanctity' of Britney Spears' fifty-five-hour just-for-fun marriage would be destroyed, and things like that."

Everyone was looking at me intrigued. I'd only known them for about three minutes, and I couldn't quite gauge if the looks meant they were impressed or annoyed.

"Sorry, I guess I shouldn't walk up to a bunch of strangers and start talking about the two most taboo topics ever, sex and politics," I laughed.

"No, don't apologize. You're fiery," said one of the guys who it turned out was named Adam.

"I'm just very opinionated about politics, particularly sexual politics."

"Ok, so you got me curious. What exactly is 'sexual politics?' I've never heard that before."

"It's when private sexuality topics become political, governmental, legislated, like marriage equality, abortion, things like that. Or, when these topics become a part of the social discourse, for example, the topic that interests me most is the way society treats female sexuality versus male sexuality and how society doesn't want women to enjoy sex or masturbate otherwise she'll be punished by being called a 'slut,' but men can all they want."

"Whoa! Oh shit. She's talking about masturbating," said

the third guy, Jeff, who was only half joking.

"Yes, I am. It's an important subject. We should talk about it."

"Yes, let's talk about it," he added enthusiastically but still joking.

"No, seriously..."

"Ok, Jill, you lost me. I think that's a stretch to say that 'society doesn't want women to enjoy sex.' I've never heard any guy say that," Adam broke in.

"It's not about saying it. It's about music we listen to, the news that we watch, the words we choose that subtly, and sometimes not so subtly, send this message. Hear me out. 'Beat the meat,' 'jerk off,' 'choke the chicken.' Slang phrases for masturbation overwhelmingly refer to men masturbating, but not women," I said.

"And these are expressions you've heard of, heard men mention doing...shit, it was even manifested in a major motion picture with Jason Biggs and one very abused pastry. Could you imagine a movie about a parent helping teach a teen *girl* how to get herself off? Men masturbate. They admit it. They talk about it. They enjoy. But you ask a woman if she masturbates and the scenario becomes quite a bit different. When I talk to girls, half respond 'No, never,' and the other half cop to it but swear it has been awhile and isn't a regular occurrence. Now what, you might ask yourself, is the cause of the discrepancy between men and women?"

At this point, the whole gang was staring at me intently again, but this time I could read their facial expressions. They were loving it. I was provocative but classy, sexually confident but smart and articulate. I had their undivided attention as I continued to lay out my theory on female masturbation. The two female students who were studying at a nearby table must have overheard me and found their way over to our circle of couches, leaning up against the armrest as they listened in.

"On the surface, it makes no sense. The tendency to pleasure oneself is innate," I continued. "Even fetuses have been

195

known to touch their genitals. The positive outcomes are countless, from reducing stress to discovering what turns you on to curing insomnia; and let's face it, it feels good, right?"

Everyone let out a nervous giggle, especially the girls, who were clearly embarrassed to be agreeing in front of the boys that masturbation felt good. Admit to enjoying sexual pleasure? Imagine that!

"Maybe it's not that women aren't doing it," I continued, "maybe it's that they're too ashamed to admit it. So where does this shame come from? To understand why both sexes are engaging in natural behavior, but women are too uncomfortable to acknowledge it, you have to look at the sexual societal context. Here's a classic scenario, a man has sex with three women in one month. He got lucky. He's a pimp. He's a player. His actions are celebrated. A female engages in the same activities, and she's a slut. She has no self-respect. Men don't think she's worthy of value and would only be interested in her if they wanted to become number four.

"Pop culture exacerbates this double standard every day. Male musicians are free to write about sexual fantasies, sexual violence, and conquest. Remember that song from high school, *Back That Ass Up*? and the line 'after you back it up then stop and drop it like it's hot,' implying getting rid of the girl after having sex with her. The response was that it was one of the most aired songs of 1999. And *Yeah,* by Usher, is a more recent example of a popular song that is about nothing except the desire for no-strings-attached sex for pleasure. He's talking about getting a little 'VI,'…Vaginal Intercourse, 'get 'em in their birthday suits,' and then, you guessed it, 'put 'em on foot patrol.'

"I don't think there is anything wrong with these expressions of lust, but can you imagine if a female singer was like, 'I just need some dick, I just want to find a guy on this dance floor I can take back and strip naked, and then kick out when I'm done?' She'd be lucky if her career wasn't tarnished. Madonna has tried to communicate her sexuality through her music and videos, and do you remember the responses over the years? MTV banned her *Justify My Love* video, stores sold her *Sex* book concealed in a brown paper bag, and Pepsi cancelled her commercial after she released a sexy video. All because she writhes around looking like she's enjoying her sexuality and she's a woman. But Usher can blatantly sing about going out on the hunt for vaginal sex with a woman he can throw out when he's done, and this song is played at middle school dances. The unfair truth is that society does not want women to enjoy sex. It's not tolerable for females to enjoy multiple men, or even our own hand. And before you interject and disagree..."

"No, please, continue. I actually find this very insightful," said Adam.

"Good. But I was going to say, it's not just men. The concept that a woman enjoying sexual pleasure means she is a slut/whore/skank/easy/dirty and so on, is so deep-seated in our culture, even women fall prey to the stigma. This is very evident in the way we use expressions of anger and frustration and equate them to female sexuality. Cunt, a word referring to female genitals, is often considered the most offensive term in the English language. Think about that. The most offensive thing you can say, the most horrible insult you can give someone, is to call them a vagina. Vaginas are bad, insulting things? Pussy is another such term, and how is it used? Someone tell me."

"Well...not to be...but, you know, it's sometimes used to call someone a wimp," said Jeff.

"Thank you. Men call other men pussies to accuse them of being wimps or weak. There is a book in my sex library I LOVE called *The Guide to Getting it On* by Paul Joannides, which at one point questions why we associate cowardice with being a woman or having a woman's genitals, and conversely being brave and strong means 'having balls' or male genitals. I don't remember the exact quote obviously, but he tells the story of a young girl yelling 'suck my dick' to another child who was bothering her in the school yard and notes that even an eight-year-old knows that the way you insult someone in our society is to tell the person to take the woman's place when she is having sex. The author gives more examples such as 'screw you' and 'get fucked,' and others as being the way of saying 'you're the woman in sex, you piece of garbage.' I'm not saying that male masturbation is completely accepted. We're a very erotophobic, puritanical society in general. I'm just trying to elucidate that the sex and masturbation taboo is much harsher for women."

I was heated. My heart was pounding, my breath ever so slightly labored from the high of helping others become self-reflective and challenge what they'd been taught about sex.

I noticed it while I was talking, but I was on such a roll that I didn't allow myself to process it. But now that I had concluded and was able to take a breath, I felt my cheeks pull back a big, humble grin. The small group of five ballooned into twenty-two; people passing by from their dorm rooms on their way to the bathroom, people with towels coming out of the shower, others just passing through to see if any other friends were in the lounge. People from everywhere stopped what they were doing, where they were going, and were three people deep in a circle around me, listening in on my impromptu presentation on female masturbation.

"You have a fire in your belly, and people respond well to those types of things," Adam said to me as chatter opened up among the crowd.

"Well thank you," I responded, still with a shit-eating grin on my face.

"I'm one of the editors for the student run newspaper on campus. If you write even half as well as you speak, I'd love for you to write a column for me. Would you consider it?" he asked.

"Wow, really? Like a weekly sex column? I'd love to!" I was thrilled. I chatted some more about non-sex and non-political topics with all of my new friends, then called it a night at six in the morning, went back to my dorm room, and typed up my first article, a near replica of the speech I had just given. I titled it "Masturbation and Other Dirty Words." In the weeks following I wrote about oral sex, circumcision, breasts, homosexuality, and gender identity, all with a sex-positive tone and an educational flare intertwined with an informal writing style dotted with the occasional curse or provocative word to keep it funny, young, and relevant, all with an underlying theme of challenging the status quo.

I incorporated interviews with other students, references to pop culture, academic research, personal experiments, and professional interviews. One article promoted the legalization of prostitution and included an interview I had done with employees at a Nevada brothel. In an article on the association between nudity, sexuality, and body image, I set up a male/female research team and went door-to-door in my residence hall talking to people about how they felt nude and inviting them to get naked in public to ascertain the difference between how much people are willing to admit societal pressures affect their comfort with nudity (sixty-eight percent said they would be perfectly comfortable being naked in public, thirteen percent actually got naked). Looking back, I said some sex-negative things in my articles, and in some ways it's embarrassing, but at the same time, it helps me realize that sex-positivity is something that must always actively be worked on, because in our erotophobic society, it's so easy to be sex-negative.

The column was popular from the beginning, but once the article on nudity hit the press and the campus learned that I had people running around naked in Laurel Residence Hall, defying social norms, challenging thinking about how we were raised with body oppressive beliefs that continue to affect us, everyone ate it up, launching me as a campus celebrity.

I started receiving regular fan mail from other students. Some asked for digital copies in addition to the print copy from the paper so they could email them to friends back home. I got stopped in the hallways, the Quad, in my classrooms, the dining hall. Once a girl walked passed me talking on her cell phone and stopped to say, "Every week I read your article to my coworkers, who are still in high school. They say they cannot wait for college so they can be free to speak their mind too. I can tell you spend a lot of time on them, and I love to read them!"

Even faculty followed along. My former Marriage and

Family professor asked if she could photocopy my article on gender and sexuality for her students as required reading. The Director of Health Education used my article critiquing the abstinence-only education agenda, while a Residence Hall staff person in another dorm said at least four of her residents had my first article on female masturbation hanging on their dorm mini fridges.

If I was psyched back in high school when I was building my business plan and an adult coworker asked me for sex advice, I was in heaven now. There was buzz. People were talking and thinking and feeling things they never had before I came along and provoked their liberation. I loved it.

And knowing I had this loyal base, I decided to finally take the final leap into the persona of outspoken sexologist provocateur by publically advocating that which had humiliated me for so long and at the same time made me hell-bent on doing this for a living – clitoral stimulation from bodies grinding. It was so taboo. It was so *not* talked about that I thought I'd made the thing up until I read it in a book in my high school library. No one talked about it because it's embarrassing to admit enjoying something so inferior to the almighty penis-in-vagina sex, the only time it was even slightly acceptable was as a temporary third base for young lovers working their way up to something "better." But I knew the truth, and I was ready to shed any harboring embarrassment and tell the world – dry humping is not just for horny teens! And suddenly, the campus was abuzz with dry humping.

One night I was waiting in the notoriously long line for the bathroom at an underage house party when I saw it. There it was; my latest article "Dry Humping Not Just For Horny Teens," from the school newspaper had been clipped out and was adorning one of the fraternity brother's bedroom door. Forget imitation, seeing your feminist manifesto hang on the walls of a frat house with black electrical tape is the sincerest form of flattery.

My nineteenth year was filled with turning my little world called East Stroudsburg University upside down by advocating sexual liberation. It worked out well. That year was also filled with advocating for larger social justice issues and attempting to turn the whole world upside down. Revolutions, impassioned debates, marching, canvassing. I worked the polls on Election Day 2004. It didn't work out so well, and George W. was reelected. And no matter what I was doing, at the end of the day, when I was finished researching the week's sex column, registering classmates to vote, and partying with my new friends, I thought of Pat.

After the election, after facing four more years of George Bush and the Republicans, I solidified a decision I had been privately mulling over. In high school, I was completely in the dark about higher education, but after two years of living it, I was more confident. I thought there was no such thing as a sex major, but that was because I didn't know where to look. American schools didn't offer a sex degree to undergraduates, but Canadian schools did. During my research for different class assignments and for my column, I came across St. Jerome's University, which is federated with the University of Waterloo in Ontario, Canada. It offered the North American continent's only bachelor's degree in sexuality. Since I'd learned of it I had wanted to transfer there but I had nestled in so well at my little Pennsylvania state college, I couldn't bear to pry myself away. Now after the election, moving to Canada seemed much more appetizing. I applied, secured funding, and got in. At nineteen years old I had made the decision to move to a foreign country to formally study sex and follow my dream.

As if I wasn't living the life already, the second semester was even more picture perfect. The weather was getting warmer. I wore fewer clothes, showing off my new confidence and sex appeal. I loved my classes. As the last semester started to wind down I loved the carefree days of hanging out with my friends before I would move away and probably never see them again.

Earth Day that year was on a Friday, full of rainy skies and a cool spring nip in the air. I attended the Earth Day festival on the Quad, played a game of Ultimate Frisbee, and then made yet more friends when I joined some people around a bonfire listening to The Dave Matthews Band. I really loved the college life!

As the evening went on and the air got colder, the campus started emptying. My little group, huddled around the warmth of the flames, were the only humans in sight on campus, and then one by one, they started packing up too. No one was partying. My roommate was gone. It seemed that everyone was home for the weekend except me.

I went back to my quiet residence hall, hearing every creak of my footsteps echo down the empty halls, and got cozy, alone in my room. I felt comfortable and naughty, the same way I felt in those early days of talking to Pat on the phone all night, protected in the little world of my bedroom. Wrapped in a blanket, I sat at my desk and logged onto Facebook.

It was April, 2005, and Facebook had barely been out for a year. It was so different than it is today. It was only for college students, and you could only create an account if you had a valid college .edu email address. There was no newsfeed, no photo albums. Just poking, a wall, one profile picture, and the ability to join groups. Michael Higgins poked me. "Are you serious?" I thought. "Michael Higgins from eighth grade?"

We exchanged wall posts back and forth, chatting about how much has changed since we kissed in high school. Then he asked for a chance to redeem himself. When I told him no he got fresh and I realized nothing had really changed since that time. Facebook was an addictive world of stalking and snooping, voyeurism and exhibitionism. It had led me to Michael Higgins for goodness sake. Ugh. Who else would it lead me to?

At this point, in the elementary days of Facebook, the left panel on the screen listed every college where you had a friend. For about a month in time, the coolest thing was to have a long list of colleges and universities on your Facebook page. It was better to have only one friend at twenty different schools than to have more than one hundred friends at just your own school. So I picked a random college, found their list of groups, clicked on the anti-Bush group for that school (someone had started one at every school in America, it seemed), sifted through the list of members, and hit "add to friends" for the attractive males. It was complete middle-

202

school silliness, but I figured if I was going to bulk up my list of colleges where I had "friends" it might as well be filled with cute boys. So I clicked Temple, Bloomsburg University, Penn State, and St. Joseph's. I'm not sure what I was thinking, except that I was bored and alone on a dreary dark campus on a Friday night, and I was having one hell of a fun time scouring Facebook.

One person who I randomly friended wrote to me, "I'm sorry I'm not placing your face. How do we know each other?" His name was Justin Duerr.

"Well, actually we don't know each other," I typed awkwardly, realizing how creepy and stalker-like it sounded when I wrote it out. "I saw that you were a member of 'Bush: A Stupid Piece of Shit' group at St. Joe's...and...well...yeah." To my surprise, he thought it was great. We chatted and typed, and the next thing I knew, six hours had passed.

The next day I typed another Facebook message to Justin.

Do you always talk online for six hours to girls who randomly Facebook you, or am I special? ☺

We chatted again that whole Saturday, and again all day Sunday. We spoke on the phone, and he was so...different than Pat. He was a grown-up. Pat and I had one extreme view of sex – it was too special to do before marriage. Others I knew at school took the opposite view, that it was meaningless. But Justin had a mature outlook. He'd loved. He'd been heartbroken. He'd had sex. Sex wasn't meaningless, but it didn't mean everything either. And he listened when I talked about why I was obsessed with the specialness of sex and waiting for that one special person.

Me: I think I'm going to end up marrying my high school boyfriend.
Justin: Oh?
Me: Yeah, it's not really working right now. He's traveling the world and he's a born-again, fundamentalist Christian, but we were meant to be together. In twenty years I think we'll just find each other and realize it has to be and we'll get married.
Justin: Yeah, I know what you mean. I've felt that way.

203

He was understanding and not threatened by my discussion of Pat. He didn't seem uninterested in me even though I said that I would not have sex with him unless he married me, which was absurd to think about seeing that we had never actually met. He was romantic and sent me kisses over the phone. He was driven and obsessed with achieving big things in his future. He was passionate about liberal politics. He was sensible, and because his mother was a theology professor and biblical scholar, he had a healthy question-and-critique relationship with religion. I liked him a lot.

Justin wrote to me on Facebook one day:

I am ever so glad that you randomly Facebooked me…No really I am. Over the past few days our mutually liberal political banter and all the discussion we had have definitely been enjoyable. Good thing you are so random or I would never have gotten the chance to know this special stranger.

When we spoke on the phone that night, my roommate had returned and was in her bed reading a textbook as I lay in my bed with the phone, snuggled under blankets with a warm spring breeze blowing through the window. It was safely familiar.

Justin: I want to play you a song. It makes me think of you.
Me: Aw that's sweet. Ok, let's hear it.

He took a few moments to situate his phone next to his computer speakers. But within a moment an old guitar was strumming.

> *Well, she can dance a Cajun rhythm*
> *Jump like a Willys in four wheel drive.*
> *She's a summer love for spring, fall and winter.*
> *She can make happy any man alive.*

Me: Sugar Magnolia makes you think of me?
Justin: You're like my summer love, but it'll last so much longer.

Me: You like the Grateful Dead?
Justin: Of course!

Instead of pulling teeth trying to get Pat to appreciate the soul and rhythm and acoustic sounds of anti-establishment rock 'n' roll music, here was Justin not only dedicating this music to me, but introducing me to more I hadn't yet heard of yet, like OAR and Keller Williams. He played me music for quite awhile.

Justin: Hey Special
Me: Special?
Justin: Yeah...you're the special stranger. I'm going to start calling you that.
Me: I like it!
Justin: Well it fits you fine, because you really are a special person and I was thinking...we should meet.

I was so thrilled, but nervous. I was nervous about meeting a man from the internet. I was worried about falling in love and forgetting Pat. But I was excited and giddy, and I wanted to run to Justin and wrap my arms around him.

Me: Ok, let's plan this.
Justin: Yes, let's. Where will we meet?
Me: On a busy street. And you should bring some friends and I'll bring some friends. Just in case either of us is a serial killer.
Justin: Good plan. Will there be a...kiss hello?
Me: Um...I don't think so. There can be a hug hello though!
Justin: That's good, I like hugs.
Me: When you hug, do you put your head to the right side or left side?
Justin: I think the right.
Me: And with the right arm over their left shoulder?
Justin: Yeah I think.
Me: Ok, then I'll do the same. Because I think it's so awkward when you hug someone and you do that bob back and forth thing

because you're both trying to go to the same side. And I don't want our first encounter to be awkward.
My Roomate: Are you two choreographing your meeting?
Me and Justin: (laughing) Yes, I guess we are!

He didn't bring a friend. He claimed none were free. And at the end of the night, after our no-kiss agreement, as my friends George and Scarlet, who did accompany us on our first date turned their backs to head to the car, he cornered me.

"Can I have a kiss?"

"Uh…"

"I know we said we wouldn't, but we had a really great time, and don't you think we should end it on a good note?" he pleaded.

I was pretty uncomfortable. I didn't want to, but I liked him and didn't want to rock the boat. I gave him a quick tight-lipped peck on the mouth and ran after my friends. It left me with a momentary feeling of nervous puke butterflies, which in retrospect I realize I probably should have interpreted as red flags. But I ignored the feeling and saw him every night for the next several nights. It was the end of the year, and one night he drove up to East Stroudsburg University and helped me back up my dorm room to move back home. Another night we went to a movie. We went to an amusement ride park. We had known each other for two weeks and were now officially dating, even though we lived three hours apart. I didn't take it too seriously. I was crushing on Justin, but my heart was still all about Pat.

Then one night, he asked me casually over the phone, "What's one thing you have always wanted to do?"

I thought about it for a minute. I thought of all my grandiose plans. I wanted to own a business. I want to be a famous speaker, expert on sexuality, I wanted to travel the world with a "Female Orgasm" tour or have a little office hosting small discussion groups. I wanted to write books. I wanted to do a lot of things but for some reason, I chose a fairly ordinary thing. A thing that yes, on a backburner in my brain, I'd always wanted to do but it was never actually any kind of special goal. I said, "I'd like to go to California."

"Well then we should go," he responded.

"I'd love to, but don't be one of those people who says 'oh, let's do this,' but when push comes to shove you don't have money, you can't get off work, you're parents won't let you, blah blah blah. Whenever I talk about protesting, people get so excited and say 'Let me know the next time you go and I'll be there,' but when I say, 'We're getting up at four o'clock and driving to D.C. for a protest,' they have a million excuses. So... don't pretend to make these crazy plans just for the fun of talking about it. I'm not a talker; I'm a doer. You'll learn that about me."

Justin laughed. "Special, I'm not just talking. I think we could really do this. I'll wake up early and drive down to your house tomorrow. I'll be able to get there by noon. We'll plan it all out." I loved that he called me Special.

Sure enough, early the next afternoon he showed up at my house with a map.

"I have something better than just a visit to California. What if we drive, take a cross country road trip?" he offered with a smirk. "How amazing would that be?"

So, just like that, I packed up my tiny little Hyundai with three weeks' worth of clothes, nonperishable food, and a tent, hopped in the driver's side next to this man I'd met on the internet just a few weeks prior, and set out for California.

George: You are not serious.
Me: Oh, but I am.
George: I don't believe you.
Me: George, it's happening. I already have all the groceries bought. The car is packed. I'm going. Spending three weeks in a tiny car and a tiny tent with Justin. We're going to either come back ready to kill each other or completely in love.
George: You don't even know this person!
Me: Do you remember when I spent most of my teen years cooped up in my bedroom writing papers for nothing? No scholarship, no

help with college whatsoever? And me, you, and my dad had that talk in his Buick and he said I should be living life, "Visiting new places and going on adventures, and climbing mountains, and riding roller coasters, and swimming with dolphins?" Well, I'm doing that.

And I did. I climbed The Rockies in Colorado. I rode roller coasters in Virginia. I swam with dolphins in California. I crossed the Mississippi River. I drove through the Mohave Desert and couldn't get a single radio station as I drove farther and farther into the middle of nowhere. I travelled Route 66. I backtracked twenty-six miles out of my way just to get a picture of the "Welcome to Kansas" sign. I accidently drove away from a gas pump in Arkansas with the nozzle still in my car and ripped it out of the ground. I looked out from the top of the arch in St. Louis. I hiked the Grand Canyon in Arizona, got chased by bulls in Texas, swam with wild seals in San Diego, saw the Hollywood sign in L.A., almost drowned when I was thrown from my river raft in Phoenix, and touched Elvis' grave in Memphis, all with Justin by my side.

If you're wondering if we had sex, we didn't. Justin, a clit enthusiast, knew how to keep those nights in the tent good for both of us while keeping his "no sex until marriage" promise. When we returned from this epic journey, we were completely and insatiably in love.

Chapter 19

Me: Hello.
George: I'm surprised you answered your phone.
Me: Why's that?
George: Because apparently you're a celebrity now. Christ, you were on the evening news and the front page of the paper, and I got bombarded at work today with everyone saying, "Doesn't your best friend own that shop that's on the news? I can't believe that church is being so ridiculous to her."
Me: What has happened to my life?
George: Oh, you love it.
Me: You got me there!

George was right. I was incredibly flattered by all the verbal support and positive publicity. In fact, it completely counteracted how downtrodden and defeated I felt after reading terrible things about myself, like that I was responsible for social ills like child abuse and teen pregnancy. I knew it was absurd and that the opposite was true, but hearing it all did wear on me.

Everything was different now. Folks all across the country had heard about the crusade against sex in West Chester's council meeting and were vocally on my side, and all my negative feelings evaporated. I was so confident because of my parade of supporters,

I even found a way to respond to that email I had received that said "I can't believe you are determined to destroy the morals of our young people. Shame on you! This will only bring the downfall of family life and perversion for you and all concerned. May God help you see the light."

Before, negative energy had coursed through me. I didn't know what to do with it. I wanted to respond *somehow* and get the feeling out, but I knew that anything I said would either be dismissed or be turned against me. But with many of the people of West Chester and beyond behind me, I felt empowered to think of a perfect, clever, up-your-ass response. I decided to respond by having t-shirts printed up that read "Feminique Boutique: Destroying Morals 1 Vibrator at a Time." I turned the negative into a positive as dozens of people walked around in t-shirts mocking the erotophobic people who wanted to shut down my store while advertising it at the same time. It was a deliciously satisfying act of sticking it to The Man.

After I hung up the phone with George, a woman came in looking for a vibrator. I was thrilled! A sale of deliberate intention, not just a passerby who I convinced to buy a little $12 bottle of massage oil on a whim. Someone had actually driven to West Chester specifically to shop at my store!

"I've been needing to replace my old vibrator, which is older than old. It's like...older than you," she said as she approached my sale counter.

"Well sounds like you got your money's worth out of it," I responded with a smile. She laughed. I led her back to the Pleasure Room where the sex toys are housed and extended my hand, "I'm Jill, by the way."

She shook my hand enthusiastically and said, "Oh I know who you are, and that's why I'm here. I was needing to replace my old vibrator, and I was going to go down to that sex shop in Delaware, but then I read in the paper about the town and the church giving you a hard time. I thought 'how convenient, I work in the next town over, I'll just swing by Feminique Boutique.' Plus I wanted to support you. I never come into West Chester and never would have even heard about you if it wasn't for that church making a big stink." She placed her hand on my shoulder and chuckled before picking up the demonstration model of a vibrating tongue sex toy that looks and laps like a real tongue for simulated oral sex.

"Wow!" she exclaimed. "What will they think of next?"

"If you think that's nuts, check this one out. It plugs into your iPod and vibrates to the beat of the music!" I handed her a sleek high-end vibe.

"Oh my goodness. I am so glad I found you!"

Soon after, my first return customer came in. A few days before I had sold her Butterfly Wings, a little vibrator that flutters against the clitoris, has an extension for hitting the G-spot, and vibrates in a pattern so that when you orgasm, the vibration keeps the pelvic muscles contracting in rhythm, extending the length of the orgasm. It was a top seller at my Sex Toys 101 in-home party presentations, and it was doing well at Feminique too.

"Remember me?" she said with a friendly warm smile.

"Oh course I do!" I said.

"I just have to tell you," continued the woman, a suburban mom in her mid-thirties. "That vibrator changed my life! I've been married for twelve years, and we could never find my g-spot, and when we used that thing it was just the perfect angle."

"That's wonderful!" I was so happy for her. These were the moments that made sexology the world's most rewarding profession.

"I grew up in this town so I know how small it can be. My neighbor, this older gentleman, was trying to gossip to me about you. He said, 'Can you believe that awful adult store?' and I said, 'Hey! Don't say anything bad about that woman! She is smart and brave and principled, and I had the best sex of my life because of her!'"

"You did not say that!" I exclaimed, blushing.

"I sure did!"

"You told him about having good sex?" I was so flattered that this adorable young mom had stood outside her house and told

211

her neighbor about her sex life to defend my honor.

"Well, it's nothing to be ashamed of, right? Isn't that what you're all about?"

The next several days were similar, and I went through each with a smile on my face as blogs and emails and comments continued to buzz about my dilemma. The controversy over my store should have been old news at this point, and yet it continued building momentum, starting its own grassroots marketing phenomenon completely without my participation.

A blogger at exploringintimacy.com, based in the Washington, DC area, encouraged readers to put their sex-positive money where their mouth was and help me triumph over the crusade against sex by spending money at Feminique and insuring my survival, saying "If you find yourself in the area of Feminique Boutique, be sure to stop by and drop a few dollars, and tell her thanks from us for keeping things classy and pleasurable."

The comment section on a website that compiles interesting news stories from around the country reposted the NBC affiliate's news coverage, and the phenomenon emerged again.

"We supporters should start signing a 'Keep the Boutique in West Chester' petition and organize a fundraiser to raise funds for possible legal challenges by the church and other extremists," wrote one person thirty-something comments down.

"I'll be the first in line to sign my name!" responded another. Yet a third person typed, "Hey man, sign me up!!!!! If any local church holds a protest in front of this store I will organize a protest in front of that church! It's time someone lets the sheep know they are being brainwashed! Let's organize!! And also patronize her shop, on like a 'Panties Tuesday' and EVERY ONE of her supporters pledge to buy a pair of panties (or two) for themselves or significant others. We need to make sure she can not only beat the religious heat, but also have enough sales to stay in business. I don't know how she's doing so far (hopefully, quite well), but I'm sure selling a few hundred panties on a given day would help..."

I continued to be floored, sitting at my computer spending

hours and hours reading these posts and remarks after a long fourteen-hour day of self-employment. The feeling was euphoric. I had often felt like the lone soldier on the defense against the Crusade Against Sex. A multibillion-dollar, thousand-year-old institution and a powerful government with the ideology that sexuality should be repressed together against a twenty-two-year-old woman with a sexuality advocacy business opened on an $8,000-limit credit card and a dream. The Crusade could not have been more stacked against me. But while I still may have been the underdog, David against Goliath, I now had a fighting chance because the people were ready to revolt!

But then, of course, there was a new setback, a new hurdle, a new oppression; a new level in the Crusade Against Sex. I opened up Feminique one morning and saw a manila envelope had been slipped under the door. Inside was a formal letter from the Borough of West Chester, printed on the same high-quality crisp paper they had mailed my original permit denial. I immediately felt nervous, puke butterflies of panic fluttered in my stomach once again. What could it possibly be this time?

The letter stated that West Chester residents had filed a formal appeal of my business permit, and although it was already known to all that the thirty-day appeal window had passed, the letter from Anthony Ciccerone stated, "We will not be defending the building permit. You may want to seek legal counsel."

The envelope contained a photocopied paper printed on St. Mary's letterhead and signed by the Monsignor, two nuns, and a congregant. It was a letter addressed to Ciccerone stating that they found West Chester's issuance of my business permit illegal and against Chapter 112 Article II of the zoning code:

An establishment wherein live displays of the human body without a covering on the specified anatomical areas are conducted or…materials depicting or describing specified sexual activities or specified anatomical areas for observation by patrons therein.

Nervous puke butterflies are an understatement! That moment was paralyzing, probably the hardest of the whole debacle for me. I could not believe it. We had, with my attorney, already determined that Feminique Boutique did not fit that legal description. We had, in front of the news media and a room full of a hundred and fifty people, already determined that it was too late to appeal. If despite this West Chester was going to allow this legal maneuver to happen, telling me I'd have to hire a lawyer to defend their laws myself, allowing me to be steamrolled by the deep pockets of the Catholic Church, I had officially lost any faith in justice. This was just plain bullying and cronyism.

In the beginning, I had mocked Anthony Ciccerone's "letter of the law" persona. But now, the letter of the law was in my favor. The law of West Chester was that Feminique Boutique was allowed to exist. So how could they get away with this?

I figured the bureaucrats in charge of running West Chester wanted this whole church/sex shop mess to go away as fast as possible, and so they sided with the one they thought would make the biggest headache for them if they didn't get their way. I was out of money, and without being able to afford my attorney I was likely to go away quietly. St. Mary's, on the other hand, had deep pockets and could rile up their base of loyal lifelong members. St. Mary's, West Chester Borough likely assumed, could elicit a bigger uprising and cause them the bigger headache. They were wrong.

Instead of calling my attorney and fighting this matter in a court of law, I decided to call the press and let the case be fought in the court of public opinion.

Chapter 20

When Justin and I returned from our monumental three-week road trip across the country, there was no way life could return to normal. But summer was under way and again Pat and I were home together. We sat on his couch. He told me about all of his wonderful world travels, and I told him all about mine.

"I want to be honest with you Pat."

"Ok…"

"I'm dating someone, and I'm totally in love. And I'm so happy," I said.

"That's great, Jill. I'm happy for you. You know all I've ever wanted is for…"

"Me to be happy. I know. I'm just really excited because I thought I could never love someone to the full extent, with all the zeal that I had for you. But I do. I thoroughly, thoroughly love him," I replied with a smile.

"And what's this guy's name?"

"Justin."

"Well," Pat offered, "I'm incredibly happy for you and Justin. But remember, I'm always here for you. If he ever hurts you I will be there, and no matter what, I'll always want you in my life. You're still one of the most important people to me, Jill."

An avalanche of bricks had been lifted. I had wings, and I was ready to keep breaking the chains that had held me oppressed for so long. School, work, boys – anything and everything. Never again would I martyr myself. Never again would I sacrifice my happiness by pouring endless time and effort into something that was not worth the time. I decided that if I didn't like a job, I'd quit. If I didn't like a class, I'd drop it. If I didn't like a boy, I'd dump him.

After spending every single moment together on the trip, being three hours apart back home was something Justin and I hated. We decided to move in together in his off-campus apartment.

He had three other roommates but they were all home for the summer, giving us free reign of the house. I felt so grown-up. We went grocery shopping together, cooked together, curled up watching TV together, and every night snuggled together in our own bed, in our own apartment. We had a huge loft bed right next to a bright sunny window, and I loved waking up late nose to nose with Justin, having hours of playful pillow talk and light smooches before we finally got out of bed around noon.

"I love you so much, Special," Justin said. "You're too perfect. You eclipse perfection."

One day a few weeks into our cohabitation, after a round of reciprocal oral sex, we settled in with a movie. We propped up pillows in our bed and turned all the lights out, with only the glow of the small old-fashioned TV to illuminate the space. I was so satisfied and comfortable, physically and in my heart.

"Hey Special, do you want some popcorn?" Justin asked.

"Sounds great," I said, and I kissed him.

"I'll be right back. Extra melted butter on that, right?" He knew what I liked and tried so hard to please me with the little things in life. I felt that warmth, that glow.

"No, that's ok. I know you don't like it with that much."

"You're the special one, Special, and you should have it the way you like it. So lots of extra melted butter it is."

He scooted down the ladder of our loft bed and a few

minutes later came back with a bowl of deliciously aromatic steaming hot popcorn. He handed the bowl to me, then climbed back up the ladder to bed.

"Oh, I forgot to ask you to bring back a glass of water," I said.

"I'll go get it," Justin offered cheerily.

"No, that's okay."

"Special, I'll do it. You're comfy, and besides, I'm closest to the ladder anyway," and he climbed down the ladder again.

"You are the sweetest boyfriend ever!" I shouted after him as he made his way to the kitchen. When he returned we lay in bed and chatted for awhile, and he playfully flirted with me by throwing kernels of popcorn at me. I tossed some back, and we continued trying to land a piece of popcorn in each other's mouths. One time it missed and got stuck in his hair. I giggled as he patted his head to get it down and kept missing it.

"It's still there!" I laughed.

"I love this," he said, finally picking the kernel out. "We were watching a good movie, and I don't even want to finish it because I am just having so much fun talking to you, looking at your beautiful face." I smiled. "And…throwing popcorn at your beautiful face," and he threw more at me, this time a small handful.

Looking back now, the moment reminds me of the night of the carnival, when Pat and I started our playful romance by throwing the powdered sugar from a funnel cake on each other. I must have a thing for food and flirting. But I did not see the comparison at the time. I absolutely was not thinking of Pat at that moment. I was all about Justin. Besides, Pat would *never* do what Justin did next.

I got him back by dipping my finger tips in the glass of water and flicking some droplets at him. I laughed. I thought he was laughing too, when he retaliated with more popcorn, this time a fistful. I picked up the glass and said with a flirtatious smile, "How would you like it if I dumped this on you?"

"You better not," he said, playfully trying to wrestle the glass out of my hand. I didn't want the whole glass to spill, which was likely with all the horsing around, so instead I dipped my wrist to let a shot glass amount spill on him and then put the glass down. My laughter was suddenly alone and echoing on the low ceiling as we sat high in the loft bed.

"What the FUCK is wrong with you, Jill?" he said in a slow, drawn out and deliberate tone designed to be disdainful and belittling. I couldn't determine what made me feel sick the most. That he cursed at me, that he called me Jill instead of Special, or that tone. "What. The FUCK. Is wrong. With you. Jill?" Yes. It was definitely the tone and not the words that made me feel the sickest.

"I'm sorry," I said. "I didn't think I dumped that much. I was just playing. It's just water. It will dry. I didn't..." I kept rambling as he stared at me with a hate-filled glare. It was menacing, and it shook me.

"Good one, Jill. Fucking BRILLIANT! We don't have any clean sheets so I guess we're either going to sleep on wet sheets or a bare mattress!"

He didn't yell. He didn't have to. The growl of hatred was worse than yelling. Then he started tearing the fitted sheet off the corners of the mattress, which he couldn't do with me still sitting on them.

"Get up."

"Excuse me?" I said, now pissed off.

"GET. UP. And look what you did!" he added as he peeled the sheet back and saw that the mattress was also damp. "The mattress is probably going to have to be thrown away now. It's going to grow mold and bacteria, and I'm going to have to buy a new mattress. But don't worry about it, Jill. I'll buy it. I know you probably don't have the money."

My muscles felt tingly and hot. I didn't like being cursed at. I didn't like being demeaned. I wasn't having any of it.

"I'm out," I said coolly, avoiding looking him in the eye. I jumped off the bed, not even using the ladder, and started speedily throwing my clothes in a bag, clean folded clothes mixed with dirty rumpled clothes. I grabbed whatever was mine from the closet and bedroom floor and threw it in the bag. At first he did nothing. He said nothing. Then it must have struck him that I was really leaving because he too jumped down.

"Special, I'm sorry," he said with a pathetic look on his face.

"I don't want to hear it. I'm leaving" I retorted.

"Just to cool down, right? You're not leaving forever, are you?"

"Yes," I said with a blank, emotionless glare. "Forever."

He erupted into tears. I rolled my eyes. This was textbook abuse; manipulation, random explosions, followed by sweet talk and an attempt to gain sympathy.

"Please don't go! It was one mistake, and I was so wrong and I am so sorry. I can be better for you, and you know I can. You know I can be perfect for you, Special. Please, I'm begging you; please don't throw away what we have. We have something really beautiful. Our road trip, remember, Special? Remember how magical it was. Please don't throw that away." Tears welled in his eyes and flooded his thick, long lashes. It was so hard to say no.

"Listen, it was magical. But it's not magical right now. I'm not going to stay just so you can fly off the handle some other time in the future."

He shook his head back and forth as I spoke.

"No. It will never happen again, Special. Never."

"Well how do I know that? These things always happen again." I turned away and continued packing. As I did he fell to his knees in front of me.

"I'll never do it again."

I looked down at him on his knees on the ground, his big pleading eyes looking up at me.

"And what if you do?"

"But I won't."

"But what if you do?"

"But I won't."

"Yes, but let's say, you do. What should I do then?" I demanded. "Then I would have wasted however much more time

219

of my life between now and then."

"If it happens again, even though it won't, but if it does," Justin stated, still on his knees in front of me, "I'll understand if you leave. No questions asked."

"No begging and crying?" I questioned.

"No, but it won't happen."

I acquiesced. I didn't really want to leave. I could feel the heartbreak coming on every time I tossed another article into my bag, and I wasn't ready for another round when I had just finally healed from Pat.

The rest of the summer went swimmingly and without further incident. He returned to his sweet, romantic, great conversationalist self, and I chalked the outburst up to a bad day.

That fall I packed up all of my worldly possessions and put them in the back of my car and prepared to move to Canada for two years to get a bachelor's degree in sexuality. At the border I showed them my acceptance letter to St. Jerome's of the University of Waterloo and received a student visa. I continued driving several more hours and arrived on campus. I parked my car in the lot behind my dorm room, opened my car door, and looked around. I was alone. In a foreign country. Not knowing a single human being. To study sex. Who does this? I chuckled aloud.

Despite my still annoyingly perfect college grades and the extracurricular activities I had on campus during my two years at East Stroudsburg University such as writing the sex column and my political involvement, I was still not offered a dime of scholarship or grant money to finance my education. Worse yet, because I was studying abroad, I couldn't even take out a low interest federal school loan. To become a sexologist, I had to take out a $52,000 personal bank loan, insuring that in two years I'd have two things: a degree in sex and a mortgage payment. This is the cost of following your dreams.

The first weekend in Canada was boring. I decorated my dorm and unpacked my things. I wasn't making many friends, and I was lonely. I was beyond excited when class started because the courses were nothing but sex. My sex program was housed in the small Roman Catholic section of the college. St. Jerome's was tiny and had only small classrooms, so the most popular, high enrollment classes were held in the only room that could fit over two hundred people, the chapel.

On Sunday mornings, Catholic students and area families attended Mass there. On Tuesday and Thursday mornings it transformed into a lecture hall where I learned about the history of the vibrator, the pulpit became my professor's lectern. In Christian Sexual Ethics we saw a slide show of Renaissance art pieces depicting Jesus with an erection to show his humanity. In Sexual Anthropology I learned about the Sambia tribe in Papua New Guinea, which initiates boys into adulthood by having them ingest the semen of older men. In The Dark Side of Sexuality, a course on AIDs, rape, incest, sexual sadism, prostitution, and pornography, there was a final exam question about "the money shot," the occurrence in porn films of men ejaculating on the face and mouth of a woman.

It fascinated me that these scholarly debates and critical thinking investigations into subjects too shocking and controversial for most were occurring at a Catholic school, and in a chapel no less!

I loved my classes and the academic freedom I had, but I was very lonely. I had transferred during year three when everyone had already made their friends, plus, I was the foreigner. I felt so alone. Justin and I talked so much we racked up a $3,000 phone bill the first month apart, so we switched to love letters. This kept me yearning to be with him, and our love grew stronger.

Dearest Special,

With every passing day I love you more than the day before. It is really not fair because I also miss you more too, but all the same my love for you grows continuously. What I have been noticing more and more lately is that not only are you an amazing person, not only are you wondrously beautiful, but also that you really know how to love perfectly. All those little things you do and say, how talented you are at expressing emotion and the genuine kindness and passion that radiates from your heart all make me think and say not only do I love you, but I love the way you love me. Thank you so much, Special, for being you...

"When I go home for break, I think I'm going to have sex," I said to my roommate, who, like many people, was a bit perplexed about my chosen career path, the fact that there was an air of sexuality in my dress and body language and yet I was a "virgin." But she also understood that clitorises are awesome and that there was a perfectly robust sexual repertoire in lieu of vaginal sex.

"I thought you were waiting until marriage?"

"I was, but it just seems so arbitrary anymore. I do everything else. I'm the 'everything but' girl. And I love him and I'm ready and you know what, I don't think this will take away from it because I'm not married. The whole point of waiting was for it to be special and to be with only one special person and this will be. Everything is lined up perfectly, so to not do it would be unnatural."

I told Justin about my idea. Every time he called I brought it up. One day I'd say, "I'm totally horny. I totally love you. This is totally right and good and normal, we have to do this." The next day I was freaking out because the more I built it up in my head the more nervous I was. It was like the nervousness of my first kiss when I wondered if I should turn my head to the right or left. What if we went the same direction and bumped noses? I didn't want my first vaginal sex experience to be similarly awkward. Finally the day before I was set to visit him during a school break, I called Justin.

"So I'm thinking sex will *not* be happening tomorrow," I started. "It's too built up now, and I feel like if I just take the pressure off myself and say 'it's not happening,' then I can just relax and let it happen naturally, if at all. So, no sex."

"Whatever you want, Special," he said with a chuckle at my neurosis, and when I made the eight-hour drive home to our apartment, the sex thing had completely left my mind. I was so focused on seeing him and hugging him because it had been over a month since we'd seen each other.

When I pulled up to the apartment late at night, he was waiting for me on the porch with flowers. I had a mild case of nervous puke butterflies because I'd realized when I saw him standing there that it had been so long I had nearly forgotten what he looked like. Of course I had an image of him in my head, but in person I almost didn't recognize him.

Once inside, we stared at each other and cuddled for awhile, and then we were kissing and full body gyrating and had an intensely passionate session of clitoral rubbing. I fell asleep utterly satisfied with my decision for no sex. This was definitely good enough.

When I awoke the next morning, in the big comfortable bed high in our own loft oasis, with the early morning sun brightening the room with a warm glow, it happened. I was no longer a virgin. It wasn't a big production. It wasn't scandalous or dramatic, or particularly noteworthy. In fact, there's nothing much to write about it other than it was…nice. In hearing high school friends and college friends talk about their first experience with intercourse, it was awful, awkward, painful, forced, or the result of unrelenting hormonal passion and fervor. For me, it was none of these things. Simply the right person, the right time, just…nice. I wish everyone's first time could be like that.

George: Hey, what are you up to?
Me: I'm driving back to Canada.
George: How was your long weekend home?
Me: Well…I had sex with Justin!
George: Really?!
Me: I know, surprising.
George: Well how was it?
Me: It was good, but I gotta tell you…it unleashed a beast.
George: Oh I gotta hear this.
Me: George, I learned that while clitoral stimulation is still the best thing ever, vaginal stimulation is a very, VERY close second.

We had sex nineteen times this weekend.
George: Holy shit. Must have been good Filet Mignon sex?

George and I had a whole rating system for sexual encounters based on cuts of meat. Filet Mignon was the top.

Me: And then guess what happened?
George: I'm afraid to wager a guess…
Me: This morning he walked me to my car and before I drove away I rolled the window down to give him one last kiss goodbye and he said to me, "I know how much you cherished the idea of sex being with one special person, and I just wanted to let you know that I get it, and I value it and what we have." So just in case there was any doubt in my mind that I did the right thing, which there wasn't, he confirmed that he understood the weight I placed on it and didn't take the whole thing lightly either.

Justin and I continued on with the rest of our third year of college completely starry-eyed and completely hypersexed. I could write the book on international phone sex.

Chapter 21

The legal troubles brewing with my local Catholic Church were ones I could not afford, so I decided to use creative, grassroots, and, most importantly, free ways to rally my supporters and give St. Mary's the battle they were looking for.

First, I created a petition to keep Feminique open and free from attempts to close it down; both online via a free website and a paper version that was available in the shop, both free to me. Second, I wrote on my whiteboard sidewalk sign something to the effect of "Church wants to bring me to court and close me down. Come sign my petition!" Also free to me! Last, I called up the reporters who covered the initial story to tell them the latest twist and about my petition. All three covered the story: the news station with a thirty-second news story, *The Daily Local* with another front page, top of the fold write-up, and *The Philadelphia Inquirer* with a full page article and two color photos in the Sunday paper. All FREE to me. If I had had to pay for this type of advertising, if I had had to produce and run a thirty-second local commercial, a front page ad in the local paper, and a full page color ad in the Sunday Inquirer, it would have cost me $34,000. But since "Catholic church sues young blonde sex shop owner" makes a great headline, it was all free.

The Philadelphia Inquirer broke the story first on June 1, 2008. A reporter and photographer came to Feminique to interview me, clients, and shoppers, and take photos for the Sunday paper. I particularly loved the story because the reporter interviewed the local priest who signed the appeal, as well as Ashley O'Malley, the politician running for state legislature, and Anthony Ciccerone. The article started like this:

The prom-dress-pink store, with strips of ribbon dangling in the windows and a breast-cancer-awareness sign out front, looks like any girly gift shop in West Chester's bustling business district.

But the Feminique Boutique, a new adult novelty store, has triggered a tempest, with a local pastor and a candidate for state representative saying the shop does not belong in the heart of downtown and, more important, one block from a Catholic school.

"It's corrupting the morals of children," said Msgr. _____ of St. Mary's Church, who alerted his parishioners at Sunday Mass.

His curiosity had been piqued by the name and the bright pink facade. And while he did not take a peek inside, "I knew what was going on," he said. "It was an adult something-or-other. And it's cheapening human sexuality."

Once again, I needed to say nothing and instead let supporters of sexual freedom say it for me. People standing in line at Feminique to sign my petition were more than happy to speak up to the reporter from *The Inquirer*:

Customer Sam Dickerson 54, a truck driver for West Chester University, said: "We put sex in the wrong box. Sex keeps you healthy. We need all this stuff, especially when you get older and things are slowing down."

Strangers stop by to offer a kind word.

"I'm worried about her. All this is ridiculous," said Charlie Silvestri, who works down the street.

226

The Daily Local also interviewed the Monsignor about his appeal, quoting him as saying, "There is no place for such a boutique in this town that cheapens human sexuality," and like *The Inquirer*, the local paper also couldn't help but report on the growing number of community members standing in line at Feminique to sign the petition.

The day was long and busy managing the hundreds of people who suddenly had taken an interest in Feminique Boutique, but whenever I had a second to stop and reflect on it, I just couldn't believe it. A few days before I had been a brand new business struggling to get my name out there, advertise, and get people to walk in the door. Now I had a line like Toys R Us two days before Christmas.

Since (the Catholic parish) has come out against the store, the shop has been the focus of a steady stream of curiosity seekers wondering what McDevitt was selling and whether it really is offensive.

By midday Wednesday, more than 170 people had signed a petition to "Keep Feminique Boutique Open."

John Erdek, an attorney in the borough, dropped into the shop Wednesday to give support to McDevitt.

"Any Victoria's Secret catalogue is more offensive than this," said Erdek, looking around the shop at sexy lingerie on one wall and a display of body oils on the other. "The idea that Catholic school kids are coming in here and being corrupted is ridiculous."

By the end of the day, the news reporters from both papers had long since departed when a woman standing in line to sign the petition said angrily, "I'd like to sign your petition. This is such bullshit, it makes me angry. Those pervert hypocrites picking on you, a young lady just trying to run her own business. This is a free country! They should be ashamed of themselves!"

She became more and more flustered as she spoke, and

after signing she abruptly fumbled through her purse, pulled out a $20 bill, and handed it to me. "Take this. Put it toward your legal defense," then she gave me a hug and walked out the front door of Feminique. I was touched. Most of my entire sexology career I had been met with illogical opposition. Finally, and in large quantity, sensible people gathered in one spot and spoke the truth. It restored my belief in the power of rational people and rational thought. After receiving other requests, I opened a "Feminique Boutique Legal Defense Fund" bank account, and people mailed checks to the hosting bank.

The free grassroots battle snowballed online. Comments on each of these three news pieces were in the hundreds, which caught the attention of yet more bloggers. The more that was written, the more attention it attracted, and the more attention it attracted, the more that was written. Liberal feminist bloggers and conservative pro-small business bloggers, two groups of folks who might otherwise have nothing in common, suddenly did; they both were vocally wishing me victory against the Crusade Against Sex. And there were more; atheist bloggers, American civil liberties advocate bloggers, sex education bloggers, small-time personal journal bloggers. There was even a blog that other than the words "West Chester, Pennsylvania," "Feminique Boutique", and "Jill McDevitt," was written entirely in French. I also received an email of support from someone claiming to live in China. Did that mean this small town scandal had actually become an *international* news story? I was humbled, but still ready to let the battle wage on.

"A skirmish in the culture war between those who believe in sexual empowerment and personal freedom versus the local West Chester, PA religious establishment, escalated into a full scale legal battle," wrote a blogger at lazygeisha.com, based in California.

The next battle zone was the letters to the editor where supporters and naysayers hurled insults at one another about their respective opinions about my store and larger sexuality issues. One freelance writer for the Daily Local newspaper, named Gene Sellers, wrote a satire op-ed piece called "Where is That Sleazy

Sex Shop?" in which he mockingly wrote about coming in Femique Boutique to investigate the "sleaze" that everyone was so upset about.

Knowing that my duty to you, my devoted readers, absolutely required me to march through that doorway – regardless of what hellish sights I might see in there – I took a deep breath and pushed my way through the unlocked portal to confront the pornographers who were threatening to corrupt our children's morals.

Surprisingly, there was only one pornographer on duty when I walked in, and he was a she.

And I'll admit that for a sleazy purveyor of filth, she was actually surprisingly low-key.

But let's look at the positive side of this thing: After so many years of horrible publicity, it's great to see the Catholic Church finally making the front pages with stories about sex that don't involve child-molesting priests or church officials who transferred them to other parishes.

Another person wrote a response letter to the editor titled "Sex Shop Must Be Taken Seriously," and hurled personal insults at Gene saying, "*His credibility just fizzled out, in my opinion, with his investigative reporting of West Chester's newest and controversial store on North Church Street, Feminique Boutique...He negates the impact and importance that high standards and morals have in our families and this community, and makes light of the new store as though it is not such a bad place, and even compliments the owner about how clever she was in displaying (or hiding) things. He also jokingly writes insulting comments about how women should be comfortable with their sexuality.*"

My first response was wow, how very sad that this person finds it insulting for someone to advocate that women should be comfortable with their sexuality. My second thought was that I felt badly for Gene, because even though the editor of the paper was supportive of Feminique, writing in his column "Controversial store follows rules, has right to exist," the fact that Gene had mentioned the rape of children by priests caused controversy on top of controversy. Gene was forced to publically apologize, saying "I now feel that the reference to the priest sex-abuse scandal may have been inappropriate in this particular column. I thus wish to sincerely apologize to anyone who was offended by this reference, including my good friends at St. Mary's."

Despite the apology, rumor has it he was no longer used as a freelancer by the paper.

I was pretty incensed about the response, Gene's loss of work, and the apology to anyone "offended by this reference" to the scandal in the Catholic Church. Do you know what I find offensive? That some priests rape children and then get shuffled around parishes to protest them from prosecution. It's more than wrong, and yet apparently, dissent can be career ruining. The incident reinforced that I was right when I decided not to publicly make that point myself because it would just get turned against me, and ruin my career. *They* were condoning the rape of children. *They* were attacking my sex shop and education center where I was working to create a view of sexuality that made it valued, pleasurable, and less conducive to sexual violence. And yet, this man lost his freelance gig and was forced to apologize for offending *them*.

The peace-loving hippie in me knows the ineffectiveness of the "us versus them" mentality, but boy, was it difficult to remember at that moment that many religious people are loving and compassionate. It was more than anger-provoking; it was downright frightening to see the power that religion has. I'll never get over having to read someone's apology for pointing out that raping children and covering it up is wrong.

After the Letters to the Editor section of the paper, the next battleground was St. Mary's Monsignor and Ashley O'Malley personally.

I started receiving emails from people that said things to the effect of, "I just wanted you to see the letter I sent to St. Mary's," with an attached strongly worded document addressed to the Monsignor. Others sent me copies of the letters they'd sent to Ashley O'Malley, many of them inflammatory and stirring up decades-old political scandals involving him. In addition to a letter to O'Malley, one gentleman brought me a piece of paper he had handwritten notes on. Like everyone who'd taken up my cause, I'd never met this man before.

"I've been working at the public library all day," he said, showing me his list. "I've been researching how you can handle this. Here's some information about laws that pertain to your struggle, precedent court cases, and the contact information for the ACLU."

"That's...unbelievable," I stammered back. "Thank you so much for taking the time to do that for me."

"I'm not just doing it for you, I'm doing it for all of us," he said.

This all took place in a forty-eight-hour period, and at the end of the two days, I had over four hundred and fifty signatures on the petition.

Chapter 22

After my third year of college in Canada, I moved home for the summer. And by "home," I mean back into Justin's off-campus apartment. Again we joyfully played house, pretending the large four-bedroom home was ours alone while his roommates were gone for the summer. Again it started out blissfully. And again it turned ugly. But it wasn't just the cursing, and the belittling, and the hot tempered tongue-lashing that would randomly rain molten lava and hate filled insults upon me; it was his absence.

"I was thinking of cooking dinner. When are you coming home?" I asked Justin. I worked a part-time job at the local mall as well as a part-time gymnastics coaching job and still had plenty of time for summer fun – the beach, the pool, the amusement parks – as well as time to attempt to learn to cook.

"I should be home around 5:30," he responded. Justin was a marketing major in college and was pretty business savvy. His part-time job was running an office as a salesman. He found and rented an office and hired and trained a staff. He was so proud of his successes. On the nights I tried my hand at cooking real food, as opposed to microwaving mac and cheese, we sat together at the kitchen table while eating, and he would talk the entire meal about his business sense and sharp sales skills and slick management style. Sometimes I couldn't get a single word in during the whole meal.

I began to notice his love of work becoming more and more obsessive. He was obsessed with talking about it and obsessed with doing it. That summer, it was not uncommon for dinner to be ready at 5:30 p.m., cold at 6:30 p.m., and thrown in the garbage at 9:30 p.m. when he still wasn't home.

"If you're not going to be home for dinner, fine, but could you at least be honest about it? Don't tell me you're going to be home for dinner and have me sit around for hours doing nothing. My time is valuable, and I have better things to do."

But he never listened. He missed my birthday that summer because he was so many hours late to the party it was over by the time he showed up.

I tried to pass the time with Scarlet and my sister, but Justin worked to convince me that they were trying to sabotage our relationship. Every time one of them called he rolled his eyes and started rambling about how they were no good for me, of course in a voice loud enough that they could hear. After listening to his rants about them so often I kind of lost contact with them. He didn't have a problem with George though, so every day for hours at a time I talked to George on the phone. We became very close during this time.

In retrospect, I see that it was classic emotional abuse. He was mean and insensitive, tried to isolate me from my friends and family so that I'd be emotionally dependent, and then left me alone for extended periods of time so that I would grow lonely and need his company more. I didn't notice the abuse at the time, I just thought he was a dick, so we'd get into a fight and I'd pack up my shit and head toward the door to leave, but he'd stand in front of the door to block me and beg and sob and fall to his knees and cry until I felt sorry for him and stayed.

Meanwhile, I was already applying for real-world jobs, preparing for graduation from college with a bachelor's degree in Sexuality, Marriage, and Family. Part of me thought we would be married just because we had been dating for over two years. But part of me also sat at my school desk applying to jobs in New York City, Michigan, and California, knowing he wasn't graduating yet and wouldn't be able to come. I didn't lose an ounce of sleep over this.

I also worked more ardently on my business plan. I designed a workshop on how parents can talk to their children about sexuality, and I had a chance to practice it on a group of moms during my senior year internship. They loved it, and, like the feeling I had in high school when I helped my classmates or had great response to my sex column, the best way I can describe my feelings after giving that presentation is as a high. I was euphoric because I'd given an empowering message and my audience understood it. I broke taboos by suggesting parents accept their young children as sexual creatures and not punish or dissuade them from sticking their hands down their diapers. I was so ready to start my career!

Justin saw things differently.

"You can't just start a business right away. You just can't do that. You're going to have to work in the field for ten or fifteen years first, make a name for yourself before you can start expecting people to want to bring you in as a speaker or trainer," Justin insisted.

I tried to ignore him and plan my dream. I liked figuring out the little details. The pink and brown business color scheme and the business name. I hadn't decided if it would be best to have a venue where I would hold seminars, in which case I had already devised a calendar and workshop schedule, or just a home office and book traveling gigs. In this case I had already researched the contact information for college organizations, women's groups, and entertainment venues that might be interested in booking me. I had a list of retirement communities for my sexuality and aging workshop, I had the addresses for a host of different hospitals for a training for medical professionals about sexuality. I was rip-roaring ready.

I was not having much luck with the resumes, and when I graduated and moved back to Justin's apartment in Pennsylvania, I barely took a day to unpack and relish in my amazing achievement of earning my bachelor's degree. I went right to work with building the business, but I kept hearing about it from Justin.

"Trust me, I know marketing. I'm an independent contractor, which is like having your own business, plus I've gone to school for this. You've never even taken a single business class in your life. Did you know that fifty percent of businesses fail within the first three years? Did you know that, Jill?"

I was so confused. That meant that fifty percent of businesses were successful after three years. Why was he trying to bring me down?

As usual, I called someone I knew would support my wild and crazy ideas.

Dad: Hello, First Born.
Me: Hey.
Dad: You excited about your upcoming graduation party?
Me: I am. What's my budget? Because I was thinking of going really crazy with this one. Because of my degree, I want to have a sex themed graduation party. A penis cake and vagina cake. And I came up with a sex trivia game. We'll divide everyone up into teams to play, and I'll buy prizes for the winners; a Playboy, lube, a vibrator, a sex book, etc. And I want to buy a ton of condoms and use the packets to make streamers and blow some of them up for balloons.
Dad: Just buy what you need and send me the bill.
Me: You're awesome, Dad!
Dad: Yeah, yeah…
Me: But, this is what I'm thinking. I've had it in my head and I can't get it out. I'm thinking of starting my business now. I know I don't really know what I'm doing, but it's all in my head. I'm thinking…
Dad: Do it.
Me: But I don't really have money and…
Dad: This is why God invented business loans. Or maybe find some investors. And…I still haven't determined what I wanted to

give you as a graduation gift so maybe I could help out. But it could be great! You could do your workshops and train a team of minions and get a cut of everything they do. The possibilities are endless, and with someone like you, with your drive and ambition, the sky's the limit.

Part of me really wanted to do it; I fantasized about it when I was driving, in the shower, lying in bed before falling asleep. If I was alone and able to play in my own head, I was on stage entertaining, educating, and empowering a group of women about their sexuality. But part of me was somewhat realistic. I tried to find work, and thanks in large part to Justin's discouragement, I put the sex business on the back burner, as part of the "ten-year career plan." I sent out hundreds of resumes and went on my first interview, that disastrous interview where the woman picked her dirty fingernails as I spoke.

I kept playing with the business idea as the lack of options in the workforce made me feel increasingly panicked that despite Justin's two cents on the matter, this business might be my only option, not ten years from now, but now. After I was passed over for the job handing out clean needles to IV drug users in North Philadelphia because I didn't at the time have a master's degree or speak Spanish, I was frustrated, and fantasies of sexology entrepreneurialism bubbled in me again. Justin tried one more time to break my spirit.

"Jill, I'm telling you it won't work. You're twenty-one years old. You have no real work experience. You have no start-up capital. You have nothing but a crazy pipe dream," he reminded me.

And that was it. No longer was I going to let this loser hold back my reigns. I dumped him, dumped the job search, moved back home with my dad, and started a company.

Chapter 23

Within a three-week period I had opened a groundbreaking feminist sex-positive, shame-free sex shop after surmounting countless setbacks, slowly fighting a Crusade Against Sex. I was verbally assaulted and strung up, followed by being stampeded with a legal offensive by a Catholic parish. I was putting myself through graduate school to study Human Sexuality Education. My name and struggles were fodder for bloggers and pundits and West Chester residents I could overhear as they walked by the shop front. I was also the fodder for the morning commute on my beloved classic rock radio station.

The DJ remarked, "Babies in black, stockings, and heels, if you're in West Chester this morning I don't know how much longer you'll be able to go. I can *not* believe that story. There's this little shop in West Chester called what? Feminique Boutique. It's owned by this twenty-two-year-old woman. I saw her on TV; she seems like a very intelligent woman…"

His sidekick chimed in, "She's a certified sexologist, she's going for her master's…."

And he continued, "And it has a little sign hanging that says 'Feminique Boutique' that's it. And in the front is some lingerie, and in the back room there are…"

A third sidekick helped out, "Novelty items."

"Adult sex toys. And the church is in an uproar about this, 'oh there's a school three blocks away', and I'm like 'don't these people have a calendar? It's 2008! Why are you getting upset about this in this day and age?"

"And there's no display in the window, just a little sign that says 'Feminique Boutique,' the co-host added.

I had listened to this man on the radio tens of thousands of times, and I couldn't believe my ears as I heard him talking about me. Everyone was talking about me. I was even invited into the studio for a live interview with Michael Smerconish, a conservative political pundit with a nationally syndicated show. Conservative, and still a supporter against the Crusade.

Sensing the building support and intrigue in both the controversy and in me as a young recent college graduate with a degree in sex and a love of pushing the envelope, the papers took to writing articles that were not just about the latest number of signatures on my petition, but about me.

The Philadelphia Inquirer interviewed my family.

Her grandmother, in whom she first confided her ambitions, encouraged her.

"I said, 'You go girl,' "said Joyce McDevitt of Clifton Heights, who works in a day-care center. "I also said, 'Be prepared, because you're probably going to get trouble.'"

If the complainers went into the store, they might not object to what they saw, said McDevitt's mother, Sarah McNelly, a nurse from Cinnaminson.

"They're picturing some of those sex stores in Philly," she said. "It's not like that."

Other news outlets reported on my high school and college years and the story of how my business developed.

After the parish filed the legal complaint stating that West Chester had illegally issued my business permit, I mentioned two things off the cuff to the press that ended up being additional bombshells. First, when a reporter asked about my college education, I mentioned I graduated from St. Jerome's University. Again, I didn't have to talk negatively about my opponents. Readers could see for themselves the foot-in-mouth revelation that I had spent four years and $70,000 to learn a career from one Catholic institution only to have another Catholic institution attempt to destroy that career.

The second bombshell was that all the press and viral online support had made sales double. This little fact, this little twist of irony, of stick-it-to-The-Man, of a victorious bullied underdog, was eaten up by the masses. The publicity had helped sales, and this fact became further publicity and fodder for the bloggers.

One headline from About.com said, "Oops! Catholic Church Helps Adult Store's Business." It read in part,

These good Catholics decided that an adult boutique should not be allowed to exist in West Chester. Granted, other adults might want to buy things there, but that just goes to show how depraved they are and thus that their judgment can't be trusted.

What the St. Mary's Church Catholics didn't expect, though, was that their efforts to shut down a store they didn't like would actually lead to increased business for that store. According to McDevitt, her business doubled after the church started publicizing their opposition to the existence of store.

Some people were probably alerted to the presence of a new store they were unaware of (free advertising!) while others may have simply gone to the store as a form of counter-protest.

Tyler, whose new three-week relationship with me had entirely consisted of this chaos, also offered a nose rubbing laugh at the fact that the fabricated controversy was helping me and was in fact the miracle I needed to kick-start my sex-positive revolution.

I don't know if it was the knowledge that I was capable of

bringing out the public to support me, my doubled business sales, the angry letters St. Mary's had received, or the nonstop chatter throughout the community, but only two days after they filed the appeal, Anthony Ciccerone pulled up behind me one morning in a white West Chester borough SUV as I walked up North Church Street to open Feminique Boutique.

"Jill," he called out. "I have something for you. St. Mary's has dropped their appeal." He handed me a manila envelope from the car window and drove off.

I was overjoyed! I had won. Maybe not the Crusade Against Sex, but I had won this battle. I could carry on with my dreams, free to deliver my message of sexual liberation. But then I stepped back for a second. Had Anthony Ciccerone smiled? Was he actually…happy for me?

Excitedly, I tore open the envelope and read the photocopied letter from the Monsignor redacting his appeal. It was all over. But one paragraph gave me pause.

"While we continue to believe that there are legal issues regarding the issuance of, and compliance with, the referenced permit, we also believe that our energies, resources and efforts at this point are better utilized in continuing our dialogue with the borough on amendment of the ordinance…"

I was following and complying with all the ordinances. For crying out loud, I'd had to give away that beautiful piece of art with the "glutteal cleft." I hoped this line wasn't another attempt to shut me out, and just in case decided to keep the petition available for further signing.

A blogger at classicalvalues.com, quoting *The Philly Inquirer*, captured perfectly the satisfying way in which the Monsignor and Ashley O'Malley, the state legislative candidate, gave up, scampering away with their tails between their legs.

When a struggling adult boutique found itself under attack by a local church, the opposition created a backlash of sympathy that was like manna from heaven:

A week after opposing the permit for a downtown West Chester adult boutique, a nearby Catholic church has withdrawn its appeal and the store owner has learned that while sex sells, opposition makes it sell even better.

Jill McDevitt, 22, owner of Feminique Boutique, said business had doubled since St. Mary's Church filed an appeal on May 29 to revoke her permit, issued March 31.

Even a politician who had campaigned against the store was forced to utter some kind words, and admit the campaign had backfired:

Ashley O'Malley, a GOP candidate for the state House's 156th District who has opposed the store, said he heard McDevitt on Michael Smerconish's radio show.

"She seems like a great person; hats off to anyone who's opening a small business in this economy," he said. "I just have a problem with the location so close to a school."

The school is located on the 200 block of West Gay Street and the store is on the 100 block of North Church Street, perpendicular to Gay Street.

O'Malley, who said he has heard dozens of complaints about the shop's location while campaigning, labeled the subsequent publicity "unintended consequences."

"She is possibly the luckiest small business owner in West Chester," he said.

A woman who answered the church phone yesterday said the pastor was not available and not commenting.

The newspaper also quoted Anthony Ciccerone as saying he saw nothing "lurid" about Feminique Boutique, and *"If you stand outside and look at the building, you would go, 'What's the problem there?'"* he said. McDevitt *"has guts to face the lions,"* he added, noting she sat quietly Tuesday as about 150 people,

241

many from the town's four parishes, criticized her shop at a Planning Commission meeting.

I breathed a sigh of relief. That night, I took my first night off since the whole thing started, the Memorial Day weekend that I'd spend with Tyler, oblivious that hell was breaking loose at Feminique Boutique. We went on a date, a picnic in a nearby park. Dusk was coming, and the crickets began their nightly song. As I enjoyed the moment, my phone buzzed and lit up with a number that looked a bit familiar, but didn't recognize.

"Hello?" I asked.

"Michael Smerconish, huh?" asked the voice on the line. It was Justin. "I couldn't believe it when I heard it," he said. "I'm driving to the office, and he said his next guest was a young woman, a sexologist, and I thought 'no, couldn't be,' but then I heard your voice."

I felt so awkward. Here I was, in the arms of the man who in the short time that I'd known him had volunteered his time to help me paint, had supported my dreams, and shared my frustrations and triumphs, listening to another man who found joy in stamping those dreams out. It was momentarily uncomfortable but in the end, the single most satisfying "up yours" of the whole ordeal.

"That's really impressive," he continued on. "That you have started a business and got invited on Michael Smerconish's show. I'm like wow, Jill. Just wow. And hearing your voice got me realizing that it took me so long to get over you. You are such a special person and..." as he started crying I interjected.

"I'm not doing this." And hung up.

"Who was that?" Tyler asked with his arms wrapped around me.

"No one special," I responded.

Then *Cat's in the Cradle* came on the little radio.

A child arrived just the other day
He came to the world in the usual way

But there were planes to catch and bills to pay
He learned to walk while I was away…

I denied the urge to change the channel as I'd done each time I heard this song throughout my entire life. As I listened to it I suddenly exclaimed, "I know why this song makes me cry!"

The song is about a man who puts off all of the important things in life until it is too late. There are so many people who put off the little miracles that make life, like cuddling, shouting out answers to Jeopardy, college ramen noodle dinners in throwaway bowls by candlelight, a weekend in Vermont, because they're too busy picking up dry cleaning and balancing the checkbook. It's one of the saddest things I can think of, which is why that song always made me cry.

And maybe because I'd just been talking to him, I thought of Justin. What a waste of life. My biggest fear for him is that he will wake up a lonely old man and realize he pissed away a wonderful girlfriend and his youth and the better part of his life because he had to stay late at the office shuffling papers.

Hearing that song just then made me so thankful that finally I was doing what *I* wanted to do, what I'd been dreaming about since I was a sophomore in high school. I wasn't doing it because school required it or social mores dictated it, or boyfriends demanded it. Not because powerful institutions refused it. I had Tyler, but I didn't need him or depend on him. I had Feminique Boutique, and everything else was just frosting.

A few days later I called Pat, and I told him all about my small town scandal and being on the news; about the church, and borough, and the politician. At first there was a chilly silence. It was awkward and emotionless. But then he laughed and said, "This, coming from someone who freaked out at the word 'vagina?'" That quick memory was all we needed to lighten the conversation.

"Well," Pat said. "You're living the dream. You said you wanted to teach people how to love, and you're doing that. I'm proud of you, Jill. I really am. You know all I ever wanted is for you to be happy." And I was happy. Really, really happy.

About the Author

Jill McDevitt has bachelor's and master's degrees in human sexuality and is currently working on her Ph.D., which upon completion in spring of 2013 will make her the only person in the world with all three of her degrees in sex! She opened Feminique, a sex shop and education center, at 21 years old, and currently travels to colleges, conferences, and living rooms across the country conducting sex-positive workshops. She documents her adventures and misadventures in her blog "A Day in the Life of a Sexologist." She can be found at www.thesexologist.org, www.facebook.com/JillAtFeminique or jill@thesexologist.org.

CPSIA information can be obtained at www.ICGtesting.com
Printed in the USA
BVOW070025011111

274905BV00005B/2/P

9 780983 875017